EROS CRUCIFIED

Bringing contemporary philosophers, theologians, and psychoanalysts into dialogue with works of art and literature, this work provides a fresh perspective on how humans can make sense of suffering and finitude and how our existence as sexual beings shapes our relations to one another and the divine. It attempts to establish a connection between carnal, bodily love and humanity's relation to the divine.

Relying on the works of philosophers such as Manoussakis, Kearney, and Marion and psychoanalysts such as Freud and Lacan, this book provides a possible answer to these fundamental questions and fosters further dialogue between thinkers and scholars of these different fields. The author analyzes why human sexuality implies both perversion and perfection and why it brings together humanity's baseness and beatitude. Through it, the author taps once more into the dark mystery of Eros and Thanatos who, to paraphrase Dostoevsky, forever struggle with God on the battlefield of the human heart.

This book is written primarily for scholars interested in the fields of philosophical psychology, existential philosophy, and philosophy of religion.

Matthew Clemente, PhD, is a Lecturer in the Woods College of Advancing Studies at Boston College specializing in existentialism, philosophy of religion, and contemporary Continental thought. He is the associate editor of the *Journal of Continental Philosophy and Religion* (Brill) and the co-editor of three philosophical volumes: *The Art of Anatheism* (2017), *misReading Nietzsche* (2018), and *Richard Kearney's Anatheistic Wager* (2018).

PSYCHOLOGY AND THE OTHER

DAVID M. GOODMAN
Series Editor

BRIAN W. BECKER   DONNA M. ORANGE   ERIC R. SEVERSON
Associate Editors

The *Psychology and the Other* Book Series highlights creative work at the intersections between psychology and the vast array of disciplines relevant to the human psyche. The interdisciplinary focus of this series brings psychology into conversation with continental philosophy, psychoanalysis, religious studies, anthropology, sociology, and social/critical theory. The cross-fertilization of theory and practice, encompassing such a range of perspectives, encourages the exploration of alternative paradigms and newly articulated vocabularies that speak to human identity, freedom, and suffering. Thus, we are encouraged to reimagine our encounters with difference, our notions of the "other," and what constitutes therapeutic modalities.

The study and practices of mental health practitioners, psychoanalysts, and scholars in the humanities will be sharpened, enhanced, and illuminated by these vibrant conversations, representing pluralistic methods of inquiry, including those typically identified as psychoanalytic, humanistic, qualitative, phenomenological, or existential.

Series Titles:

Unconscious Incarnations
Psychoanalytic and Philosophical Perspectives on the Body, 1st Edition
Edited by Brian W. Becker, John Panteleimon Manoussakis, David M. Goodman

Schelling, Freud, and the Philosophical Foundations of Psychoanalysis
Uncanny Belonging, 1st Edition
By Teresa Fenichel

Race, Rage, and Resistance
Philosophy, Psychology, and the Perils of Individualism, 1st Edition
Edited by David M. Goodman, Eric R. Severson, Heather Macdonald

Eros Crucified
Death, Desire, and the Divine in Psychoanalysis and Philosophy
of Religion, 1st Edition
By Matthew Clemente

For a full list of titles in the series, please visit the Routledge website at: https://www.routledge.com/Psychology-and-the-Other/book-series/PSYOTH

EROS CRUCIFIED

Death, Desire, and the Divine in Psychoanalysis and Philosophy of Religion

Matthew Clemente

Duo,   12.25.19

Your friendship has seen me through
some very trying times and some times when
I've made a real ass out of myself.
You are the truist form of friend and
I couldn't be more grateful.

MS Cl

Routledge
Taylor & Francis Group

LONDON AND NEW YORK

First published 2020
by Routledge
52 Vanderbilt Avenue, New York, NY 10017

and by Routledge
2 Park Square, Milton Park, Abingdon, Oxon, OX14 4RN

Routledge is an imprint of the Taylor & Francis Group, an informa business

Library of Congress Control Number: 2019952729

ISBN: 978-0-367-28048-2 (hbk)
ISBN: 978-0-367-25939-6 (pbk)
ISBN: 978-0-429-29938-4 (ebk)

Typeset in Bembo
by Deanta Global Publishing Services, Chennai, India
Printed and bound by CPI Group (UK) Ltd, Croydon, CR0 4YY

For John Panteleimon Manoussakis
Ad eum autem ducebar abs te nesciens, ut per cum ad te sciens ducerer.

Test everything. Retain what is good

~ St. Paul

CONTENTS

A BRIEF DISCLAIMER

Knowing that you know not, or how to read philosophy

In this work I wear many masks. At times I seem to reject a thinker's premises only to take them up again a few pages later. At times I seem to accept an argument only to cut it down in a subsequent chapter. I give a good amount of space to extended quotations, allowing thinkers to express themselves in their own words rather than doing violence to their ideas with my commentary. It is not always clear which position I hold, which thinkers I agree with and which I reject.

This, I'm told, is a flaw. One which detracts from the integrity of work. Upon reading a draft of this book, a dear friend lamented, "It's not a detective novel. You need to state explicitly the positions you hold." But for me, a good work of philosophy is very much like a detective novel. And a good reader must approach it as such. When I began writing this book, my ideas were very different than they are now that I am done with it. (An observant reader might be able to track the changes in thinking from the first chapter—originally drafted over three years ago—to the last). At different points I agreed with, or at least honestly entertained, every idea put forth. (Now I wonder whether I agree with any of them). But the writing of this book changed me. It changed how I think. It changed what I think. I am still changing today.

I have come to believe that a philosopher ought never to be fixed in his ideas. Fixed ideas are the end of philosophy. They are the end of thinking altogether. *It is a capital mistake to theorize before you have all the evidence. Insensibly you begin to twist facts to suit theories, instead of theories to suit facts.* So says our greatest sleuth. Why have we philosophers been so unwilling to hear him? Why do we rush to conclusions even as new evidence abounds? Is it perhaps because we lust for clear and distinct ideas? Do we need the control that comes from knowing?

But we live in a world in which nothing is certain. A world which contains more things than we philosophers could ever know. Being a philosopher, then, means learning to live with ambiguity. It means being open to the fact that your ideas will change, being willing to let them change. The worst thing a reader of philosophy can do is approach a text expecting that his first reading (or his tenth) will tell him what the author means. Rather, it will tell him what *he* means: which ideas he is willing to entertain and which he is too closed off even to consider. Or, it might tell him that—if he lets it. The key is to stop reading philosophy from the perspective of *one who knows*, and to begin reading it as one who wants to know—that is, to play the part of the detective.

PREFACE

Christianity gave Eros poison to drink; he did not die of it but degenerated—
into vice.

~ *Beyond Good and Evil* (§168)

This single aphorism expresses the essence of the critique leveled by Nietzsche against Christianity. It is a critique which Nietzsche rightly asserts is directed at the foundations of Christian thinking itself. Christianity as rationalism, Christianity as Platonism, Christianity as fleshless spiritualization and puritanical creed—certainly the history of Christian thought lends itself to such interpretations.[1] That the followers of the man who declared "I came so that they might have life and have it more abundantly" (John 10:10)[2] readily adopted the art of death and dying (*Phaedo* 64a), that believers in the resurrection eagerly aligned themselves with a thinker who openly despised the body, who viewed the material world as a prison (*Phaedo* 64e), that those who were instructed "Be fertile and multiply" (Genesis 1:28) saw no inconsistency with ascending away from sensuous desire toward "higher" intellectual pleasures (cf. *Symposium*/*Phaedrus*) can be legitimately interpreted as a second betrayal of Christ—only this time without the carnality of the kiss.

For Nietzsche, "there has been only one Christian, and he died on the Cross."[3] All of the good philosophical thinking done in the name of Christ has only served to move us further from the life he lived and the death he suffered. (Does not all philosophizing distance us from the raw brutality of life and death?) Indeed, the death of Christ—the crucifixion of his tangible, touchable, corporeal flesh—has remained, as Paul prophesied it would, foolishness for serious philosophers (cf. 1 Corinthians 1:23). (Think, for instance, of Hegel's desire to transcend the messiness of Christ's bodily death by means of a pure concept.)[4] Yet those of us foolish enough to want to take seriously the scandal of the incarnation, those who would try to answer Nietzsche's critique without merely dismissing it, must "begin by reminding ourselves of this simple truth: 'the Word became flesh'—it was not the flesh that became word, it was not the carnal that became spiritual or must become spiritual."[5]

Arguments that have stood at the basis of many Christian philosophies—trifling over the immortality of the soul, primary causation, unmoved movers, and the like—begin by neglecting this first foolishness.[6] In doing so, they miss the radical realism of what Bonhoeffer calls the "profound this-worldliness" of Christianity.[7] It is *this* life, this physical, carnal, human life that matters. All abstracting away from the world in which we live—the world of bodies and of blood, of sex and hunger, of desire, depravity, and death—all thinking that leads us from the real world, our world, the only world we experience, the one world we can know, denies the simple, scandalous truth that God became man and made his dwelling among us (John 1:14).

Many Christian thinkers have mistakenly moved away from the world of the body. Many have followed the Platonists into the unreal realm of ideas. (As a good friend recently quipped: "Christianity is not Platonism for the masses, but masses of Christians are Platonists.") To do so is to fail to realize that spiritualizing the flesh and its affections "simply amount[s] to getting Christianity backwards—it … mean[s] to undo Christianity and worse 'in its name.'"[8]

Yet as I sit at my desk writing these words, only a week removed from the celebration of God's scandalous birth, I cannot help but to think that the foolishness of Christ's flesh has not been entirely forgotten. Today we celebrate the Feast of the Circumcision. And it is worth noting that the Church has always seen this day as marking the first time that Christ shed his sacred blood for the redemption of man. He redeemed man by being a man, by becoming a body with all of the parts of a body—even the most intimate and the most profane. Are we capable today of thinking what this means? Do we understand, do we *value*, the corporeality that God has made his own?

No, if anyone has given Eros poison to drink, it has been *us*. We who find ourselves caught between a sterile restlessness and a restful sterility,[9] we who reduce sex by our obsession and seek to remedy our obsession by calling sex obscene, we who spiritualize the flesh, who long to *see* rather than *touch*, to transcend rather than incarnate, we who know nothing of Eros save the pornographic and the puritanical, the shameful and the ashamed—we have poisoned Eros. (And *we philosophers*—who peddle unreal concepts—*we* most of all.)[10] By remaking Eros in our own cracked image, by degrading him with our gaze, by refusing to see him as he is and instead clothing him in our shame, we have made for ourselves an empty idol—one that satisfies our voyeuristic need for spectacle (pornography) or provides us with a legalistic moralism that allows us to feel justified even when we refuse to love (puritanism).

Eros has become for us an idol: a false love erected in the place of the living God. But Eros himself—not the Eros of our making—is a jealous lover. He will not leave us to our own devices. He will not allow us to feed on ashes and pretend we have found the bread of life. We have given Eros poison to drink. He has taken it from us. He has drunk it for us. He has degenerated and he has perished. But on the third day he rose again. And with the taste of the grave still fresh on his lips, he offered us the very chalice we forced upon him, asking: "Can you drink of the cup that I drink?" (Mark 10:38).

MSC
Boston College
Feast of the Circumcision of Christ
January 1, 2018

Notes

1 As Heinrich Heine, anticipating Nietzsche, argues:

> The historical manifestation and development of [the idea of Christianity] in the real world can already be seen in the first centuries after the birth of Christ, especially through an impartial investigation of the history of the Manicheans and the Gnostics. Although the former were declared heretical, and the latter denounced and damned by the Church, they still retained their influence on dogma.... At base, the Manicheans are not very different from the Gnostics. A characteristic of both is the doctrine of the two principles, good and evil, which battle each other.... [E]verywhere we see the doctrine of the two principles in evidence: opposed to the good Christ stands the evil Satan; the world of spirit is represented by Christ, the world of matter by Satan; our soul belongs to the former, our body to the latter; and the whole world of appearance, nature, is thus originally evil; ... it is essential to renounce all sensual joys of life, to torment the body, Satan's fief, so that the soul can rise aloft, all the more nobly, into the lucid sky, into the bright kingdom of Christ.
>
> (On the History of Religion and Philosophy
> in Germany, *12–13*)

2 Unless otherwise stated, all biblical references come from the *New American Bible Revised Edition*.
3 Nietzsche, *The Anti-Christ*, (§39).
4 He goes so far as to propose that we "re-establish for philosophy ... the *speculative* Good Friday in place of the historic Good Friday." Hegel, *Faith and Knowledge*, 191 (emphasis mine).
5 Manoussakis, "On the Flesh of the Word," 306.
6 As Pascal says:

> The metaphysical proofs for the existence of God are so remote from human reasoning and so involved that they make little impact, and, even if they did help some people, it would only be for the moment during which they watched the demonstration, because an hour later they would be afraid they had made a mistake.... That is the result of knowing God without Christ.
>
> (Pensées, *[XIV, 190]*)

7 As quoted in Kearney, *Anatheism*, 69.
8 Manoussakis, "On the Flesh of the Word," 306.

9 Cf. "Love, such as our culture has fashioned it, walks between two abysses: restless desire, and a hypocritical wish for constancy—a harsh caricature of fidelity." Ricoeur, "Wonder, Eroticism and Enigma," 141.
10 Cf. Nietzsche, *Twilight of the Idols*, "Reason in Philosophy," (§1).

Bibliography

Hegel, GWF, *Faith and Knowledge*, trans. Walter Cerf and HS Harris, (Albany: State University of New York, 1977).

Heine, Heinrich, *On the History of Religion and Philosophy in Germany*, ed. Terry Pinkard, trans. Howard Pollack-Milgate (Cambridge: Cambridge University Press, 2007).

Kearney, Richard, *Anatheism: Returning to God After God* (New York: Columbia University Press, 2011).

Manoussakis, John, "On the Flesh of the Word: Incarnational Hermeneutics," in *Carnal Hermeneutics*, eds. Richard Kearney and Brian Treanor (New York: Fordham University Press, 2015), 306–316.

Nietzsche, Friedrich, *Twilight of the Idols: or How to Philosophize with a Hammer and the Anti-Christ*, trans. RJ Hollingdale, (New York: Penguin, 1990).

Pascal, Blaise, *Pensées*, trans. AJ Krailsheimer (New York: Penguin, 1995).

Ricoeur, Paul, "Wonder, Eroticism and Enigma," in *Sexuality and the Sacred: Sources for Theological Reflection*, eds. James B Nelson and Sandra P Longfellow (Westminster: John Knox Press, 1994).

ACKNOWLEDGMENTS

The act of writing often feels like a solitary venture. In point of fact, however, nothing could be written—or, indeed, thought—without the time, care, support, and love of other people. This work bears the unmistakable marks of those who have so generously given themselves to me. I will here acknowledge but a few whose friendship and influence were instrumental to the writing of this book. Still, the list of those who deserve my recognition and gratitude extends far beyond the names contained herein and it is important to me to express my sincere thanks to everyone who, in ways big and small, has helped to make me the thinker, the writer, the human being I am.

First I would like to express my sincere gratitude for the generous support of the Boston College Philosophy Department, the Graduate School of the Morrissey College of Arts and Sciences, and the Woods College of Advancing Studies. I would like to thank Richard Kearney whose close and careful reading of this text has made it stronger than it ever would have been without him; David Goodman whose friendship made this book possible; Brian Becker without whom I may never have been able to formulate explicitly the central thesis; William Hendel who has read more drafts of my writing than anyone ever should; Scott Reznick and Brian LeBlanc for acting as sounding boards for my more absurd ideas; Vanessa Rumble and John Manoussakis for their notes on this work; Sir Christopher Ricks whose keen critical eye immediately recognized the need for a better subtitle; Bryan Cocchiara, Melissa Fitzpatrick, Teresa Fenichel, Stephen Mendelsohn, and Greta Turnbull for their friendships and for keeping me sane over the many years it took write this book; Kyle Broderick who has been a good student and friend; and, most importantly, my wife Tracy without whose patience I would not have completed this project and without whose love I would know nothing of the subject matter. Thank you all.

INTRODUCTION

Sex and death

What is the relation between sex, death, and the divine? This question, which is of vital importance to Plato and which Freud tacitly takes up by turning to the *Symposium* at the end of *Beyond the Pleasure Principle*, can be seen as standing at the foundation of philosophy, theology, and psychoanalysis. It ought not to surprise us, then, to observe the vibrant conversation going on between Continental philosophers, theologians, and psychoanalysts today. This attempt to untangle and analyze the intersection where the "Heavenly Powers"[1] of sex and death converge with the divine is that which allows Julia Kristeva to state, during a recent interview with Richard Kearney, that of all "the human sciences and the social sciences, the only rational approaches to human beings, psychoanalysis … come[s] closest … to the experience of faith."[2] It is that which enables Lacan to assert that "Saint Augustine … foreshadowed psychoanalysis"[3] and to insist that psychoanalysts ought to "become versed in Augustine."[4] It is that which compels thinkers like Emmanuel Falque—who advise philosophers of religion to speak first and foremost about "*finitude*, the consciousness and horizon of death"[5]—to write books on Freud and philosophy.[6] And it is that which drives the work being undertaken today.

The purpose of this project is to approach once more the dark mystery of Eros and Thanatos which, to paraphrase Dostoevsky, forever struggle with God on the battlefield of the human heart. In order to broach this topic, we will attempt to establish a connection between carnal, bodily love and man's relation to the divine. To do so, we will rely upon and further develop what Paul Ricoeur has called "the nuptial metaphor"—the recurring biblical motif that portrays God's relation to man as a kind of love affair, neither reductively sexual nor legalistically marital, but passionate, romantic, protective, desirous, even jealous.[7] We will begin with a phenomenological consideration of the movement of Eros in and through the relationship between lover and beloved. By considering how that relationship advances from language (word) to touch (flesh) to unity (spirit), we will hope to show that, in many ways, the progression of the erotic life on the human level mirrors the self-revelation of the divine through the drama of history.

Like God, human beings long to offer themselves, to present themselves, to give themselves, to make themselves known. Yet this revealing, this presenting of oneself to the other, is never straightforward but always masked, disguised, concealed even as it reveals. For this reason, the erotic or nuptial relationship—which depends upon play, desire, distance, dance, a thirst for that which can never be possessed or fully known—offers a fitting metaphor for our experience with the divine. Yet the analogy becomes clearer still when we observe that the erotic relationship's movement from word to flesh to spirit bears a striking resemblance to the three distinct yet interwoven movements by which God is revealed in and through history: creation, incarnation, and eschaton.[8] For, if we accept that the world was created through the Word (John 1:3), that that Word was incarnated in the flesh (John 1:14), and that the Spirit will one day unify our disparate fleshes into one eschatological body (cf. Ephesians 4:1-4; 1 Corinthians 10:18), then we will have to admit that in the nuptial metaphor we find not only what Aquinas calls the *analogia entis*, but perhaps even the *imago dei*, the mark of our Creator.

To say this, of course, contradicts much of the traditional discourse about the dangers that carnal love poses to the spiritual life. In addition to the Platonic ascent away from the body—for instance, Socrates's reiteration of Diotima's erotic ascent in the *Symposium*—we can think here of Gregory of Nyssa's view that "God created the consequences of disobedience—sensuality, and especially sexuality—along with human nature in his foreknowledge of sin."[9] Yet the connection that we hope to draw between carnal, bodily love and the divine is not without precedent. Consider, for example, the statement by Ignatius of Antioch from which this work derives its title—"my Eros has been crucified"—which Pseudo Dionysius reads as a supreme affirmation of divine desire.[10] (Let us not forget that, for Dionysius, it is the corporeal body of God with all of its wants, desires, and wounds that is crucified.) John Manoussakis, commenting on this link between the carnal and the spiritual, writes, "The desire for God is not independent from the desire for the other human.... One who has not felt the latter rarely and with difficulty would seek the former."[11] I would add that, as Jean-Luc Marion argues in *The Erotic Phenomenon*, one who *has* felt the latter has perhaps already experienced the former, if only in a veiled way. Thus, where Freud reads the desire for God as a sublimation of the sex drives, I would suggest the opposite: erotic desire often reveals a deeper, more fundamental longing—a longing for the divine.

And yet, Freud might counter, one must consider not just Eros but Thanatos as well. How does the desire for death factor into this religiously-inflected reading of the drives? That human sexuality implies both perversion and perfection, that it brings together man's baseness and his beatitude, is one of the most important insights offered by Freudian drive theory. As Freud himself notes, "The highest and the lowest are always closest to each other in the sphere of sexuality."[12] But why this is the case remains for Freud a great mystery. Here, I would suggest, is where philosophy of religion can make an important contribution. To do so, it will have to take seriously the challenges posed by thinkers such as Nietzsche and Freud—and perhaps even adopt some of the major elements of their philosophies. To that end, it is worth reconsidering the traditional understanding of Eros as the (masculine) god of ascent, the drive toward unity, wholeness, and truth.

Offering a new understanding of Eros[13]

Richard Kearney, whose work is situated in the space where psychoanalysis and philosophy of religion overlap, tells us that "the life-drive Eros" manifests itself as "a desire for its other."[14] Immediately, this raises a question: how can Eros—"which seeks to push together and hold together" separate organisms[15]—preserve otherness while at the same time pursuing unity? For Freud, Eros is a drive which opposes otherness, one which swallows up alterity in its unending quest for wholeness. As Lacan captures with his famous formulation "There's such a thing as One" (*Y a d' l' Un*): "[I]n Freud's discourse ... Eros is defined as the fusion that makes one from two, as what is supposed to gradually tend in the direction of making but one from an immense multitude."[16] This drive toward oceanic oneness, toward a primal unity which can never be fully achieved, is at every moment contested by "another factor that poses an obstacle to this universal Eros ... Thanatos, the reduction to dust."[17] (Whether or not these two drives actually oppose one another is a question to which we will return to in the pages to come.)

But if "Eros is defined as the fusion that makes one from two," where then is the other? And, conversely, if Eros emerges as the drive that desires "its other," what justifies the rejection of the Freudian view? In this text, we will propose a new understanding of Eros, one which counters Freud's by linking the pursuit of an illusory past of oceanic oneness to Thanatos, which sees in the (phallic) Eros of old—the Eros of Plato and Freud—a god of wholeness who cannot account for the "jouissance of the body" that exists "beyond the phallus," the "something more" (*en plus*) of female desire.[18] This erotic *surplus*—which Kearney (and Lacan)[19] links to the love of God, the God who "is relation," who is the "Trinitarian dance" of *perichoresis*[20]—is a love that pours itself out, a love that forgoes power, that refuses to objectify, subjugate, grasp, a love of divine recklessness and divine abandonment, of surrender, vulnerability, powerlessness, self-gift.[21]

It is no secret that the history of philosophy has often neglected the feminine, feared it, suppressed it, relegated it to the realm of the irrational and untrue. (For Lacan, this is because "in her essence" woman "is not-whole"—that is, she cannot be contained by "the nature of words"[22] but exceeds the limits of language, experiences the ineffable: "that woman knows nothing of this jouissance ... is underscored by the fact that in all the time people have been begging them, begging them on their hands and knees ... to try to tell us, not a word!")[23] Yet Nietzsche, of all people, surprises us by pondering: "Supposing truth is a woman—what then?"[24] And he follows this startling query up with the assertion that "Perhaps truth is a woman who has reasons for not letting us see her reasons."[25]

This feminizing of truth is an implicit and essential aspect of the revaluation of Eros which we will posit in this text. For if truth is a woman, then he who is "the way and the truth and the life" (John 14:6)—the one who we will later identify as *Eros crucified*—will reveal to us a far different understanding of Eros than we have heretofore garnered on our own.[26] As we will see, it is this insight which will allow us, in our sixth chapter, to posit a "basic similarity between human love and Trinitarian love,"[27] to assert that "bodily love is intrinsically linked to, and even a sign of, the Trinitarian relations."[28] But before we get there, we will have to ask what this new understanding of Eros—this Eros of the extra (*en plus*), this Eros of feminine *jouissance* (which, incidentally, Lacan links to the face of God)[29]—looks like.

Nietzsche, in *Beyond Good and Evil*, tells us that "What inspires respect for woman, and often enough even fear, is her *nature*, which is more 'natural' than man's."[30] He admires her "inner wildness, the incomprehensibility, scope, and movement of her desires and virtues" and notes that "she appears to suffer more, to be more vulnerable, more in need of love, and more condemned to disappointment than any other animal."[31] This combination of "fear and pity," which for Nietzsche reaches its climax in woman, "tears to pieces as it enchants."[32] That Nietzsche uses the essential elements of Greek tragedy—fear and pity—to define the nature of woman should give us pause and perhaps cause us to reconsider the standard readings of his purported misogyny.[33] Who, after all, could miss the resonances between his understanding of the feminine—"which tears to pieces as it enchants"—and the "dismembered god" of Greek tragedy, the god of mystery, intoxication, overfullness, agony, ecstasy, joy: the suffering Dionysus who was himself "torn to pieces ... and now is worshipped in this state"?[34]

Understanding Eros in these more "natural," carnal, womanly terms moves us in a very different direction than Plato and his disciples are wont to go. It leads us away from the disembodied intellectualizing of the philosophers—whose God of purity and oneness remains alien to this world, uncontaminated by the desires of the flesh—and brings God down to earth, situating him "as the third party in the business of human love," the unexpected other in the "*ménage à trois*" of human intimacy.[35] More than that, it supports our central thesis that what must be crucified is the Eros of Plato, the Eros of Freud, the Eros which strives for wholeness, stasis, peace, the return to an illusory Eden of oceanic oneness and truth. *That* Eros, we hope to show, is no more than Thanatos in disguise. It must be granted the unmaking it so cunningly strives for. It must be allowed to die.

And once that Eros has been crucified? Might it be injected with new life? Might there be a rebirth, a resurrection? It is our contention that the Eros we seek, the triune Eros of relation, unity (not identity) between self and other, initiates a "metamorphosis" of Eros (to use Falque's language) which brings about an encounter between the finite and the divine. But—and this is the essential point—that encounter takes place within and by means of finitude, not in some celestial realm beyond the heavens, beyond all being. Like Kierkegaard's knight of faith—whose "absolute relation to the absolute"[36] represents a "leap into life,"[37] who remains "in finitude" and learns to "delight in it as if finitude were the surest thing of all,"[38] who "belongs entirely to finitude ... belongs entirely to the world"[39]—like the knight, the descent of Eros reveals that "Temporality, finitude—that is what it is all about!"[40] It reveals, contrary to our expectations, that "the gesture of choosing temporal existence, of giving up eternal existence for the sake of love ... is the highest ethical act of them all,"[41] that in order to ascend, one must be willing to descend, to become a servant, the last of the last, the lowest of the low (Mark 9:35).

Why God?

It will be asked, first, whether the reader must accept the tenets of faith—that God is love, that that love is Trinitarian in nature, that God became man, etc.—in order to entertain the arguments put forth in this work; and, secondarily, why bring God in at all, why not confine oneself to the limits of reason, the *lumière naturelle* of the philosophers? To address these concerns in order, I would suggest first that, just as one need not be a Marxist to find the reading of *Das Kapital* a worthwhile endeavor nor a Thomist to draw life from Dr. King's *Letter from Birmingham Jail*, so too can one find fruit in the work of a Christian existentialist without ending in prostration before the altar. Whether one is a Christian or not, one must admit that the Freudian understanding of love leaves little room for love in that it makes no room for the other. If one would object to this solipsistic view of the human person, one would do well to seek support wherever he can find it. ("Whoever is not against us is for us" [Mark 9:40]—a wise saying reserved not exclusively for Christians.) Augustine tells us that in order for there to be love, there must be "three things: the lover, the beloved, and the love."[42] Freud's understanding of Eros closes off this possibility. One could, I think, side with Augustine without necessarily accepting his recourse to the divine.

To answer the question why bring God in at all, I would remind readers of Ricoeur's famous criticism of the attempts to radically separate philosophy and theology; he calls them a kind of "controlled schizophrenia." For me, such a divorce is never fully attainable. And if it were, I am not sure it would be advisable. According to Nietzsche, philosophy is the attempt to articulate and make sense out of one's perspective, one's experience of the world. Well, theology is something one experiences in the world. Questions about the nature and existence of God, about the problem of senseless suffering, about the quasi-mystical pull of violence and depravity, about the unnamable, unspeakable beauty that resides at the heart of things, the miraculous encounter with kindness, self-sacrifice, and love—these too are things found in the world. The idea that philosophy is somehow made purer or more philosophical by excluding them is, I think, rooted in a false premise about what philosophy is and what it does.

Philosophy, according to the stoics, is therapy for the soul. (A theologically charged assertion in its own right). But if the philosophy I espouse is going to be therapeutic—that is, if it is going to offer some degree of consolation for the traumas of life—it can only be so by embracing the problems of life, the problems that life presents, including theological ones. Never has there been a man who lived without the question of God. Indeed, it is a defining characteristic of man that he alone questions God. And to pretend that this is not the case in order to obtain some sort of quasi-scientific objectivity is a betrayal of philosophy's first and most important dictum: *I know that I know not.* Or, put differently, I know that I only know the world through my limited, finite perspective.[43] I am not God. But by speaking of him I can perhaps guard against my propensity to deceive myself into thinking that I am.

This is one reason to allow philosophers to take up and consider theological questions—philosophy is, after all, concerned with truth and this fundamental truth ought never to be lost. But there are other reasons as well. William James, for instance, sees philosophy as having the potential to "redeem religion from [the] unwholesome privacy" of religious sentiment. "Feeling," he tells us, "is private and dumb, and unable to give account of itself."[44] Philosophy, therefore, is necessary if one is to make sense of and articulate the experience of faith.

> We are thinking beings, and we cannot exclude the intellect from participating in any of our functions.... Both our personal ideals and our religious and mystical experiences must be interpreted congruously with the kind of scenery our thinking mind inhabits. The philosophic climate of our time inevitably forces its own clothing on us. Moreover, we must exchange our feelings with one another, and in doing so we have to speak, and to use general and abstract formulas. Conceptions and constructions are thus a necessary part of our religion; and as moderator amid the clash of hypotheses, and mediator among the criticisms of one man's constructions by another, philosophy will always have much to do.[45]

Put simply, we cannot but philosophize about our personal experiences; consciousness and communication demand it. And religious experiences are experiences, just like any other. As Manoussakis has recently argued, the attempt to bifurcate experience into religious and non-, sacred and profane, makes little sense when we consider that

> we have no other recourse to the world than experience ... and, therefore, we cannot justifiably talk of religion as if religion constituted, or rather was

constituted by a predetermined set of phenomena other than that single experience through which we are in-the-world.

We cannot speak of multiple experiences even if experience is always manifold. Experience as such cannot be more than one thing. Surely, one may object, we have an experience of more than one thing. Yes, but whether one experiences the most trivial and mundane thing or the *mysterium tremendum*, experience is experience... . To the one, then, who would like to know as to what kind of phenomena we are willing to admit within such a phenomenology of religion, our answer is *all*. All phenomena are religious for no exclusion can be justified, and therefore all philosophy is a philosophy of religion, if one still wishes to designate it so.[46]

Thus, to dismiss the theological questions that arise naturally from experience or to try to exclude them from philosophical discourse is as foolish as it is impossible. In so far as philosophy is a tool for helping us to understand our lives, it must not shy away from even the most speculative lines of inquiry—for, speculation too is born of that singular experience we call life.

A different yet not unrelated reason for allowing philosophers to engage in theological discourse stems from the hermeneutic insight that no thinker thinks impartially. Every philosopher, we must admit, has a story—a history of lived (and read) experience that he brings to thought. The cogito does not exist in a vacuum. Thought is always already formed and informed by what comes before, what precedes it. Ricoeur's often cited introductory question—*d'où parlez-vous?* Where do you speak from?—reminds us that we all speak from somewhere, none of us is capable of uttering the first word.[47] And if, as Manoussakis argues, "the language of the community within which I am born or reborn"—the language that "predates me"—always structures my understanding of both myself and the world in which I live, then the question *where do you speak from?* must be answered at a personal level if one is to be honest about the philosophy one puts forth.

As a Catholic philosopher writing in the wake of the death of God but also after the theological turn in phenomenology, I find myself in the precarious position of trying to discern how to live in and understand the contemporary world while at the same time remaining separate from it. I am a student of Kearney's and Manoussakis's, a beneficiary of the Second Vatican Council, an inheritor of both the emancipation and destruction wrought by the sexual revolution. My thinking bears witness to these inescapable biographical facts—as it does, I am sure, to countless others. Yet this does not strike me as a knock against the philosophy I propose. To engage with the world in which one lives and to work to see that world made anew is the obligation of every person of faith. To attempt to better understand oneself, one's motives and desires, what prejudices one has acquired simply by living, is—or ought to be—the goal of every philosopher. Where these two objectives meet in me is in the approach I have adopted for practicing philosophy.

Balthasar famously called for a theology "of adoration and prayer," a theology practiced "on one's knees."[48] His meaning, I think, was this: theology is not theology if it is not worship, speaking *to* the one it is speaking *of*. But prayer, we are told, is to be done with the door closed, offered in the secrecy of the bedroom (Matthew 6:6). It is my contention that such an understanding of theology opens the space for another mode of thinking: a philosophy that is lived and acted out, that concerns itself with the cares of this world, a philosophy of the streets. What would such a philosophy look like? The answer, I think, will depend upon the philosopher who lives it. But such a lived philosophy will invariably represent what Falque has called the "quest for a common name," the attempt to express and explore what is "common for all people."[49]

> For me, the Natural Reason of Thomas, the Natural Light of Reason, is nothing but the quest for a common name.... Instead of saying "you need reason in order to be able to ascend to God," he says: "with the Jews I have the Old Testament in common, with the heretics I have the New Testament in common, but with the pagans I have nothing in common so I need to find this *common* thing I call *reason*." My hypothesis, then, is this: one does not have to follow Thomas Aquinas to the letter, but one should be true to his spirit.... I understand [his spirit] as an openness to the novelty of one's time (for Thomas that was the introduction of Aristotle), transforming it in the light of Christianity.[50]

If theology begins with God's self-articulation, with his expressed plan and purpose for the world, philosophy has a different starting point. Unlike the theologian, the philosopher begins with this world—the world of experience, the world that is "common for all people"—and, finding it lacking, he may ultimately end at God. Or he may not. But if he does, the glimpse of God garnered will be very much shaped by, seen through the lens of, creaturely existence.

I said a short time ago that faith requires of us that we work to see the world made anew. But in order to do so, one must be willing to meet the world where it is and not expect from the world that it has already been made anew. And the philosopher, more than any other, must begin by understanding where this world is. According to Falque, "what we have in common today is no longer reason as it was for Aquinas. We think after Nietzsche, after Freud, so what we have in common is *finitude*, the consciousness and horizon of death."[51] Thus, he insists, "If it is finitude that we all—believers and nonbelievers, Christians and pagan alike—have in common, then it is about finitude that we should first talk."[52] To this possible starting point, Kearney adds another: "Eros is what Christians have in common with the Greeks, the atheists, and so-called pagans. A sort of erotic *lumière naturelle*."[53]

Sex and death. Eros and Thanatos. The "Heavenly Powers" of life and destruction. For the philosopher living in the world, such topics are unavoidable. That examining them should lead one to the question of God need not be the case.

But for those of us who already carry that question with them, those who wrestle with God like Jacob wrestled with the angel, examining the most mysterious and monstrous aspects of the human condition could not lead anywhere else.

Notes

1   Freud, *Civilization and Its Discontents*, 128.
2   Kristeva, "Mysticism and Anatheism," 81.
3   Lacan, *Ecrits*, 93.
4   Ibid., 742.
5   Falque, "An Anatheist Exchange," 90.
6   See, Falque, *Ça n'a rien à voir* (2018).
7   See LaCocque and Ricoeur, *Thinking Biblically*, 265–303.
8   Manoussakis, in his reading of Augustine, notes that "the overlapping symmetry between history (from creation to eschaton) and the personal history of each one of us is the idea that provides the *Confessions* with its structure and thematic unity." Manoussakis, *The Ethics of Time*, 90.
9   Balthasar, *Cosmic Liturgy*, 187.
10   See, Dionysius, *The Divine Names*, (IV.12.709B).
11   Manoussakis, *The Ethics of Time*, 105.
12   Freud, *Three Essays on Sexuality,* 162.
13   I am incredibly grateful to Brian Becker of Lesley University whose careful reading of my work helped me to make explicit its central thesis which was, prior to his feedback, only expressed implicitly.
14   Kearney, "God Making," 4–5.
15   Freud, *Beyond the Pleasure Principle*, 97.
16   Lacan, *Encore: Seminar XX*, 66.
17   Ibid.
18   Ibid., 74.
19   See Ibid., 68.
20   Kearney, "God Making," 5.
21   It is essential to note here that the love that offers itself to the other, that makes itself vulnerable, powerless, capable of being accepted or rejected, is *not* a form of masochism (which is really just a disguised lust for power). Masochism, as Freud says, is "Sadism which cannot find employment in actual life" and is thus "turned round upon the subject's own self." Freud, *Three Essays on Sexuality,* 158, n. 2.
22   Lacan, *Encore: Seminar XX*, 73.
23   Ibid., 75.
24   Nietzsche, *Beyond Good and Evil*, "Preface."
25   Nietzsche, *The Gay Science*, "Preface," (§4).
26   As Kearney reminds us, the Wisdom of God—who, Paul tells us, *is* Christ (1 Corinthians 1:24)—is called "Sophia (a feminine noun)." Kearney, "God Making," 5.
27   Sweeney, "Bodily Love and the *Imago Trinitatis*," 117.
28   Ibid., 119.
29   Lacan, *Encore: Seminar XX*, 77.
30   Nietzsche, *Beyond Good and Evil*, (§239).
31   Ibid.
32   Ibid.
33   Countering such readings, Teresa Fenichel observes:

> Although his views on women are generally acknowledged to be the most dated aspect of his thinking, Nietzsche is quite prescient here. The great error of the women's movement, he tells us, is its underlying assumption that woman ought

to be the same as man; that any *difference* between man and woman is something to be overcome, made up for, rather than respected and preserved. What concerns Nietzsche above all is not whether woman *deserves* equality, whether she is capable of manly pursuits; he cannot understand how woman could possibly want such a thing. It was just such an idea of progress, as Nietzsche so painstakingly details, that resulted in man's decline into a domesticated, anemic and corrupted creature. And we should read Nietzsche's famous line from *Thus Spoke Zarathustra*, spoken through the mouth of an old woman, as corroboration: 'Are you visiting women? Do not forget your whip!' (Z, 1, 18). Nietzsche holds out hope that woman, unlike man, might still be capable of inspiring fear—wild enough, alive enough to still be in need of breaking!—and thus still deserving of love, of admiration.

("Pussywhipped," 37–38)

34 Nietzsche, *The Birth of Tragedy*, (§10).
35 Lacan, *Encore: Seminar XX*, 70. Compare this with our later discussion of Graham Greene's *The End of the Affair* in the last section of Chapter 6.
36 Kierkegaard, *Fear and Trembling*, 56.
37 Ibid., 41.
38 Ibid., 40.
39 Ibid., 39.
40 Ibid., 49.
41 Žižek, *The Puppet and the Dwarf*, 13. The connection between Žižek and Manoussakis on this point is striking. Compare Manoussakis's central thesis in *The Ethics of Time* that—contrary to the philosophies which assert that time is the ultimate prison preventing us from reach eternity—beatitude can only accomplished by means of the movement of time with Žižek's insistence on the import of temporality: "The Event of 'incarnation' is not so much the time when ordinary temporal reality touches Eternity, but, rather, the time when Eternity reaches into time."
42 Augustine, *On the Trinity*, (9.2.2).
43 By reformulating the wisdom of Socrates in the terms of perspectivism, Nietzsche was able to breathe new life into a truth that, for many readers, had lost it arresting charge. For more on this, see Clemente, "Disciple of a Still Unknown God" in *mis-Reading Nietzsche*, especially pp. 156–158.
44 James, *The Varieties of Religious Experience*, 432.
45 Ibid.
46 Manoussakis, "Sacred Addictions: On the Phenomenology of Religious Experience," 43.
47 Manoussakis's meditation on the prayer that opens the *Confessions*—"Great are you, O Lord, and exceedingly worthy of praise ..."—elucidates the point:

> To begin with a prayer—as the *Confessions* do by combining a number of verses from the Psalms—is to circumvent the problem of the beginning, for a prayer is never mine. It predates me.... Yet, what does it mean that the words of my prayer predate me, if not that they speak me before I speak them? The language of prayer, which is also the language of the community within which I am born or reborn, comes before me, and makes the effort to my own beginning already vain. For if I am to begin *speaking* ... I will have to do so in someone else's words. No one invents one's own language and such a language, as strictly private, would have also been strictly *idiotic*. Thus, the very words that one may use to affirm his autonomy fail him and betray his dependence in what is always prior and anterior than the self: language. God has spoken first and humanity's word, whether one realizes it or not, comes always as a response to that first word. Humankind's language is responsorial.

(The Ethics of Time, 40–41)

48 Balthasar, *Explorations in Theology*, 206.
49 Falque, "An Anatheist Exchange," 90.
50 Ibid.
51 Ibid.
52 Ibid.
53 Ibid., 99.

Bibliography

Augustine, *On the Trinity*, trans. Gareth B Matthews (Cambridge, UK: Cambridge University Press, 2002).

Balthasar, Hans Urs von, *Explorations in Theology, vol. 1: The Word Made Flesh*, trans. AV Littledale and Alexander Dru (San Francisco: Ignatius, 1989).

Balthasar, Hans Urs von, *Cosmic Liturgy: The Universe According to Maximus the Confessor*, trans. Brian E Daley, SJ (San Francisco: Communio, Ignatius, 2003).

Clemente, M Saverio, "Disciple of a Still Unknown God or Becoming What I Am," in *misReading Nietzsche*, eds. M Saverio Clemente and Bryan J Cocchiara (Eugene, OR: Pickwick Publications, 2018), 151–165.

Dionysius the Areopagite, *Divine Names in Pseudo-Dionysius: The Complete Works*, trans. Colm Luibhéid, ed. Paul Rorem (New York: Paulist, 1987).

Falque, Emmanuel, "An Anatheist Exchange: Returning to the Body after the Flesh," in *Richard Kearney's Anatheistic Wager: Philosophy, Theology, Poetics*, eds. Chris Doude van Troostwijk and Matthew Clemente (Bloomington: Indiana University Press, 2018a), 88–110.

Falque, Emmanuel, *Ca n'a rien a voir: Lire Freud en philosophe* (Paris: Les Éditions du Cerf, 2018b).

Fenichel, Teresa, "Pussywhipped: Unteaching Nietzsche on Woman and Truth," in *misReading Nietzsche*, eds. M Saverio Clemente and Bryan J Cocchiara (Eugene, OR: Pickwick Publications, 2018), 29–41.

Freud, Sigmund, *Three Essays on Sexuality* in *The Standard Edition of the Complete Psychological Works of Sigmund Freud*, trans. James Strachey, vol. VII (London: Hogarth, 1953).

Freud, Sigmund, *Beyond the Pleasure Principle*, trans. Gregory C. Richter, ed. Todd Dufresne (Peterborough, ON: Broadview Editions, 2011).

Freud, Sigmund, *Civilization and Its Discontents*, trans. James Strachey (New York: WW Norton, 1962).

James, William, *The Varieties of Religious Experience: A Study in Human Nature* (London: Longman, 1905).

Kearney, Richard, "God Making: Theopoetics and Anatheism," in *The Art of Anatheism*, eds. Richard Kearney and Matthew Clemente (London: Rowman & Littlefield, 2017), 3–28.

Kierkegaard, Søren, *Fear and Trembling*, trans. Howard Hong and Edna Hong (Princeton: Princeton University Press, 1983).

Kristeva, Julia, "Mysticism and Anatheism: The Case of Teresa," in *Richard Kearney's Anatheistic Wager: Philosophy, Theology, Poetics*, eds. Chris Doude van Troostwijk and Matthew Clemente (Bloomington: Indiana University Press, 2018), 68–87.

Lacan, Jacques, *Encore: The Seminar of Jacques Lacan Book XX: On Feminine Sexuality, the Limits of Love and Knowledge*, trans. Bruce Fink (New York: WW Norton, 1999).

Lacan, Jacques, *Ecrits: The First Complete Edition in English*, trans. Bruce Fink (New York: WW Norton, 2007).

LaCocque, André and Paul Ricoeur (eds.), *Thinking Biblically: Exegetical and Hermeneutical Studies*, trans. David Pellauer (Chicago: University of Chicago Press, 1998).

Manoussakis, John, *The Ethics of Time* (London: Bloomsbury, 2017).

Manoussakis, John, "Sacred Addictions: On the Phenomenology of Religious Experience," in *the Journal of Speculative Philosophy*, vol. 33, no. 1 (2019), 41–55.

Marion, Jean-Luc, *The Erotic Phenomenon*, trans. Stephen E. Lewis (Chicago: University of Chicago Press, 2007).

Nietzsche, Friedrich, *The Birth of Tragedy*, trans. Walter Kaufmann (New York: Vintage, 1967).

Nietzsche, Friedrich, *The Gay Science*, trans. Walter Kaufmann (New York: Vintage, 1974).

Nietzsche, Friedrich, *Beyond Good and Evil*, trans. Walter Kaufmann (New York: Vintage, 1989).

Sweeney, Conor, "Bodily Love and the *Imago Trinitatis*," in *God and Eros*, eds. Colin Patterson and Conor Sweeney (Eugene, OR: Cascade Books, 2015), 107–122.

Žižek, Slavoj, *The Puppet and the Dwarf* (Cambridge, MA: MIT Press, 2003).

PART I

Creation: A theological aesthetic

For my beloved

If touch awakens flesh and soul
And touching part touches the whole
Then wake me with your sacred flesh
And bless me with your love-caress.

Kiss with mouth both chaste and true.
Whisper songs ancient and new.
Nurse with overflowing breasts.
And in your arms give restless rest.

With lilac perfume earth and air.
Let song birds nest within your hair.
Your belly, plump and ripe with fruit.
Your body sings. Your lips are mute.

With toes and teeth and finger tips
A child wraps about your hips.
He knows the mystery inside.
Mother. Lover. Holy Bride.

1

OEDIPUS AND ADAM

The genesis of Eros and the infancy of man

During a recent reading of *Beyond the Pleasure Principle*, I was struck by the fact that, as the final pages approach, Freud shifts from a scientific analysis of drive theory to a more philosophical musing on two ancient myths. First, he discusses the Platonic myth found in the *Symposium* which links the drive for sexual union with a desire to return to an earlier state of human existence, a time when a third type of human—neither male nor female but fully both—walked the earth. Then in a footnote, he quotes from a similar narrative found in the *Upanishads* which describes the splitting of Yājñavalkya—an individual "so large as man and wife together"—into two separate individuals: a husband and wife. What attracted my attention was not Freud's decision to include these stories; as he himself notes, both myths hint at the regressive character of the drives, the need to restore an earlier state, the compulsion to repeat. In this context, his choice to use them for the purposes of illustration makes sense. What interested me, however, was that with these two lesser-known myths, Freud opts not to mention a third, more prominent one—one which also points to the desire to restore an earlier state. I am speaking, of course, of the Adamic myth found in the Book of Genesis.

In a 1911 letter to Jung, Freud questions the credibility of the Adamic myth. Commenting on the narrative which serves as the foundational text for the three Abrahamic religions, Freud calls the myth "a wretched, tendentious distortion devised by an apprentice priest."[1] He asserts that it is nothing more than the remnants of two separate stories woven together to form a single narrative, observes that "there is something very strange and singular about the creation of Eve," and later concludes that "the surface versions of myths cannot be used uncritically for comparison."[2] Here, one might think, we find Freud's reason for not employing the Adamic myth when analyzing the drive to repeat. The creation of Adam from inorganic clay, the creation of Eve from the rib of Adam, the prelapsarian paradise in which they live, their subsequent banishment from that paradise, the constant search in the Abrahamic tradition for a Messiah who will return man to his earlier, unblemished state—all of this seems analogous to Freud's theory of the regressive nature of the drives. Yet perhaps he neglects these obvious connections because, as he states, he believes the author of the myth to be biased and untrustworthy.

No. For, Freud himself notes that the myths which he does include are of "a fantastical kind,"[3] that they are merely "analogies,"[4] and that, like all thinkers who seek to answer ultimate questions, he is not impartial but "dominated by deep-rooted internal prejudices."[5] He plainly acknowledges that the narratives used are meant to shed a poetic light on the scientific reality of the regressive nature of the drives. And he openly admits to using "figurative language" in order to get at truths which are not yet biologically verifiable. (An admission, by the way, which many devotees of sciencism—today's most prevalent religion— refuse to make; namely, that scientific "truths" can only be expressed through, and are thus subject to, metaphor and language).[6] If this is the case, why then does Freud neglect the Adamic myth? Why does he avoid a narrative which appears to be wholly analogous to his claim that the essential character of the drives is regressive?

The primacy of death: At the limits of philosophy

In *Beyond the Pleasure Principle*, Freud asserts that the biological progression of all life can be seen as the movement from nonliving matter to living being to death, a return to the inanimate state from which life first arose. The drive to repeat, then, is a movement back toward a lifeless beginning, a repetition which leads the living organism closer to its primary, inorganic stasis. According to Freud, the state which the repetition compulsion unconsciously seeks to recapture is "an old state, an original state that the living being has left at some time, and toward which it strives to return through all the detours of evolution."[7] Yet for Freud, there can be no state older, none more originary, than the lifeless itself:

> If we may accept as an observation without exception that every living being dies for *internal* reasons, returning to the inorganic, then we can only say that *the goal of all life is death*, and, looking backwards, that the nonliving existed before the living.[8]

All life tends back toward the death from which it came.

From a Freudian perspective, then, death is primary. Life represents a brief interruption in the inorganic—death—but it inevitably returns to its original, inanimate state. This, we must admit, is not only a philosophically defensible position but represents *the* philosophical position on the origin of life, the one to which those who wish to remain within the confines of philosophy must adhere. Indeed, at the very foundation of philosophy, just prior to the death of Socrates, we find it being argued in the most empathic of terms that "what comes from being dead … is being alive" (*Phaedo* 71d) and all subsequent philosophies have taken death—corruption, degeneration, falling away (think of the Plotinian *katastrophē*)—as their starting point. According to Freud, life arises out of nonliving matter "through the influence of a completely inconceivable force."[9] And whether you call that force "the Good," "the One," or "the Unmoved Mover" matters little, the point remains the same: life comes from death and longs to return to it.

It is for this reason, I suspect, that Freud neglects the Adamic myth. For, while the Greek and Hindu understandings of the cosmos give credence to this assumption—in Greek mythology Chaos, the primordial void, precedes the existence of the world; in Hindu Vedic cosmology, time is cyclical, existence arises out of nothingness and fades back to it in a constant ebb and flow—the Genesis narrative stands in stark opposition to it. Contrary to the philosophical perspective, Genesis asserts that the world was created by a personal, loving Godhead with a definite plan and purpose and, what is more, that it was created good. (Though, of course, we could say that because God created the world *ex nihilo*, nonexistence is in a very real sense the deepest reality of the created world, that ours is a world "bordering on nothingness.")[10] Thus while the Freudian assumption is that death is primary—that existence moves from death to life back to death—the Abrahamic tradition posits that life is primary—that existence moves from the fullness of life in God to created life which is subsequently interrupted by death back to the fullness of life, the redemption of creation by its Creator. One view is purely philosophical. The other is theological. The first is attained through reason, the second through revelation.

From the first pages of this work, we have made it clear that, though we speak as philosophers, we will not shy away from theological speculation. Indeed, as Nietzsche often reminds us, we must "guard against the snares of such contradictory concepts as 'pure reason,' 'absolute spirituality,' 'knowledge in itself.'"[11] Rather, it is better to admit with Freud that "each person is dominated by deep-rooted internal prejudices"[12] and that none of us have a monopoly on the truth, especially when it comes to matters as mysterious as the origin of life.[13] Let us then acknowledge our willingness to take up and consider thoughts that come from beyond the boundaries of pure philosophical thinking. Let us say that, "given the present obscurity in the theory of drives, it would be inadvisable to reject any idea that promises to enlighten,"[14] even if that idea comes from scripture. Let us utilize the myth that Freud himself neglects, the Adamic myth found in Genesis, and consider what, if anything, it can tell us about the insights garnered from philosophical and psychoanalytic thought.

The primacy of life: Beyond the limits

In *Beyond the Pleasure Principle*, Freud picks up and further examines the dualistic theory of the drives which is prevalent throughout his corpus. As his views evolve, develop, and become more nuanced, he begins to see the drives as existing between the poles of Eros, the sexually charged life drive, and what later commentators would term Thanatos, the purely destructive death drive.[15] Recounting the progression of his thought, Freud writes:

> [T]he sex drive transformed itself for us into Eros, which seeks to push together and hold together parts of a living substance.... These speculations then have Eros operating from the beginning of life and acting as a "life drive" in contrast to the "death drive," which arose through the animation of the inorganic. These speculations seek to solve the riddle of life by assuming these two drives struggling with each other from the very beginning.[16]

For Freud, Eros is a drive which serves to further life by seeking the union of separate beings—be it the union of cells which make up a living organism or the union of organisms which reproduce life in their offspring. The death drive, on the other hand, seeks the oblivion of the living being by returning it, through death, back to its original, inorganic state. Thus from a Freudian perspective—a perspective which holds that existence moves from death to life to death—Eros acts as a "detour to death" which interrupts Thanatos's regression back to nonbeing. Death, the end of all tension, is pleasurable. Eros, which awakens tension in nonliving matter by awakening life, is beyond the pleasure principle.

If, however, we reexamine Freud's drive theory by altering its premise, if we begin with the scriptural assumption that the movement of life is from Creator to creation through death to Creator, then we will conclude upon an entirely different understanding of the drives. For, if the Alpha and the Omega, the first and the last, the beginning and the end of all things is Life itself (see, Revelation 22:13; John 14:6), then we must conclude that Eros and not Thanatos is the regressive drive. After all, the regressive drive seeks to reproduce an old state, an original state which the living being left at some time. If, then, we accept the assertion that all life comes from the Godhead, that the Godhead is the source of life, then we can only say that *the goal of all life is life* and, looking backwards, that the living existed before the nonliving.

That we have now offered a hypothesis which represents the exact opposite of the one expressed by Freud ought not to surprise us. After all, we began our analysis by inverting his base premise. More surprising, however, may be our next assertion. For, if we hold Eros to be the regressive drive because the beginning of all life is God who is Life itself and thus any movement toward life must necessarily be a regressive movement, then we must maintain, simultaneously and paradoxically, that Eros is also progressive. For, God stands not only at the beginning but also at the end of all life. Thus the erotic tendency is one which seeks to repeat an earlier state—the Alpha, the first, the beginning of all things—but it is also one which looks forward to, progresses toward, prefigures a final state the Omega, the last, the end of all things. Eros longs to recapture prelapsarian existence while simultaneously striving toward eschatological beatitude. It is the life drive and the goal of all life is life.

At first glance, it may seem that our discovery of the paradoxical nature of Eros as a drive which is simultaneously regressive and progressive has undone the Freudian duality mentioned above. To some extent it has. But ought we now to conclude that there is no death drive? If the life drive is both regressive and progressive, ought we to assert that Thanatos has been done away with? Not at all. For, like Freud, we must acknowledge that the existence of a purely destructive drive toward death is experientially verifiable. Episodes such as war trauma attest to its reality.[17]

But what is the function of this death drive? Where does it come from and how does it operate? If the beginning and end of life is life and death is an interruption into life then death must be assumed to be derivative. Unlike Freud, who sees Eros and Thanatos as "struggling with each other from the very beginning,"[18] we now assert that death has inserted itself into life as a perversion, not an equal.[19] But in order to understand how this came to be, we must return to an earlier state. We must begin at the beginning. Thus we will leave our discussion of the death drive here and detour, by way of the Adamic myth, back to a time before death entered the world, to the paradisal existence of the Garden—an existence which we all long to recapture.

Myths of origin

In *Totem and Taboo*, Freud posits a hypothetical account of how the Oedipus complex may have first manifested itself in the human psyche. Theorizing that the complex originally resulted in the patricide of a primitive, dominant father at the hands of his sons, he writes:

> One day the brothers who had been driven out came together, killed and devoured their father and so made an end of the patriarchal horde. United, they had the courage to do and succeeded in doing what would have been impossible for them individually.... The violent primal father had doubtless been the feared and envied model of each one of the company of brothers: and in the act of devouring him they accomplished their identification with him, and each one of them acquired a portion of his strength. The totem meal, which is perhaps mankind's earliest festival, would thus be a repetition and a commemoration of this memorable and criminal deed, which was the beginning of so many things—of social organization, of moral restrictions and of religion.[20]

We will return to this Freudian myth shortly. For now, however, we ought to note that Freud opts once again to neglect the Adamic narrative; he chooses to construct a speculative account of the first manifestation of the Oedipus complex rather than testing his theory on the already prevalent story of origin.

While the connection to the scriptural narrative is less apparent here than it is with the regressive theory of the drives, we see indications from the first mention of the creation of man—"the Lord God formed the man out of the dust of the ground and blew into his nostrils the breath of life, and the man became a living being" (Genesis 2:7)—that a Freudian psychoanalytic account of man's constitution can be applied. At the moment of his creation, man saw himself as at one with all that existed. As a product of the earth, he was linked to the whole of creation.[21] Unlike the world itself, which was created *ex nihilo*, man was created out of creation. Thus from his beginning he was tied to that from which he was made (see, "you are dust, and to dust you shall return" (Genesis 3:19)). But in addition to this connection with creation, man also shared a unique bond with his Creator. After all, it was God's breath that filled his nostrils and provided him with life. Thus the Genesis text makes clear that the prelapsarian man's original constitution was one of intimate connectedness with the entirety of existence, both created and uncreated.[22]

How does this sense of undelineated unity experienced by the first man relate to Freudian psychoanalytic thought? Freud begins *Civilization and Its Discontents* by relating a critique of his *The Future of an Illusion* offered by his friend Romain Rolland:

> [Rolland] entirely agreed with my judgment upon religion, but … he was sorry I had not properly appreciated the true source of religious sentiments. This, he says, consists in a peculiar feeling, which he is never without, which he finds confirmed by others, and which he may suppose is present in millions of people. It is a feeling which he would like to call a sensation of 'eternity,' a feeling as of something limitless, unbounded—as it were, 'oceanic.'[23]

This oceanic feeling, Freud later concludes, is nothing more than a regression by the individual to his most infantile state.[24] It is a longing for and movement toward the primary stage in the development of life, a time when one experienced "a more intimate bond between the ego and the world about it."[25] In the earliest experiences of infancy, an individual does not yet identify himself as distinct from the outer world. Rather he feels a sensation of "eternity," an unbounded connection with all things: "originally the ego includes everything, later it separates off an external world from itself."[26] "An infant at the breast does not as yet distinguish his ego from the external world as the source of the sensations flowing in upon him. He gradually learns to do so, in response to various promptings."[27]

For Freud, the oceanic feeling described by Rolland is nothing more than a return to the mode of existence that preceded such promptings, a movement back toward the unboundedness of infancy. This feeling of limitlessness which Freud believes to be experienced in the infancy of the individual is described in Genesis as having been experienced in the infancy of mankind. Just as a newborn neglects to distinguish himself from his mother's breast (the outside world), so too did the first man neglect to individuate himself from the entirety of existence. In the Genesis text, the Adamic figure is not identified as distinct, separate, or alone until after God has handed down his command not to eat from the tree at the center of the Garden (Genesis 2:18). Prior to that, he had felt himself to be at one with all that existed.

Law and individuation

As was stated above, Freud's oedipal theory posits the introduction of various external promptings as the main cause for the individual's first recognition of himself as distinct from the outer world. Of these promptings, the earliest and most significant is the imposition of the law by the child's father. After birth, the infant seeks the full gratification of his desires through unrestricted access to his mother's breast. But this unrestricted access is restricted when the father intervenes; he imposes a law upon the child in the form of a prohibition by saying "No" to the child's desire for full gratification. He restricts the child's unlimited contact with the mother. Once the imposition is put in place, the infant is confronted by the raw otherness of his mother—his mOther, as Lacan famously put it. The infant no longer sees himself as at one with her breast. Rather he begins to distinguish his ego from the external world. In doing so, he recognizes his uniqueness from the rest of existence and develops what Freud terms the "original *reality-ego*," an ego which "distinguishes outer and inner by means of a sound objective reality."[28]

This account of the genesis of the individual is strikingly similar to the account found in Genesis of the first man's recognition of himself as distinct from the rest of creation. In the scriptural text, the Adamic man is confronted by his first external individuating encounter when "The Lord God gave the man this order: You are free to eat from any of the trees of the garden except the tree of knowledge of good and evil. From that tree you shall not eat; when you eat from it you shall die" (Genesis 2:16–17). In the command handed down from God we clearly see a parallel to the Freudian theory of the imposition of the law by the oedipal father. The first man—the child in oedipal terms—was originally constituted with an oceanic feeling of unrestricted access to the whole of existence. He felt intimately connected with all things and thus saw no difference between himself and the outer world.[29] But once he encountered the restriction placed upon his desire for infinite gratification by God—the oedipal father—he immediately distinguished himself from the rest of creation.[30] And it was at this point that the drive to restore an earlier state, the regressive side of Eros, was first felt by man.

This becomes all the more evident when we consider that, immediately following his decree, God observed, "It is not good for the man to be alone. I will make a helper suited to him" (Genesis 2:18). Prior to the imposition of the first law, there is no textual mention of the fact that the man was alone. Rather, he saw himself as united to the earth from which he was made and to the God from whom he received the breath of life. Following the emergence of the law, however, the Adamic man began to distinguish himself from everything else. (For instance, in Genesis 2:19 he names the various animals formed by God. The naming of creatures is a clear recognition on the part of the first man that those creatures are external to, and not at one with, his existence. Only after he sees that they are separate from him does he feel the need to give them distinct names). Moreover, it was at this point that Eve—the suitable partner with whom the first man could be united and thus mimic the union he had previously felt with the whole of existence—was created.

It now becomes clear that, in oedipal terms, the imposition of the law by God (the father figure) acted as an external prompting which caused the first man (the infant) to recognize himself as distinct from the entirety of existence thus destroying his oceanic feeling of connectedness with the whole world (his oneness with his mother's breast). Just as the child first recognizes his own autonomy because of the restriction imposed upon him from without, so too did the Adamic man first understand his isolation and individuation after God commanded that he not eat from the tree of knowledge.

The sins of space and time

For Freud, the restriction placed upon the child's unimpeded access to his mother by his father marks not only the first instance of individuation for the child but also the first instance of internal conflict. Never before has the infant been told "No." Never before has he been restricted. He must now deal with the frustration brought on by the fact that his father has stolen from him that which he desires most: full gratification. In doing so, his father has forced particularity and limitation upon what had previously seemed like an infinite existence. Hatred wells up in the child. He desires to kill his father. And yet something within him still loves and admires the man who protects him. Turmoil rages within. This inner conflict constitutes much of the individual's mental life. From his infancy through his adulthood, his internal constitution consists of dealing with this perpetual struggle.

Although the *Genesis* narrative neglects to explicitly mention whether or not the Adamic man harbored conflicted feelings toward God, it is clear from his actions that, following the imposition of the law, the first man's constitution was radically altered. The moment he was made aware of his own uniqueness was the moment he became conscious. And that moment marked both the beginning of man's existence as body and the beginning of his temporality.[31] It introduced man to the distinctions of space and time. First, it individuated man in space. Because God's command marked off a single tree from every other—"From *that tree* you shall not eat"—it revealed to man the otherness of each individual thing, unsettling the quasi-Thalesian unity he had previously known. The introduction of the law made man *the one who shall not eat from the tree*, thereby underscoring his radical alterity and isolating him from the world around him, the world that was not him, a foreign world, unfamiliar, alien, unknown.

But in addition to this physical individuation, God's decree also sparked in man the awareness of his finite temporality. For, when the law was imposed, man was awakened to the fact that he exists at an in-between. He exists in time. After the imposition of the law, he first recognized a past—the time before the law—and became aware of a future—his desire to ultimately restore a past which no longer existed. He was not at the beginning nor had he reached his end but was in the middle, in time, finite, limited, isolated, alone.

In note 29 of this chapter we see that for Augustine, God's imposition of the law revealed to man the fundamental experience of his primordial separation, the sin of his being distinct, other, separate from God. Manoussakis, commenting on the *Confessions*, draws our attention to "Augustine's emphasis on the literal meaning of infancy, as his 'unspeaking stage' in life" in order to clarify this very point.[32] Certainly it was an odd choice for the Bishop of Hippo to begin his *Confessions* with a discussion of "my earliest days and my infancy, which I do not remember."[33] Why, one might ask, would Augustine find it necessary to confess that which he had done as an infant? Why confess that of which he has no memory, that for which he cannot reasonably be held responsible, that for which he ought to feel neither shame nor guilt?

Like Freud, Augustine insists that we never possessed the type of mythical purity we often associate with infancy.[34] For both men, our attempt to recapture a youthful innocence which we once experienced but have since lost is a vain illusion. (Listen to the facetious tone Freud takes on when summarizing the dominant cultural view: "Children are pure and innocent, and anyone who describes them otherwise can be charged with being an infamous blasphemer against the tender and sacred feelings of mankind. Children are alone in not falling in with these conventions").[35] We were never pure. We were never good. The infant's "oceanic" feeling is just that: a feeling.[36] It was never a reality. No infant is actually one with all that is. Each of us is always already separate, always already alone: "Who is there to remind me of my infancy (for sin there was: no one is free from sin in your sight, not even an infant whose span of earthly life is but a single day)?"[37]

According to Manoussakis, Augustine sees man's separation, fallenness, sin as manifesting itself first "in the distinction within/without, inside/outside.... The first experience of fallenness is the separation from others, in terms of a distance in space."[38] That which is not God is separate from God. And space is the most obvious sign of man's separation. (Think of how Augustine's inability to conceive of God in anything but spatial terms distances him from God).[39] For Augustine, the infant's existence in space, his distinctness, his individuation inhibits him from being at one with the other (especially the divine Other). Space implies distance. I am me and not you because I am here and you are there. If I were here and you were here—if we were to both occupy the same space— then we would both be me or we would both be you. The distinction between self and other would collapse. But this is impossible. Space separates. It isolates. It forces us apart.

For Augustine, the infant is the least equipped to deal with such isolation because, as his name implies, he is "incapable of speech." The one who cannot speak, the *in-fant* (Latin), is the one most secluded within himself. "Little by little I began to notice *where* I was and I would try to make my wishes known to those who might satisfy them; but I was frustrated in this, because my desires were *inside me*, while other people were *outside* and could by no effort of understanding enter my mind."[40] It is this recognition of *where he is* that causes him to begin to identify his otherness from the world around him. The infant finds himself in sin when he notices that others, who are not where he is, exist outside, that they are not him, and that they cannot intuitively know his desires, they cannot enter his mind.

Yet if space is that which divides us from the other, it is not the sole individuating factor. "To this one, immediately, Augustine adds a second one: the separation from oneself, in terms of a distance in time."[41] For Augustine, the second sign that the infant is fallen and thus in sin is temporality. "My infancy has been so long dead now, whereas I am alive. But you, O Lord, are ever living and in you nothing dies, for you existed before the dawn of the ages and before anything that can be called 'before.'"[42] Here Augustine draws our attention to the radical dissimilarity between his own temporal being and the eternal being of the ever-living God. For God, "to be and to live are not two different realities, since supreme being and supreme life are one and the same."[43] But this cannot be said of man. For, if man's being and his life were the same then Augustine would not only remember his infancy, but would find his infancy still present to him today. The fact that man is in time and time is in man means that man is separated from God who is timeless,[44] from others ("our ancestors") with whom he shares continuity but not unity, and from himself—a self "so long dead," continually dying as it fades further and further into a nonexistent past.

Augustine sums up the sin of separation made evident by our individuation in space and time when he asks, "And if I was even conceived in iniquity, and with sin my mother nourished me in her womb, *where*, I beg of you, my God, *where* was I, your servant, ever innocent? *Where,* Lord, and *when?*"[45] The answer to this question, as we have seen, is the answer provided by Freud, the answer offered by our reading Genesis—we were never truly innocent, never "limitless, unbounded—as it were, 'oceanic,'" never connected to the whole of existence as the Adamic man believed. "Both experiences, separation from others, namely space, and separation from oneself, namely time, are but two aspects of the same condition, of the *diastemic* [i.e. distanced, separated] nature of the fallen creation."[46]

Eat and you shall die: The birth of Thanatos

Following his recognition of his separation and individuation from the world outside him, from his God, and even from himself, the Adamic man was then separated further: "So the Lord God cast a deep sleep on the man, and while he was asleep, he took out one of his ribs and closed up its place with flesh. The Lord

God then built the rib that he had taken from the man into a woman" (Genesis 2:21–22). The first man was undoubtedly pleased with his father figure for having provided him with a companion—one who, by their communal life together, could help him to transcend his finite individuation and begin to satisfy his erotic drive toward unity. The language of oneness with which he describes the first woman tells us as much: "This one, at last, is bone of my bones and flesh of my flesh; This one shall be called 'woman,' for out of man this one has been taken" (Genesis 2:23). Yet though he now had a suitable partner, he did not have the full, unrestricted infinity which he desired most of all. He was still limited, still finite, still lacking. His regressive Eros still longed to recapture the time before the imposition of the law. His progressive Eros still drove him forward toward a life lived more abundantly. He could not achieve a repetition of his original state and had yet to reach the eschatological fulfillment of his perfection. He was no longer at the beginning, not yet at the end, restricted by space and time—but he longed to be as limitless as God.... Enter the serpent.

In Genesis 3 we are introduced to the story's great antagonist, the most cunning of all animals, the serpent. From the time of the earliest scriptural exegetes, the serpent has been identified with Satan. For our purposes, however, it is more important to recognize him as the one who gave voice to the internal struggle which had taken root in the heart of the first man.[47] Though the text speaks of the snake as in dialogue with the woman, it also makes note of the fact that "her husband ... was with her" (Genesis 3:6). We can infer, then, that when the serpent asked "Did God really say, 'You shall not eat from any of the trees in the garden'?" (Genesis 3:1), he stated aloud a question that had haunted the Adamic man from the moment the first law was imposed: *why has God restricted me?* The woman—who was created after the imposition of the law—replied by explaining God's command (see, Genesis 3:2–3). The man, however, remained silent. He could not speak. For, the serpent had given voice to his innermost struggle. His Creator had restricted him, cut off his feeling of unity, left his erotic drive toward the abundance of life unfulfilled—and for that he hated his Creator. Yet his Creator had created him, provided him with a companion, given him dominion over the earth—and for that he loved his Creator. The internal conflict raged on.

At this point it is important to return to the Freudian Totemic myth quoted above. We ought now to note that one of the key tenets of Freud's theory is the recognition by the child that, in the face of his father's restriction, he is helpless. Though he may be frustrated and internally conflicted, though he may hate his father, though he may even desire to kill his father, he also realizes that he is weaker than his father. And thus he is unable to resist the enforcement of the law. This discrepancy between the strength of the restrictor and the weakness of the restricted is lessened, however, when the child finds himself among companions who harbor similar resentments toward their father. Freud quotes Atkinson:

> The patriarch had only one enemy whom he should dread ... a youthful band of brothers living together in forced celibacy [i.e. with a restricted,

> unsatisfied erotic drive].... A horde as yet weak in their impubescence
> they are, but they would, when strength was gained with time, inevitably
> wrench by combined attacks, renewed again and again, both wife and life
> from the paternal tyrant.[48]

When faced with the reality that they as individuals are too weak to overcome
the restrictions put in place by their dominant father, the Totemic children join
together in rebellion. "United, they [have] the courage to do and succeeded in
doing what would have been impossible for them individually."[49] They kill their
father and—in an attempt to satisfy their oedipal drive toward oceanic oneness—
reclaim access to their mother.

Returning now to the Genesis narrative, we find that we are confronted by yet
another striking similarity. Frustrated by the fact that he had been truncated, individuated, cut off from infinity, and forced to live under the law, the Adamic man
harbored hatred toward God. Recognizing this hatred in her companion, the first
woman began to feel isolated from her partner. For, hatred is the opposite of Eros
and its drive for unity. Where Eros unites, hatred divides. The first woman thus
identified her own distinctness from the man whose rib had given her life. Upon
hearing the man's discontent voiced through the mouth of the snake, she too began
to build up resentment toward her Creator. Filled with malice, the two banned
together in murderous rebellion against their heavenly Father.

> [T]he snake [voicing the desires of Adam] said to the woman: "You cer-
> tainly will not die! God knows well that when you eat of it your eyes
> will be opened and you will be like gods, who know good and evil." The
> woman saw that the tree was good for food and pleasing to the eyes, and
> the tree was desirable for gaining wisdom. So she took some of its fruit
> and ate it; and she also gave some to her husband, who was with her, and
> he ate it.
>
> *(Genesis 3:4–6)*

This first instance of human pride constituted nothing short of the attempted
murder of God. For, what is sin but an attempt to destroy God and replace him
with the self?[50] Implicit in such an act is, of course, the assertion that God is
not the greatest good—that the will of the self is greater than the will of God.
But a God whose will could be so easily usurped is a God whose will is flawed.
And a God with a flawed will is himself flawed, destructible, subject to decay.
Thus when the first man preferred himself to his God and chose himself over
and against his God, he banned together with the first woman and the two
attempted history's first patricide—or, to be more accurate, history's first dei-
cide.[51] (As Meister Eckhart notes, to sin against God is to "do violence to God
and kill Him.")[52]

In short, the original sin was the Adamic spouses' attempt to make gods out of
themselves: "you will be like gods." But what does this mean, *to make gods out of*

themselves? It can only mean that they perverted their erotic drive by attempting to fulfill its end by their own means. Their drive for life was a drive for communion, a drive toward godliness. But godliness can only be gained through unity, connectedness, oneness with him who is Life itself. And it can only be accomplished on his terms. By attempting to bring about self-divinization, they perverted their Eros and, in its place, introduced death into the world. Thanatos was born. In this purely destructive act, the drive toward death made itself manifest. It has plagued the human psyche ever since.

Thanatos, then, is neither regressive nor progressive. It is perversion. It is sin. It seeks to accomplish the abundance of life sought by Eros on its own terms. Eros is a unitive drive. It is a drive that necessitates otherness, a drive that finds its fulfillment in communion with the other. Further, it is a drive which seeks to redeem the whole of human history. From its place in the present, its regressive nature harkens back to the moment of Creation while its progressive nature extends forward toward the Eschaton. Thanatos is a movement away from communion, a purely destructive drive which seeks to undo unity. Unlike Eros, which affirms the goodness of time, Thanatos denies temporality by attempting to bring about the end goal *here and now,* by means of itself. It refuses to allow the end to unfold in the fullness of time.[53] While the regressive and progressive tendencies of Eros are satisfied from *without*—by a God who restores man to glory and delivers him to eschatological beatitude—the perversion of Thanatos seeks self-fulfillment, self-glorification, self-actualization which can only result in self-destruction. Eros is led to life by the other. Thanatos is led to death by the self. Eros is grace from without. Thanatos is sin from within. Eros is the fullness of time and the unity of existence. Thanatos is the negation of time and the void of nothingness. And as Freud notes—sounding oddly reminiscent Milton: "It was from out the rind of one apple tasted, that the knowledge of good and evil, as two twins cleaving together, leaped forth into the world"— these two drives have struggled and will struggle in the heart of man so long as he walks this earth.

Notes

1 Freud and Jung, *The Freud/Jung Letters*, 288.
2 Ibid.
3 Freud, *Beyond the Pleasure Principle*, 93.
4 Ibid., 97.
5 Ibid., 96.
6 Rowan Williams, in the Preface to his book on Dostoevsky, does a nice job unpacking this very point. See Williams, *Dostoevsky: Language, Faith, and Fiction*, ix–xiii.
7 Freud, *Beyond the Pleasure Principle*, 77.
8 Ibid.
9 Ibid.
10 Augustine, *Confessions*, (12.7.7).
11 Nietzsche, *On the Genealogy of Morals*, (3, §12).
12 Freud, *Beyond the Pleasure Principle*, 96.

13 Freud himself gestures to the limits of his own perspective when he writes that it was "through the influence of *a completely inconceivable force* [that] the characteristics of life were awakened in non-living matter." Ibid., 77 (emphasis mine).

14 Ibid., 90.

15 "From the beginning, our conception has been *dualistic* and is today even more dualistic than before, now that we no longer describe the opposition as existing between ego drives and sex drives, but as existing between life drives and death drives." Freud, *Beyond the Pleasure Principle*, 89.

16 Ibid., 97.

17 See, Freud's detailed analysis of war trauma. Ibid., 55–60.

18 Ibid., 97.

19 As Paul-Louis Landsberg writes, "Coming as it does from a foreign sphere, death appears as *an intrusion* into our existence." As quoted in Bradatan, *Dying for Ideas*, 70.

20 Freud, *Totem and Taboo*, 141–142.

21 This point is emphasized by Genesis 2:5, which notes that prior to the creation of man "there was no field shrub on earth and no grass of the field had sprouted, for the Lord God had sent no rain upon the earth and there was no man to till the ground." Thus, prior to man's creation, the "dust of the ground"—from which man was made—composed the whole of the created world.

22 Cf. "Neither Eve nor Paradise were yet created, but *the whole world* had been brought into being by God *as one thing*, as a kind of paradise, at once incorruptible yet material and perceptible. *It was this world … which was given to Adam.*" Symeon the New Theologian, *On the Mystical Life*, 21 (emphasis mine).

23 Freud, *Civilization and Its Discontents*, 24.

24 Ibid., 29.

25 Ibid.

26 Ibid.

27 Ibid., 27.

28 Freud, "Instincts and Their Vicissitudes," 89.

29 It is important to note that the first man merely *felt* connected to the whole of existence and thus did not identify himself as separate and distinct from it. But he was not actually one with all. Thus the first law caused him to recognize his individuality. It did not individuate him because, unbeknownst to him, he was already individuated. Cf.

> Therefore we must understand that the law was given not to introduce sin [i.e. separation] nor extirpate it, but simply to make it known.… Sin [i.e. separation] … existed before the law, but did not reach its full sinfulness because there was so far no violation of a law.
>
> *(Augustine,* Earlier Writings*, 377)*

I read Augustine here as understanding "sin" as the ontological sin of being separate from God. I do not take it that he means the moral sin, "full sinfulness," of disobedience. More on this in the pages to come.

30 Cf. "Nor can the creature … ever know wherein it specifically is different from God. Only the light of revelation can draw this distinction and make this clear." Balthasar, *The Theology of Karl Barth*, 279.

31 As Manoussakis notes, consciousness both constitutes and is constituted by the "homology between the bodily and the temporal." See,

> We could say now without further delay that what makes the difference between reflective and unreflective consciousness, between the consciousness of itself, and the consciousness of the world and its manifestations, is nothing else than the *body*. Yet, we would be equally right in saying that what makes the difference

between reflective and unreflective consciousness is nothing else than *time* ... a time that is ultimately grounded in the consciousness itself.

(The Ethics of Time, *107*)

32 Ibid., 81.
33 Augustine, *Confessions*, (1.6.10).
34 For more on the connection between Augustine and Freud, see Manoussakis, *Gazing at the Medieval Unconscious: An Augustinian Retrieval* presented at the *Psychology & the Other Conference*, Lesley University (Cambridge, MA) on October 4, 2013.
35 Freud, *Introductory Lectures on Psychoanalysis*, 312.
36 Freud, *Civilization and Its Discontents*, 24.
37 Augustine, *Confessions*, (1.7.11). Kierkegaard agrees: "even though the child does not sin, because it is not conscious of its existence as such, its existence, from the point of view of the idea, is nevertheless sin, and the ethical makes its claim upon it at all times." *Fear and Trembling*, 62.
38 Manoussakis, *The Ethics of Time*, 81.
39 See,

> When I wanted to think about my God I did not know how to think otherwise than in terms of bodily size, for whatever did not answer to this description seemed to me to be nothing at all. This misapprehension was the chief and almost sole cause of the error I could not avoid.
>
> *(Augustine,* Confessions, *[5.10.19])*

40 Ibid., (1.6.8) (emphasis mine).
41 Manoussakis, *The Ethics of Time*, 81.
42 Augustine, *Confessions*, (1.6.9).
43 Ibid., (1.6.10).
44 See,

> How many of our days and our ancestors' days have come and gone in this 'Today' of yours, have received from it their manner of being and have existed after their fashion, and how many others will likewise receive theirs, and exist in their own way? Yet you are the selfsame: all our tomorrows and beyond, all our yesterdays and further back, you will make in your Today, you have made in your Today.
>
> *(Ibid.)*

45 Ibid., (1.7.12) (emphasis mine).
46 Manoussakis, *The Ethics of Time*, 81.
47 Cf. Kierkegaard's assertion that the serpent "is language, and also it is Adam himself who speaks." Kierkegaard, *The Concept of Anxiety*, 47.
48 Freud, *Totem and Taboo*, 142.
49 Ibid., 141.
50 Cf.

> [E]ven in their very sins souls are only striving for a certain likeness to God in their proud, perverted and so to speak, servile liberty. Thus our first parents could not have been persuaded to sin if it had not been said to them: "You shall be as gods."
>
> *(Augustine, On the Trinity, [11.5.8])*

51 And we must acknowledge that Freud was in fact correct in saying that this "memorable and criminal deed ... was the beginning of so many things—of social organization, of moral restrictions and of religion." Freud, *Totem and Taboo*, 142.

52 As quoted in Balthasar, *The Glory of the Lord, vol. 5*, 38.
53 As Manoussakis states:

> [F]allen imperfection is the result of our failure to accept our original imperfection, that is, the very fact of having an origin, a beginning, while, looking toward the future; fallen imperfection is the result of our impatient desire to haste the coming of eschatological perfection before its time, or rather, the desire to do away with the burden of waiting—the desire to "wipe out the duration of time and, with this, any irritating delays."
>
> *(The Ethics of Time, 108)*

Bibliography

Augustine, *Earlier Writings*, trans. John HS Burleigh (Philadelphia: Westminster, 1979).

Augustine, *Confessions*, trans. Maria Boulding (New York: Vintage, 1998).

Augustine, *On the Trinity*, trans. Gareth B. Matthews (Cambridge, UK: Cambridge University Press, 2002).

Balthasar, Hans Urs von, *The Glory of the Lord, vol. 5: The Realm of Metaphysics in the Modern Age*, trans. Oliver Davies, et al. (Edinburgh: T&T Clark, 1991).

Balthasar, Hans Urs von, *The Theology of Karl Barth*, trans. Edward T. Oakes, SJ (San Francisco: Communio, Ignatius, 1992).

Bradatan, Costica, *Dying for Ideas: The Dangerous Lives of the Philosophers* (London: Bloomsbury, 2015).

Freud, Sigmund, *Totem and Taboo*, in *The Standard Edition of the Complete Psychological Works of Sigmund Freud*, trans. James Strachey, vol. VIII (London: Hogarth, 1953).

Freud, Sigmund, *Civilization and Its Discontents*, trans. James Strachey (New York: WW Norton, 1962).

Freud, Sigmund, *Introductory Lectures on Psychoanalysis*, trans. James Strachey (New York: WW Norton, 1977).

Freud, Sigmund, "Instincts and Their Vicissitudes," in *General Psychological Theory: Papers on Metapsychology*, ed. Philip Rieff (New York: Touchstone, 2008).

Freud, Sigmund, *Beyond the Pleasure Principle*, trans. Gregory C. Richter, ed. Todd Dufresne (Peterborough, Ontario: Broadview Editions, 2011).

Freud, Sigmund, and CG Jung, *The Freud/Jung Letters: The Correspondence Between Sigmund Freud and CG Jung*, ed. William McGuire (Princeton, NJ: Princeton University Press, 1974).

Kierkegaard, Søren, *The Concept of Anxiety*, trans. Reidar Thomte (Princeton, NJ: Princeton University Press, 1980).

Kierkegaard, Søren, *Fear and Trembling*, trans. Howard Hong and Edna Hong (Princeton, NJ: Princeton University Press, 1983).

Manoussakis, John, *The Ethics of Time* (London: Bloomsbury, 2017).

Nietzsche, Friedrich, *On the Genealogy of Morals and Ecce Homo*, trans. Walter Kaufmann (New York: Vintage, 1989).

Symeon the New Theologian, *On the Mystical Life: The Ethical Discourses*, trans. Alexander Golitzin, vol. I (Crestwood, NY: St. Vladimir's Seminary Press, 1995).

Williams, Rowan, *Dostoevsky: Language, Faith, and Fiction* (Waco, TX: Baylor University Press, 2011).

2

CREATION

Eros as word

In the last chapter we saw that for Augustine, man's recognition of his finite, temporal existence—the fundamental experience of his primordial separation made manifest in the limitations placed upon him by space and time—reveals his fallenness, his fragmentation, his distance from the world, himself, his neighbor, and his God. Yet as Augustine's emphasis on the isolation of the unspeaking stage of infancy makes clear, the sins of separation are not without remedy even in this fallen world. Language, Manoussakis tells us, emerges in the *Confessions* as an "effort to cope with separation by allowing the subject to enter the world of the symbolic substitution—a world shared with other subjects whereby the communication of symbols creates a community in place of a lost unity [and] allows the subject to communicate its desires to itself and to others."[1] In language we see for the first time man's erotic striving toward unity.[2] To repeat a point made in the previous chapter, human language does not arise until *after* man has become aware of his individuation in space and time following the imposition of the law (cf. Genesis 2:19). It is that awareness—that experience of separation and isolation—that gives rise to the desire for unity which language seeks to provide.

Diastema: Language in a fallen world

Augustine, we noted above, begins his *Confessions* with infancy not only because the infant is born into the fallenness of space and time but also because the infant is the least equipped to deal with his isolation. The *in-fant*—he who is without speech—is woefully confined within himself: "I would try to make my wishes known to those who might satisfy them; but I was frustrated in this, because my desires were *inside me*, while other people were *outside*."[3] The first experience of trauma, Manoussakis writes, is precisely this "separation from others, in terms of a distance in space."[4] Yet the child is not without recourse. The unspeaking phase of human existence does not last forever. Soon the child moves beyond infancy and develops the ability to cope with his limited condition:

> I was no longer an infant who lacked the faculty of speech, but a boy who could talk.... I gradually built up a collection of words, observing them as they were used in their proper places in different sentences and hearing them frequently. I came to understand which things they signified, and by schooling my own mouth to utter them I declared my wishes by using the same signs. Thus I learned to express my needs to the people among whom I lived, and they made their wishes known to me; and I waded deeper into the stormy world of human life.[5]

"Language here, as in Freud's celebrated example of the child's game while uttering alternatively the words 'fort/da,' becomes the means to cope with and remedy a painful absence," the absence of the other.[6] Language bridges the space between self and other by reaching out of the self and making known to the other the self's wants and wishes. It also allows the other to share his desires with the self. Thus although space continues to separate and divide, language reaches across the abyss and counteracts its isolating effects.

But language not only seeks to repair the separation forced upon man by space; it also wars against the disjointing effects of time. We said earlier that time separates us from ourselves. Augustine's infancy, his past-self which is "so long dead," no longer exists. In fact, he is so far removed from that former-self that he cannot remember it at all.[7] Yet it is language—the stories told to him by those who knew him as an infant—that helps him to remember that which cannot be remembered. It is narrative—the stories he tells himself about himself—that provides some semblance of unity to his fragmented existence.[8]

Still, if language arises as a potential remedy for man's fallenness—the separation that divides the self from both itself and its other—the solution offered by language can only ever be partial. For, as a "symptom of separation," the unity that language brings is always already grounded in and regulated by man's fallen nature.[9] (As Lacan notes, "by communing in speech," we testify to the fact that we are not "one" with one another).[10] Employing the use of the concept *diastema*—a concept developed by the 4th century Church Father Gregory of Nyssa (one which Marion links to Augustine's *distentio animi*: the dissention of the soul in time)[11]—Manoussakis argues that language is necessarily limited by the "qualitatively infinite abyss" that separates the created world from the uncreated God.[12]

> [F]or the bishop of Nyssa, *diastema* is a sine qua non condition of the creation ... and the negative α-διαστατος is reserved only for the divine. The reasons for this distinction are quite apparent: one of the primary meanings of *diastema* is "dimension," in the sense we use this term today to speak of the four dimensions of our universe. *Diastema* presupposes and

requires a dimensional world (i.e. a material and temporal world) where things have length, height, depth, and duration. *Diastema*, thus understood, is translated as interval (in both spatial and temporal senses).... It is ... the insurmountable distance that separates the uncreated God from creation.[13]

"Such a separation," Manoussakis continues, "has far-reaching consequences for language."[14] For, there can be no language without the distance of space and the duration of time;[15] "the very birth of language is organized by the spatial and temporal interplay between presence and absence—the need to make present, if only in symbolic form, what is absent."[16]

Because language operates in this fallen, *diastemic* world, and as a consequence thereof, language can—contrary to its unitive intent—be the cause of disunity and pain. It is "the source of misconceptions and misunderstandings" which only emphasizes "my separation from the Other ... all the more, even while attempting to reach out and communicate oneself to another."[17] It is necessarily limited, confined by the same restraints (namely space and time) that it seeks to overcome.[18] It can be used for propaganda and manipulation, it can speak falsity and lead to self-deception, it can do violence and it can destroy.[19]

The ambiguous nature of language, Manoussakis tells us, "is centered on the supplementary function of its signification, where the absent thing is rendered present by its corresponding sign."[20] Language thus "creates an illusion of presence under which the absence of what is absent remains hidden."[21] (Think here of Plato's criticism of the poets and sophists who only *re*-present, using false images, a shadowy likeness of a truth that resists their disingenuous attempts at articulation). But the problem of language extends further still. For, if language can provide some semblance of relief for the painful isolation felt by a self trapped within itself, so too does it open up the possibility of *muteness*—a possibility which furthers man's isolation by inclosing him deeper within himself, ensnaring him in an unfreedom of his own making.

det Indesluttede: Language and the Sickness unto Death

In *The Concept of Anxiety*, Kierkegaard tells us that "[l]anguage, the word, is precisely what saves, what saves the individual from the empty abstraction of inclosing reserve."[22] For, language "does indeed imply communication" and communication implies community, a common unity between the self and others. Inclosing reserve, on the other hand, "is precisely muteness."[23] It is "the demonic": "an unfreedom that wants to close itself off,"[24] a self that "closes itself up within itself,"[25] that "closes itself off more and more from communication."[26]

> The demonic does not close itself up with something, but it closes itself up within itself, and in this lies what is profound about existence [*Tilvaerselsen*], precisely that unfreedom makes itself a prisoner. Freedom is

> always *communicerende* [communicating] (it does no harm even to take into consideration the religious significance of this word); unfreedom becomes more and more inclosed [*indesluttet*] and does not want communication.[27]

Kierkegaard, like Augustine before him, recognizes the healing power of the word. It is language that reaches beyond the self and, by allowing the self to communicate with others, frees the self from itself—a self otherwise concerned only with itself, a self isolated and alone.

Yet if freedom is always communicating, still, Kierkegaard warns, not all communication leads to freedom.[28] In fact, it often happens that the muteness of inclosing reserve is born of the failure of language. "All misapprehension," Kierkegaard asserts, "stems from speech."[29] For, "comparison is implicit in talking, especially in conversation"[30] and "All *worldly* worry has its basis in a person's unwillingness to be contented with being a human being, in his worried craving for distinction by way of comparison."[31]

While silence—especially the relational silence of the good[32]—"means nothing at all by way of comparison,"[33] the chatter of human language operates by means of comparison. (I am speaking of *this* and not *that*, she is *better* than he but *worse* than she, not *now* but *later*, etc.) To speak is to compare. To use language is to single out one aspect of existence and designate it over and against everything else. And this comparing, inescapable as it may be, causes man to become dissatisfied with being what he is.

According to Kierkegaard, when I compare myself with another, I fail to appreciate the inherent value and dignity that I possess simply by being what I am. When I compare, I become envious; I wish to be something *more* than what I am. Or I grow proud; I exalt some aspect of my being—some "distinction"— above my humanity itself. I prioritize the part over the whole, the accident over the essence, and foolishly believe that my worth lies in something beyond the simple yet glorious fact that I am a human being.

Comparison, which is inseparable from language, incloses me deeper and deeper within myself. It robs me of the freedom I am and imprisons me by convincing me that I ought to strive for the unfreedom I am not.

> [I]f a human being ... is contented with being a human being, he does not become sick with temporal things, he remains in the place assigned to him; and if he remains there, then it is true that he, by being a human being, is more glorious than Solomon's glory.[34]

But language is not content with allowing man to simply be what he is. It always adds or detracts, attempts to enhance or diminish, makes distinctions by way of comparison. Language is "sick with temporal things,"[35] comparing *this* to *that*, and craving more than the place assigned to it. (Think of our earlier discussion of Thanatos, its unwillingness to accept things as they are, its attempt to fulfill itself by means of itself.)

"Let us consider Solomon," Kierkegaard continues. "When he puts on his royal purple robes and sits majestically on his throne in all his glory—well, then there is also ceremonial address, and the one speaking says: Your Majesty."[36] Language, Kierkegaard makes clear, acts like the king's royal robes; it masks man's humanity like the fig leaves that hide the nakedness of Adam (see Genesis 3:7). Solomon, a man, becomes "Your Majesty" when compared with his subjects. He is exalted by ceremonial address just as "the one speaking" is lowered by having to address him in such a manner. And yet this—to continue the parallel with the Adamic myth—is nothing but a means of concealing his shame (cf. Genesis 2:25).[37] For, "when the most solemn term of address is to be used in the eternal language of earnestness, then we say: Man!"[38]

Man! Not "Your Majesty." Not "King." A word that situates Solomon in the exact place he is meant to be, the place assigned to him at birth. To address Solomon as a man "does not mean that we are speaking disdainfully. On the contrary, we are using the highest term of address, because to be a human being is not lower than diversities but is raised above them."[39] While the eternal language of earnestness remains silent about the superficial differences between man and man—for, such differences amount to nothing at all—human language must compare and its comparisons are most untrue. In comparing the diversity among individuals, it compares nothing to nothing. It conceals the glorious truth of man's humanity behind the untruth of superfluity. It closes man up within himself, turning his freedom into a prison, his language into a muteness which says nothing at all. "And from the spiritual point of view, that person who ... has cunningly shut himself in and thereby trapped himself, has in fact ... trapped himself unto death."[40]

For Kierkegaard, the comparison implicit in human language gives rise to the muteness of inclosing reserve, the sickness of despair. It causes man to compare himself with others, to fixate on his comparisons, to crave distinction and clothe himself in the (illusory) distinctions bestowed upon him by himself and others. More than that, it leads him to become dissatisfied with being what he is.

In *The Sickness unto Death*, Kierkegaard tells us that this dissatisfaction, this desire to be other than what one is, is precisely despair. It is the desire to rid oneself of oneself, to consume oneself, to reduce oneself to nothing at all.[41] Although despair may seem to be caused by some external thing, when one despairs, one actually despairs over being himself and over his inability to do away with himself.

> For example, when the ambitious man whose slogan is 'Either Caesar or nothing' does not get to be Caesar, he despairs over it. But this also means something else: precisely because he did not get to be Caesar, he cannot bear to be himself.... [T]his self is now utterly intolerable to him. In a deeper sense, it is not his failure to become Caesar that is intolerable, but it is this self that did not become Caesar that is intolerable; or, to put it more accurately, what is intolerable to him is that he cannot get rid of himself.[42]

Despair, the sickness unto death, is for Kierkegaard a symptom of our fallen human nature. No one is free from its crippling effects.[43] Every one of us is trapped within a prison of his own dissatisfaction. (Either one despairs over not wanting to be himself or one despairs over wanting to be himself. In the latter scenario, the self "wants to be master of itself or to create itself,"[44] "to enjoy the total satisfaction of making itself into itself, of developing itself, of being itself"[45]—which of course reveals a deep-seated discontent with what one is: a contingent being who can never possess the kind of limitless self-determination it craves.)[46]

This dissatisfaction with being a human being causes man to fixate on himself, to inclose himself within himself, to become a prisoner in the prison of the self. Here, then, we see why Kierkegaard calls language the serpent in the Garden.[47] Here we begin to understand why he refers to it as "the power of the devil."[48] For, it is language that tempts man to despair by tempting him to compare and it is language that reveals man's despair because he cannot but compare. Language is the fallenness in which man lives.[49] Or, worse still, it is root cause of the perversion of man's erotic drive toward unity.[50] It is language, after all, spoken through the mouth of the snake that gives voice to man's Thanatonic desire. It is language that convinces man: "You will be like gods" (Genesis 3:5).[51]

Proballein and *promittere*: Language sends us forth

We have dedicated a good amount of this chapter to the inability of language to heal the ruptures of space and time. The failure of language to achieve its intended aim and the dangers that follow therefrom reveal why language stands at the foundation of the erotic life and does not constitute its completion. Yet as Heidegger quoting Hölderlin tells us: "[W]here danger is, grows/The saving power also."[52] And language, we must reiterate, is the first movement of Eros's healing drive toward unity. Before they can do anything else, lovers must speak. They must express their desire—both to themselves and to one another—in words or gestures, through conversation or by speaking without speaking in a glance, a look, a biting of the lip, a running of the fingers through the hair. And if this first movement of Eros is incomplete in itself, still it gestures at and prefigures a fulfillment yet to come. Language, we have seen, is *problematic*. But language is also *promise*. It is, as Julia Kristeva has said, love.[53] Language reaches out of itself and extends toward the future, sending us forth with a desire that longs to be fulfilled.

Pharmakon: Language as poison and cure

The problem of language—that language is problematic—but also the promise—that it can be used to heal—is one of the earliest insights offered by philosophy. In the first lines of the trial of Socrates, we are introduced to the idea that language in itself is neither healing nor harmful but can be used or abused to varying ends. It has the potential to communicate "the whole truth" even when "spoken at random and expressed in the first words that come to mind;" but it can also carry us away "in spite of [ourselves]" when it is spoken "persuasively," even if "hardly anything of what [was] said is true" (Plato, *Apology* 17a). Here, Plato makes the distinction between content and style, between what is said and how it is said (a distinction that will one day lead Augustine, the accomplished rhetorician, to give up his worldly aspirations and pursue higher things).[54] This dichotomy between the proper use of language ("the excellence ... of a speaker lies in telling the truth" (18a)) and its abuse is personified in the distinction made by Plato again and again between two types of speakers: philosophers, who "put [their] trust in the justice of what [they] say" (17c), and sophists, who "toy with words" and express themselves in "embroidered and stylized phrases" (17c) in order to deceive others with their "many lies" (17a).

And yet, what does it mean to put one's trust in the justice of one's words when one readily admits that one does not know what a word like "justice" really means (*Republic* 354c)? (Have we not been warned that it is precisely the sophist who makes use of such indefinable terms in defense of his position [*Phaedrus* 263a–b])? That language (and the written word in particular) is for Plato a *pharmakon*—a drug which, though neutral in and of itself, can be used to heal by those who know what they are doing and abused as a poison by those who know not—has been demonstrated at length.[55] Of interest to our discussion, however, is the link that Derrida, in his reading of Plato's *Phaedrus*, draws between the ambiguity of language as *pharmakon* (medicine/poison) and the *pharmakeus* (magician/sorcerer/poisoner) who makes use of that *pharmakon*. For, as Derrida notes, if the drug of language in the hands of the sophist is used for sorcery, if it has the power to carry others away in spite of themselves, so too is it a bewitching agent when employed by the philosopher.[56] And if the *pharmakeus* who goes by the title "sophist" is merely a magician who toys with words, the *pharmakeus* known as "philosopher" is that par excellence.[57] After all, he alone knows that no one knows what the words they are using mean (see, *Apology* 21a–23b; *Phaedrus* 263a).

Rightly, then, has Socrates been accused of making the worse argument into the stronger and teaching others to do the same (*Apology* 19b). Rightly has it been said that he is "always in a state of perplexity," that he "bring[s] others to the same state," that he is "bewitching and beguiling ... simply putting [others] under a spell" (*Meno* 80a). Indeed, Meno goes so far as to suggest that if Socrates were to leave the city of Athens, he would be persecuted for "practicing sorcery" (80b). Perhaps this is why, with the lone exception of his mandated military service, the father of philosophy has never left the city of his birth (*Crito* 52b). Perhaps he knows that outside of the city walls, he will be recognized for what he is: a sophist of the highest order. Perhaps he has spent so much time among the men of Athens that he has bewitched them and concealed from them the face of a satyr hidden behind his philosopher's mask (cf. *Symposium* 215b–c).

For Derrida, this unintended association between philosophy and sophistry reveals a deeper truth about language itself. If the philosopher is really the sophist in disguise and thus the sophist par excellence—so convincing in his sophistry that he conceals his identity as a sophist altogether—then all discourse is sophistry, all language deception, the *logos* of the philosopher nothing more than *mythos* behind a mask. But if Derrida's reading is correct, if Plato unwittingly discloses the reciprocity that exists between Socrates and the sophist when trying to distinguish the two, why then, contrary to Meno's warning, is Socrates arrested and tried as a sophist—*in Athens*? Are his fellow Athenians so shrewd as to discover that which every subsequent reader of Plato until Derrida has missed?

No, Derrida is right to notice that the setting of the *Phaedrus* reveals something remarkable about the text;[58] he is right to read into the setting a subtle affirmation of the importance of *mythos* over and against *logos*; but he is wrong to think that Socrates's little excursion "beyond the city walls" (*Phaedrus* 230d) places him on the side of the sophists. As we will see, if Socrates the *pharmakeus* bears a resemblance to those who Plato refers to by using the same name, it is not because he is one of them but because in order to cure an illness—in this case the sickness that is the human condition—a physician must know how to administer drugs.

Logos and *mythos*: Truth and what truth is like

In his reading of the *Phaedrus*, Derrida draws our attention to the beginning of the text where Socrates is lured "outside the city walls" by Phaedrus's promise to discuss the speech of Lysias (*Phaedrus* 227a–c). That the entirety of the dialogue occurs beyond the city limits is, he rightly insists, no minor detail. "The *topoi* of the dialogue are never indifferent. The themes, the topics, the (common-)places, in a rhetorical sense, are strictly inscribed, comprehended each time within a significant site."[59] Of all the Platonic texts, the *Phaedrus* is the only one staged outside of Athens. Its setting in the countryside along the river Ilissus can thus be read as "correspond[ing] to an infallible calculation or necessity" which dictates the tone and direction of the conversation to come.[60] *Here*, Plato tells us, is the place where, according to legend, Boreas (the personification of the north wind) abducted Oreithuia, daughter of the Athenian king (229b). At the supposed site of this myth, "Socrates begins by sending myths off."[61] "To give myths a send-off: a salute, a vacation, a dismissal;" "Not in order to reject them absolutely, but, on the one hand, not bothering them, leaving them alone, making room for them, in order to free them from the heavy serious naïveté of the scientific 'rationalists,' and on the other, not bothering *with* them, in order to free *oneself* for the relation with oneself and the pursuit of self-knowledge"—this, according to Derrida, is the aim of the *Phaedrus*.[62]

Yet, as Derrida himself will note, this attempt to leave *mythos* behind is twice interrupted in the dialogue by the telling of two original Platonic myths. And what is more, by setting the conversation at the scene of a myth, Plato already gestures at the relation between philosophy and narrative, truth and the stories we tell. If, as Derrida asserts, the "hermeneutic adventure" of deciphering myths is to be left "to the sophists,"[63] how then ought we to interpret the myth-making of

Plato? What can it mean to say that "Socrates begins by sending myths off" if we know that, at the end of his life, he welcomes them back again (*Phaedo* 107a–115a)?

Let us attend to the text more closely to see if we can decipher an answer to these perplexities. "Phaedrus, my friend," Socrates begins, "Where have you been? And where are you going?" (*Phaedrus* 227a).[64] Phaedrus answers that he has spent the morning listening to Lysias's speech on Eros and that he is now going for a walk outside of the city. To this Socrates replies, "So Lysias, I take it, is in the city?" (227b). We begin already to see the contrast that Plato is drawing between Socrates and Lysias, the philosopher and the sophist. While Lysias's speeches (*logoi*) are given within the city itself, Socrates is "free to come along and listen," engaging in dialogue beyond the city walls (227b) at the site of an ancient myth (229b). Contrary to Derrida's assertion that Socrates's trip outside of Athens places him in the realm of the sophists, leaving the city actually represents a departure from the land where sophistry reigns supreme:[65]

> Phaedrus, whose name means 'bright', 'beaming' and 'radiant', which suggests presence and aligns him with *logos*, takes a walk outside the city as a respite from his fatiguing immersion in *logos*. It is here that he encounters Socrates.... Insofar as Phaedrus is associated with the *logoi* delivered *within* the confines of the city, Socrates is an *outsider* and, up to this point, is aligned with the occult and ambiguous nature of *mythos*.[66]

To further underscore the point, consider that Lysias, the sophist—one of the "intellectuals" (*sophoi*) who Socrates chides for demythologizing the story said to have taken place beyond the city walls (229c)—remains within the limits of the city while Socrates, the philosopher, has received a "divinely inspired release from normally accepted behavior" (265a) and thus finds himself outside of the *polis* among the Muses in the land of *mythos* (237a).[67]

What our reading of the *Phaedrus* now makes clear is that, contrary to Derrida's assertion, it is actually the sophist and not the philosopher who "begins by sending myths off." It is the man who calls himself wise—*sophistēs* literally means "wise man," a title which Socrates explicitly rejects in favor of "wisdom's lover" (*Phaedrus* 278d)—and not the lover of wisdom who believes he can dispense with myths by "explain[ing] them away and mak[ing] them plausible by means of some sort of rough ingenuity" (*Phaedrus* 229e). The philosopher, on the other hand, knows that he is not wise, that "human wisdom is worth little or nothing" (*Apology* 23a), and thus he has "no time for such" demythologizing (*Phaedrus* 229e). Hence, whereas Derrida reads Plato as establishing the *logos/mythos* binary, a closer reading of the text actually reveals something subtler and more nuanced—the attempt by Plato, through the creation of original myths, to transcend such binary thinking all together.[68] (That such a move anticipates Nietzsche ought, I think, to make us reevaluate the standard readings of Nietzsche.)

In order to see this, we have first to understand that, when cut off from one another, both *logos* and *mythos* are incomplete. *Logos* without *mythos* falters because it never fully captures that of which it speaks, never articulates, never expresses a truth that always transcends it; thus it depends upon story, analogy, metaphor, myth.[69] (Hence, Nietzsche's critique of the supposed objectivity garnered through scientific inquiry and logical deduction:

> When they see to their horror how logic coils up at these boundaries [of thought] and finally bites its own tail—suddenly the new form of insight breaks through, *tragic insight* which, merely to be endured, needs art as a protection and remedy.)[70]

Mythos, on the other hand, when given without reason, becomes nonsensical—meaningless, purposeless, trivial, banal. (Hence, Plato's disdain for the poets who "do not compose their poems with knowledge, but by some inborn talent and by inspiration, like seers and prophets who also say many fine things without any understanding of what they say" [*Apology* 22c].) Said differently—and to borrow a line of thinking from Kant—unreflective *mythos* is dumb, *logos* without artistry is blind. Both speak falsely. Both lead astray.

That Derrida (mis)reads Plato as merely attempting to transform *mythos* into *logos* reveals his bias: he only sees half of the picture. And while it is certainly true that "Plato succeeded in overcoming the mythical, demonic, and orgiastic character of Greek cults" with his philosophy,[71] it is equally true that his philosophy—and the philosophy of his teacher—was born of the failure of *logos*, the realization that "human wisdom is worth little or nothing," that even the wisdom of the wisest man is worthless (*Apology* 23a–b). Thus for Plato, the philosopher must make use of *mythos* and, indeed, must work to transform *logos* into *mythos*. It is the goal of the dialogues to reconcile *logos* with *mythos*, to get these two creatures who share one head to use their head to work together.

Plato does this, in part, by creating new stories. (A new art-form says Nietzsche.)[72] Not unreflective, senseless stories like the poets of his day but stories that move his readers toward an inexpressible truth by telling them what that truth is like.[73] For, although he insists that the gods alone are capable of attaining knowledge of truth in its fullness, still, he says, it is "humanly possible" to provide an analogy, an image of what that truth might be like (*Phaedrus* 246a). This *saying what truth is like*, this understanding of the analogy of being, is the wedding of *logos* to *mythos*. It is Plato's approach to philosophy itself—an attempt to overcome the failures of inarticulate *logos* and unthinking *mythos* by giving oneself over to a divine madness, the Eros that inspires the lover of wisdom to ascend from the beauty in this world toward the beauty of truth itself (249c–e).

Pharmakos: New myths, new sacrifices, a new religion

That our reading of Plato's *Phaedrus* conflicts with the reading put forth by Derrida ought not to dissuade us from borrowing freely from his work, especially when it promises to enrich our own. If we disagree with his assertion that, in the figure of Socrates, Plato inadvertently presents us with an image of the reciprocity that exists between the philosopher and the sophist—that *logos* is nothing but *mythos* in disguise—still we are forced by his commentary (and indeed by the text itself) to question why Plato chooses to use the same term, *pharmakeus*, to refer to both the father of philosophy and those descended from the father of lies. Here, Derrida's introduction of the missing term, *pharmakos*— which Plato never utters but which Derrida, by "untangl[ing] the hidden forces of attraction linking a present word with an absent word in the text of Plato,"[74] connects to *pharmakon, pharmakeus*—is particularly insightful.

As Derrida tells us, "*pharmakos* (wizard, magician, poisoner)" is "a word that can, on one of its faces, be considered the synonym, almost the homonym, of … *pharmakeus* (which Plato uses), but with the unique feature of having been over- determined, overlaid by Greek culture with another function. Another *role*, and a formidable one."[75] It is by the attending to the cultural usage of this unuttered term that we begin to make sense not only of Plato's decision to call Socrates a *pharmakeus* but also of his understanding of the role of philosophy and the unique way the philosopher administers the *pharmakon* of language.

"The character of the *pharmakos*," writes Derrida, "has been compared to a scapegoat. The *evil* and the *outside*, the expulsion of evil, its exclusion out of the body (and out) of the city—these are the two major senses of the character and of the ritual."[76] The *pharmakoi*, we are told, were typically put to death. They were offered as sacrifices to the gods for the purification of the city. Derrida quotes at length from the 12th century Byzantine poet John Tzetzes's reckoning of the matter:

> The (rite of the) *pharmakos* was a purification of this sort of old. If a calam- ity overtook the city by the wrath of God, whether it were famine or pesti- lence or any other mischief, they led forth as though to a sacrifice the most unsightly of them all[77] as a purification and a remedy to the suffering city. They set the sacrifice in the appointed place, and gave him cheese with their hands and a barley cake and figs,[78] and seven times they smote him with leeks and wild figs and other wild plants. Finally they burnt him with fire with the wood of wild trees and scattered the ashes into the sea and to the winds, for a purification, as I said, of the suffering city.[79]

That such a sacrificial offering should be made to the gods for the sake of the *polis*, the people—that "the wrath of God" might be satiated by such a sacrifice, a murder that leads to purification and unity—ought, I think, to immediately bring to mind other, more prominent ritualistic murders. (Indeed, has Derrida not shown us that a text may, and positively *does*, contain within itself not only that which it contains but also that which it excludes, that which is outside, other, the trace of everything left unsaid?) In the context of the dialogues, for instance, the resonances with the death of Socrates are obvious. Not only has the god ordered this "most unsightly" of men to sacrifice wealth and honor and even the wellbeing of his family to live the life of an impoverished philosopher (*Apology* 23b), he has placed him in the city as a "gift" and "gadfly" meant to rouse the people into reforming their impure ways (30e). And when the men of Athens refuse, they sacrifice him—forcing this *pharmakeus* to ingest a *pharmakon* the day after the annual rite of the *pharmakos* has taken place (*Phaedo* 58a–c).[80]

It is here, in connection with Plato's depiction of Socrates as a sacrificial victim put to death for the purification of the city, that we begin to make sense of why Plato ascribes to Socrates the role of *pharmakeus*. For, just as Plato creates new, analogical myths which by expressing what truth is like overcome both the reductive literalism of the sophists (*logos*) and the unreflective mythmaking (*mythos*) of those who "say many fine things without any understanding of what they say" (*Apology* 22c), so too is he able to provide an antidote to the poisons administered by two types of poisoner (*pharmakeus*) by undoing them, as it were, from within.

If the philosopher is meant to be a kind of doctor of the soul—able to heal the harm wrought by both the sophist who poisons with false words and by that older, cruder *pharmakeus*, the sorcerer, the priest—then he will need to be an expert at administering drugs. He will need to know how to lead the soul away from anything that might contaminate it—be it the untruth of lies or the impurity of lusts. But, as Nietzsche says, "The more abstract the truth is that you would teach, the more you have to seduce the senses to it."[81] And if that means employing the use of a "noble lie" (*Republic* 414b–c) or mortifying the body in order to free the soul from association with it (*Phaedo* 64a–66d), that is what the philosopher will do. He will become a *pharmakeus* of the highest order—one skilled in the use of poison, but who employs his knowledge to cure rather than harm. And if, as is often the case, his patients refuse to accept the treatment that would heal them, if they are unaware (even willfully ignorant) of the fact that they are sick, how then will he be able to reach them … if not by taking the prescription himself? Indeed, is this not what Socrates does?

In the character of Socrates, in the dialogues of Plato, we see time and again the overcoming of an old ideal by means of a new one—an overcoming which supplants the old from within. The *logos* of the sophists and the *mythos* of the poets are overcome by a new kind of *mythos*, a new art-form, one which draws readers nearer to *logos* by seducing them with *mythos*. The *pharmakeus* known as the sophist and the *pharmakeus* known as the priest are overcome by the *pharmakos* named Socrates, he who by his death reveals a deeper truth and brings a greater purification than either the intellectual or the religious has heretofore known. In the figure of Socrates, ancient wisdom and mythic religion are not done away with. They are sublimated, raised up and reborn as the love of wisdom, the ascent of the soul to the realm of the gods. From the death of Socrates, a new religion is born.[82] And with it comes, as he himself has prophesied (*Apology* 39c), an endless lineage of disciples.

And yet, before whom or what do these proselytes bow? What god is this? What kind of religion? The answer might surprise us. For, it is one with which we are familiar even today. (Though perhaps it goes by a different name?)[83] The religion that Plato invents is a religion which uses "reason to put an end to ... superstition,"[84] one which brings "purification" through knowledge, salvation by means of "pure thought" (φρόνησις), one which "is not any more *of the body*, as [were] the religious rites [of old] ... but rather [represents] a purification *from the body*, as we can now speak—for the first time perhaps—of a *purified mind* (διάνοιαν κεκαθαρμένην, 67c4)."[85] *A purified mind.* And philosophy is the means of purification: "the new *ritus* (a ritual without ritual, as it is fitting, perhaps, for this 'religion without religion'), the *disciplina*, which, when practiced rightly, ὀρθῶς ... can ensure for its adherent the attainment of pure knowledge."[86] To be sure, this *drug* is as potent as it ever was. It is the cult of truth, the cult of objectivity, the lust for certainty and power. And, subsequently, it is the cult of death, the drug administered to kill—

Thanatos: A false Eros and the language of death

The cult of death? The drug administered to kill? Yes. After all, "the one aim of those who practice philosophy in the proper manner is to practice for dying and death" (*Phaedo* 64a). "True philosophers," we are told, "are nearly dead" (64b). For them, "there is good hope that death is a blessing," even "a great advantage" (*Apology* 40c–d). Thus "a man who has truly spent his life in philosophy is probably right to be of good cheer in the face of death" (*Phaedo* 63e). He has spent his life "training for dying" (67e):

> Consider then, my good sir, whether you share my opinion, for this will lead us to a better knowledge of what we are investigating. Do you think it is the part of a philosopher to be concerned with such so-called pleasures as those of food and drink?
>
> By no means.
>
> What about the pleasures of sex?
>
> Not at all.
>
> What of the other pleasures concerned with the service of the body? ... Do you think he values these or despises them, except insofar as one cannot do without them?
>
> I think the true philosopher despises them....
>
> A man who finds no pleasure in such things and has no part in them is thought by the majority not to deserve to live and to be close to death; the man, that is, who does not care for the pleasures of the body.
> What you say is certainly true .
>
> *(64d–65a)*

This, we are told, is not a denunciation of philosophy but, on the contrary, one of the virtues of this new religion, this drug which promises to cure the ills of man.[87]

After all, "the true philosopher desires ... pure knowledge" and "'It really has been shown to us that, if we are ever to have pure knowledge [εἰ μέλλομέν ποτε. καθαρῶς τι εἴσεσθαι] we must escape from the body.' To obtain such purity of knowledge the philosopher must strive to dissociate his soul from his body as much as possible, effecting a continuous anticipation or rather mortification, during each and every day of his life, of that separation that will finally occur only at his last hour."[88]

And yet, need we to read this as a sort of covert nihilism, a concealed death drive hidden at the heart of Platonic philosophy? Certainly there is ample evidence to justify that interpretation. Yet let us, out of deference to Plato, offer another (even if we ultimately settle upon the first). For, if we are to define *death* as "the separation of the soul from the body," if we are to say that "we believe that death is this, namely, that the body comes to be separated by itself apart from the soul, and the soul comes to be separated by itself apart from the body," (64c) oughtn't we to say that *one dies every time one thinks*? Oughtn't we to assert that reason represents a kind of death, a movement away from the body, away from experience, away from life itself? Oughtn't we to insist that philosophy is death *par excellence* because to practice philosophy is to die again and again, to train oneself to leave this world and the cares of this world, to continually lose oneself in abstractions, in the unreality of thought?

An example may help to elucidate the point: A man is invited to a dinner party. He agrees to go. He takes great pains with his appearance. He bathes, he dresses, he puts on his finest sandals. He wants to look his best. Along the way, he bumps into an old friend whom he convinces to join him. He assures this friend that he will be a most welcome guest. But, as Homer says, when two men go together, one has an idea before the other and, as they walk, the first keeps slowing down, lagging behind, getting caught up in thought. Eventually he stops completely. He stands as motionless as a corpse. But all the while he is *thinking*. He is making plans, solving riddles, recollecting the past, analyzing himself, his actions, his thoughts. His body is present but his mind is somewhere else. Where it is, nobody knows. Is he even alive? Has his heart stopped beating midstride? Wherever he is, his life has passed him by. He is not in this world. He is existing *after* life, outside of it. For, while his body is here, his soul has been separated. It has separated itself. It now occupies the illusory space of thought. This man is dead to life, dead to his friend, dead to his senses and his surroundings. If someone were to call his name, still he would not come back to this world. He would remain unaware of that speaker's presence. He is existing beyond his body in the realm of "pure" thought, the Platonic otherworld populated not by persons but by ideas.

This is what it is to think. Thought removes us from experience. It distances us from life. It separates the soul from the body. For Plato, philosophy is practiced "in the proper manner" when this dying is done in the service of life, when one returns to life informed by that which he has encountered in the death that is reflection. (Thus, "the unexamined life is not worth living" [*Apology* 38a] might just as easily be reformulated: "Unless a grain of wheat falls to the ground and dies, it remains just a grain of wheat; but if it dies, it produces much fruit" [John 12:24].) Such a reading of the *Phaedo* helps to illuminate the arguments offered for the immortality of the soul; arguments which, when taken at face value, appear to be offered in jest. For, if one dies every time one thinks—if man, in so far as he is the rational animal, is *the dying animal*, the creature capable of fleeing this world whenever he reflects—then it makes sense to say that "what comes from being dead ... is being alive" (71d) and that the "soul existed before we were born" (77a). After all, every time the soul returns to the body from thought, it returns from death to life, is born again in a new body. The body of lived experience is not a static thing. It is forever changing, born and reborn at every instant. And the soul that commingles with this new body comes back to life bearing with it the trace of the death it left behind. The theory of recollection, like the Cartesian cogito, posits that "pure knowledge"—or, to use Descartes's language, "clear and distinct ideas"—can only be accessed "as long as I am thinking."[89] Wisdom can only be attained when the soul is separated from the body in thought, "when we are dead," and never when we are touching, sensing, feeling, experiencing, never "with the body," "not while we live" (66e).

If we accept this reading, what then can be said of Plato's views on death itself? What, if anything, can be ascertained about his thoughts on the final death, death defined not as "the separation of the soul from the body" but as the loss of existence, the extinguishing of all life? It is by turning our attention to another Dialogue—one concerned (or so we are told) with sex and not death—that we begin to sense our answer. In his reading of the *Symposium*, Derrida keenly observes the resemblance that the character of Socrates bears to the description of Eros given by Diotima. "Behind the portrait of Eros, one cannot fail to recognize the features of Socrates, as though Diotima, in looking at him, were proposing to Socrates the portrait of Socrates."[90] And of course, Eros too bears that famous moniker, *pharmakeus*: tempter, diviner, priest. "Neither living nor dead, he forms 'the medium of the prophetic arts, of the priestly rites of sacrifice, initiation, and incarnation, and incantation, of divination and sorcery (*thusias-teletas-epodas-manteian*)' (202e)."[91]

Does this likening of Socrates to the god of erotic love free Plato from the charge of nihilism levelled against him? Could it be that Plato comes down decisively on the side of life; that, as we have insinuated, the goal of philosophy is to learn to die in order to live more fully? Bear in mind, as you read the following, the connections we have established between, on the one hand, Socrates and Eros, and on the other, Socrates and the sacrificial victim:

> In general, the *pharmakoi* were put to death. But that, it seems, was not the essential end of the operation. Death occurred most often as a secondary effect of an energetic fustigation. Aimed first at the genital organs. Once the *pharmakoi* were cut off from the space of the city, the blows were designed to chase away or draw out the evil from their bodies. Did they burn them, too, in order to achieve purification? ... [T]hey burnt [them]

with fire ... and scattered the ashes into the sea and the winds, for a purification ... of the suffering city.[92]

Purification by means of destruction: fustigation aimed at the genitals, evil
beaten out of the body by force, the incineration of the body and the scattering of
the ashes into the sea and through the air. No, there is nothing erotic about this
immolation, this desecration of the human form. There is nothing life-affirming
about this purified ascent.

For us, Eros will be identified as he who has been crucified, he whose body
has not only been broken but exalted, lifted up (cf. John 3:14). He is the touchable, the tasteable, the carnal, the Word made flesh. For Plato, Eros ascends.
He leaves the fetters of the body behind, sacrificing the flesh on the altar of the
word, making of it a burnt offering which purifies the soul. (Note that the *pharmakos* is sacrificed for the "the suffering city," the *polis*, which is used, by way
of analogy, as an image of the soul in the *Republic*.) In him, the carnal becomes
spiritual, undone, as it were, from within. "But here lies the trap: for the philosopher-priest is already a fake priest—a self-proclaimed and (self-)idolized priest
and thus truly an idol."[93] Nietzsche's condemnation of philosophers proves true:
"[T]hese honorable idolaters of concepts ... threaten the life of everything they
worship."[94] It is they who have given Eros (Socrates) poison to drink. He died
of it. But in dying, he gave birth to philosophy: to reason, rationality, and the
world of pure ideas.[95]

Notes

1 Manoussakis, *The Ethics of Time*, 106.
2 Cf. "Here too, language ... promise[s] us the recovery that we are forced to perceive
   as a lost unity, even though one could hardly entertain a time that the self, namely
   ourselves, ever enjoyed such a unity." Ibid., 109.
3 Augustine, *Confessions*, (1.6.8) (emphasis mine).
4 Manoussakis, *The Ethics of Time*, 106.
5 Augustine, *Confessions*, (1.8.13).
6 Manoussakis, *The Ethics of Time*, 106.
7 See, Augustine, *Confessions*, (1.6.8).
8 See,

> What accomplishes the unification of a divided self? The entire narrative of the
> *Confessions* is the answer to this question. For the *Confessions* not only records
> the story of Augustine's conversion, but also illustrates the means by which this
> conversion became possible. The recollection of a self by means of narrative,
> a narrative of the ways in which the self endured over time, allows oneself to
> become one. To say it differently, the answer that the *Confessions* offers to the
> problem of a self-divided self is *time* and *narrative*. So, paradoxically, that which
> *at the beginning* appears as the effects, if not the causes themselves, of division, *at
> the end*—but only at the end—are proven to be the means of division's overcom-
> ing. The ambiguity of language is resolved by time, and the ambiguity of time is
> resolved by narrative.
>
> (Manoussakis, *The Ethics of Time*, 83)

 9 Ibid., 82.
10 Lacan, *Encore: Seminar XX*, 66.
11 See Marion, *In the Self's Place*, 218.
12 Manoussakis, *God After Metaphysics*, 98.
13 Ibid.
14 Ibid., 99.
15 "[T]o speak takes time and one cannot speak but in time. But language also 'takes'
   space: the meaning of a word is determined by its position in a sentence." Manoussakis,
   The Ethics of Time, 81. (Cf. also Manoussakis's analysis of the "space" or system in
   which language operates in *God After Metaphysics*, 79–83).
16 Manoussakis, *The Ethics of Time*, 106.
17 Ibid., 81.
18 "The limits of the *diastema* that circumscribes creation are also the limits of our
   knowledge and language ('the limits of my language are the limits of my world,' as
   Wittgenstein famously said)." Manoussakis, *God After Metaphysics*, 99.
19 Cf.

> For a long time now, our words have been part of [the liturgy of our language]:
> they have been spoken, written, cried out, and whispered. They have come to
> express agonies, fears, and desires; they caused violence, and they brought peace.
> Surely, words don't come alone. And words are not *just* words.
>
> *(Ibid., 82)*

20 Manoussakis, *The Ethics of Time*, 106.
21 Ibid., 106–107.
22 Kierkegaard, *The Concept of Anxiety*, 124.
23 Ibid.
24 Ibid., 123.
25 Ibid., 124.
26 Ibid., 129.
27 Ibid., 124.
28 One wonders if Kierkegaard not only sees "no harm" in taking into consideration
   the religious significance of *communicerende* but actually intends it to be read as the
   one form of authentic communication (*communicere* is the term used for receiving the
   sacrament of the Eucharist). Kierkegaard notes that "it will not do to represent man
   himself as the inventor of language" (*The Concept of Anxiety*, 47n2) and we know that,
   for him, the knight of faith "speaks no human language" but a higher language, "a
   divine language, he speaks in tongues" (*Fear and Trembling*, 114).
29 Kierkegaard, *Upbuilding Discourses*, 161.
30 Ibid.
31 Ibid., 171.
32 Kierkegaard insists that "the good … is absolutely able to keep silent" (*The Concept of
   Anxiety*, 125). Think, for instance, of Abraham who is able to maintain an "absolute
   relation to the *absolute*" (i.e. "private relation to the divine") even though he "remains
   silent [and] … cannot speak" (*Fear and Trembling*, 93 and 113 respectively).
33 Kierkegaard, *Upbuilding Discourses*, 161.
34 Ibid.
35 Ibid.
36 Ibid.
37 This comparison between the robes of Solomon and the fig leaves of Adam calls to
   mind a third *ad-dressing*, or, as it were, undressing: 2 Samuel 6:14–22. David, who
   refuses to conceal himself behind kingly garb or dignified language, dances before
   the Lord and in doing so exposes himself "as a commoner might expose himself"
   (6:20). There is a play here on the Hebrew word *galah* [גלה] which means both to

expose and to reveal. Thus David's nudity not only "demeans" him and makes him "lowly," but also reveals him as the true king, the one who the Lord has chosen over Saul (6:21–22). (I am indebted to Alexandra Breukink for drawing my attention to this passage).

38 Kierkegaard, *Upbuilding Discourses*, 161.
39 Ibid.
40 Ibid., 178. (Kierkegaard's use of the word "cunningly" here and elsewhere (cf. n. 50 below) should remind us, I think, of our friend the serpent—"the most cunning of all the wild animals" (Genesis 3:1)—and the link that Kierkegaard establishes between him and language itself (cf. n47 in Ch. 1)).
41 Kierkegaard, *The Sickness Unto Death*, 19.
42 Ibid.
43 "[A]nyone who really knows mankind might say that there is not one single living human being who does not despair a little." Ibid., 22.
44 Ibid., 68.
45 Ibid., 69.
46 Cf. Manoussakis's discussion of created (i.e. responsorial) being in *The Ethics of Time*, 37–50.
47 Kierkegaard, *The Concept of Anxiety*, 47.
48 Kierkegaard, *Fear and Trembling*, 61.
49 Cf.

> [A]las, in the daily association with people, in the multifarious diversity and its various connections, one forgets through the busy or the worried inventiveness of comparison what it is to be a human being, forgets it because of the diversity among individuals.
>
> *(Kierkegaard,* Upbuilding Discourses, *165)*

50 It may be asked here whether language is on the side of Eros or Thanatos, to which I would answer: "Yes." This, indeed, is the heart of the problem posed by language.
51 Cf.

> If [man] is unwilling to be contented with [being a human being], what is the something more that he demands? The something more is this: to be himself his own providence for all his life or perhaps merely for tomorrow; and if that is what he wants, then he walks—*cunningly* [!]—into the snare.... Thus he wants to entrench himself, so to speak, in a little or large area where he will not be the object of God's providence and the supporting care of the heavenly Father. He may not perceive, before it's too late, that in this entrenched security he is living—in a prison.... [T]he human being is not contented with being a human being but wants to compare himself to God.
>
> *(Kierkegaard,* Upbuilding Discourses, *178)*

52 Heidegger, *The Question Concerning Technology*, 28.
53 "Language is love, and love is language." Kristeva, "Mysticism and Anatheism," 73.
54 See:

> My interest in [Cicero's *Hortensius*] was not aroused by its usefulness in the honing of my verbal skills (which was supposed to be the object of the studies I was pursuing ...); no, it was not merely as an instrument for sharpening my tongue that I used that book, for it had won me over not by its style but by what it had to say.
>
> *(Augustine,* Confessions, *[3.4.7])*

Plato makes this same distinction more explicitly elsewhere (see, Phaedrus 234e–235a).

55 See, Derrida, "Plato's Pharmacy" in *Dissemination*, 67–186. That Derrida concerns himself specifically with the written word and not with language per se ought not to deter us from engaging with his important work.

56 Cf. "In [the *Symposium*], Agathon accuses Socrates of trying to bewitch him, to cast a spell over him (*Pharmattein boulei me, o Sokrates*, 194a)." Ibid., 119.

57 Cf.

> Although Derrida refuses to do away with all differences or to treat these differences as null and void, he demonstrates that between Socrates and the Sophists, the structure of the opposition belies not the difference that Plato would like to establish but rather the reciprocity that is suggested by the recourse to one and the same word.
>
> *(Girard,* Violence and the Sacred, *296)*

58 See, Derrida, *Dissemination*, 74–75.

59 Ibid., 74.

60 Ibid.

61 Ibid.

62 Ibid., 73.

63 Ibid., 74.

64 Socrates's question, like all language, conceals as much as it reveals. In his response, Phaedrus answers the literal question and misses the deeper one: Do you know yourself, you *who are* where you have been (your past) and where you are going (your future)?

65 Note that in the Platonic dialogues, it takes a foreigner—the stranger from Elea, not a resident of the city of Athens—to define the sophist. Only an outsider could identify that to which the Athenians themselves had grown accustomed (see, *Sophist*).

66 Spitzer, *Derrida, Myth and the Impossibility of Philosophy*, 60.

67 This reading is supported too by John Sallis's observation that, for someone who has only left the city once, Socrates knows an awful lot about the site of the ancient myth (see, 229e):

> We wonder at Socrates' acquaintance with the countryside, especially if we bear in mind (cf. *Crito* 52b) that Socrates was almost notorious for never leaving the city.... However little Socrates is acquainted with the country outside the walls, he does seem rather well informed about those features that have some connection with the kind of things told in myths."
>
> *(Sallis,* Being and Logos, *114)*

68 Cf. another instance of Socrates's upsetting of typical binary thinking:

> What a strange thing that which men call pleasure seems to be, and how astonishing the relation it has with what is thought to be its opposite, namely pain! A man cannot have both at the same time. Yet if he pursues and catches the one, he is almost always bound to catch the other also, like two creatures with one head.
>
> *(Phaedo 60b)*

69 As Camus, in his analysis of objective scientific "truths," rightly points out:

> [A]ll the knowledge of the earth will give me nothing to assure me that this world is mine. You describe it to me and you teach me to classify it. You enumerate its laws and in my thirst for knowledge I admit that they are true. You take apart its mechanism and my hope increases. At the final stage you teach me that this wondrous and multicolored universe can be reduced to the atom and that

the atom itself can be reduced to the electron.... But you tell me of an invisible planetary system in which electrons gravitate around a nucleus. You explain this world to me with an image. I realize then that you have been reduced to poetry: I shall never know.... So that science that was to teach me everything ends up in a hypothesis, that lucidity founders in metaphor, that uncertainty is resolved in a work of art.

(The Myth of Sisyphus, 19–20)

70 Nietzsche, *The Birth of Tragedy* (§15).
71 Manoussakis, "The Philosopher-Priest and the Mythology of Reason," 3.
72 See:

Plato ... was nevertheless constrained by sheer artistic necessity to create an art-form that was related to those forms of art which he repudiated.... Indeed, Plato has given to all posterity the model of a new art form, the model of the *novel*—which may be described as an infinitely enhanced Aesopian fable, in which poetry holds the same rank in relation to dialectical philosophy as this same philosophy held for many centuries in relation to theology: namely, the rank of *ancilla*.

(Nietzsche, The Birth of Tragedy [§14])

73 This is why, when attempting to understand the nature of the soul, Socrates begins by defining it philosophically—soul as "self-mover," as "source and spring of motion in everything else that moves ... [which] has no beginning" (245c)—and, finding such definitions unsatisfactory, he then proceeds to create his own myth about what the soul is like (246a). Socrates's use of *mythos* is not meant to provide a literal account of how the soul functions. Rather, it offers an image, an analogy, a glimpse at a truth that can never be captured or pinned down by words.
74 Derrida, *Dissemination*, 133.
75 Ibid.
76 Ibid.
77 See,

Frazer believes that Athens maintained a stock of ugly people to be used pre-cisely as *pharmakoi* whenever either the festival of an extraordinary occasion called to do so: "The Athenians regularly maintained a number of degraded and useless beings at the public expense; and when any calamity, such as plague, drought, or famine, befell the city, they sacrificed two of these outcasts as scapegoats."

(Manoussakis, "The Philosopher-Priest," 5)

78 "Indeed, one of the meanings of Socrates' proposal in the *Apology* (36d), namely, that he deserves to be fed on the city's expense, assumes now the more sinister character of a self-identification as a *pharmakos*." Ibid., 6.
79 Derrida, *Dissemination*, 134.
80 Derrida observes another connection:

The date of the ceremony [of the *pharmakos*] is important: the sixth day of the Thargelia. That was the day of the birth of him whose death—and not only because a *pharmakon* was its direct cause—resembles that of a *pharmakos* from the inside: Socrates. Socrates, affectionately called *pharmakeus* in the dialogues of Plato ... was born on the sixth day of the Thargelia. Diogenes Laertius testi-fies to this: "He was born on the sixth day of the Thargelion, the day when the Athenians purify the city."

(Ibid., 135)

81 Nietzsche, *Beyond Good and Evil*, (§128).
82 "We could, therefore, say that religion is born as Socrates dies; that religion is born at the same time as philosophy's emergence as the art of dying." Manoussakis, "The Philosopher-Priest," 4.
83 Cf. Nietzsche, *The Birth of Tragedy*, "Attempt at Self-Criticism," (§2).
84 Manoussakis, "The Philosopher-Priest," 5.
85 Ibid., 7–8.
86 Ibid., 8.
87 See:

> We have to see Plato's rationalism not as a cool scientific project such as a later century European Enlightenment might set for itself, but as a kind of passionately religious doctrine—a theory that promised man salvation from the things he had feared most from the earliest days, from death and time.
>
> *(Barrett,* Irrational Man, *84)*

88 Manoussakis, "The Philosopher-Priest," 7.
89 Descartes, *Meditations*, 19.
90 Derrida, *Dissemination*, 119.
91 Ibid.
92 Ibid., 133–134.
93 Manoussakis, "The Philosopher-Priest," 13.
94 *Twilight of Idols* as quoted in ibid., 1.
95 See:

> It is important to pay attention to Nietzsche's language. He speaks of a *worship* to which philosophers have dedicated themselves ... but this is not the worship of the living God, "the God of Abraham, of Isaac, and of Jacob" to use Pascal's terms, but, as one might indeed expect, the "God of the philosophers." Nietzsche is more accurate in his description: it is an *idol*, that is, a dead or counterfeit god. But how could a god die, as the madman of Nietzsche's *Gay Science* in so powerful a way declares? Religion, pagan and Abrahamic alike, has taught us that if man were to see god, man would die.... In philosophy this principle becomes reversed: when man sees god, god dies. And he dies by means of this very "seeing," by means, in other words, of what we know in Greek as the *idea*, and in German as *Begriff*. It is, at once, the crime *and* the means of that crime that Nietzsche identified by calling the philosopher an "idolater of concepts." Far from being a criticism of a religion not credible any more, as it is often assumed, Nietzsche's proclamation of "the death of God" is a powerful condemnation of philosophy itself.
>
> *(Manoussakis, "The Philosopher-Priest," 1–2)*

Bibliography

Augustine, *Confessions*, trans. Maria Boulding (New York: Vintage, 1998).

Barrett, William, *Irrational Man* (New York: Anchor Books, 1990).

Camus, Albert, *The Myth of Sisyphus*, trans. Justin O'Brien (New York: Vintage, 1991).

Derrida, Jacques, *Dissemination*, trans. Barbara Johnson (Chicago: University of Chicago, 2010).

Descartes, René, *Meditations on First Philosophy*, trans. Donald A. Cress (Indianapolis: Hackett, 1993).

Girard, René, *Violence and the Sacred*, trans. Patrick Gregory (Baltimore: Johns Hopkins University Press, 1979).

Heidegger, Martin, *The Question Concerning Technology and Other Essays*, trans. William Lovitt (New York: Harper & Row, 1977).

Kierkegaard, Søren, *The Concept of Anxiety*, trans. Reidar Thomte (Princeton: Princeton University Press, 1980).

Kierkegaard, Søren, *Fear and Trembling*, trans. Howard Hong and Edna Hong (Princeton: Princeton University Press, 1983a).

Kierkegaard, Søren, *The Sickness unto Death*, trans. Howard Hong and Edna Hong (Princeton: Princeton University Press, 1983b).

Kierkegaard, Søren, *Upbuilding Discourses in Various Spirits*, trans. Howard Hong and Edna Hong (Princeton: Princeton University Press, 1993).

Kristeva, Julia, "Mysticism and Anatheism: The Case of Teresa," in *Richard Kearney's Anatheistic Wager: Philosophy, Theology, Poetics*, eds. Chris Doude van Troostwijk and Matthew Clemente (Bloomington: Indiana University Press, 2018), 68–87.

Lacan, Jacques, *Encore: The Seminar of Jacques Lacan, Book XX: On Feminine Sexuality, the Limits of Love and Knowledge*, trans. Bruce Fink (New York: WW Norton, 1999).

Manoussakis, John, *God After Metaphysics: A Theological Aesthetic* (Bloomington: Indiana University Press, 2007).

Manoussakis, John, "The Philosopher-Priest and the Mythology of Reason," in *Analecta Hermeneutica*, vol. 4 (2012), 1–18.

Manoussakis, John, *The Ethics of Time* (London: Bloomsbury, 2017).

Marion, Jean-Luc, *In the Self's Place: The Approach of Saint Augustine*, trans. Jeffrey L. Kosky (Palo Alto: Stanford University Press, 2012).

Nietzsche, Friedrich, *The Birth of Tragedy*, trans. Walter Kaufmann (New York: Vintage, 1967).

Nietzsche, Friedrich, *Beyond Good and Evil*, trans. Walter Kaufmann (New York: Vintage, 1989).

Plato, *Symposium*, trans. Alexander Nehamas and Paul Woodruff (Indianapolis: Hackett, 1989).

Plato, *Phaedrus*, trans. Alexander Nehamas and Paul Woodruff (Indianapolis: Hackett, 1995).

Plato, *Five Dialogues: Euthyphro, Apology, Crito, Meno, Phaedo*, trans. GMA Grube (Indianapolis: Hackett, 2002).

Sallis, John, *Being and Logos: Reading the Platonic Dialogues* (Bloomington: Indiana University Press, 1996).

Spitzer, Anais, *Derrida, Myth and the Impossibility of Philosophy* (London: Bloomsbury, 2011).

3

INCARNATION

Eros as touch, caress, kiss

Language stands at the foundation of the erotic drive toward unity. Yet as we have seen, the danger of language is that it creates for us a "world of the symbolic substitution"[1]—a false world that allows us to communicate with one another by means of the use of symbols, signifiers that remove us further and further from the world in which we live. (If thought is a kind of death, it is so at least in part because thought depends upon language.) If, then, we are to resist the allure of the Platonic otherworld, if we are to silence the siren call of pure knowledge, pure ideas—which amount to pure nothingness and a purified death—we must descend into the bodily, experiencing fully this carnate, human existence, excluding nothing, not even the strangest, the most enigmatical, neither the heights nor the depths of the sacredly profane. But can this be done? Can the erotic impulse—which is first *spoken* into existence—be made manifest in and through our fragile bodies? Can the word descend? Can the language of love become flesh and dwell among us?[2]

Heidegger tells us that "the hand is, together with the word, the essential distinction of man. Only a being which, like man, 'has' the word (μύθος, λόγος), can and must 'have' 'the hand.'" He continues:

> The hand sprang forth only out of the word and together with the word. Man does not 'have' hands, but the hand holds the essence of man, because the word as the essential realm of the hand is the ground of the essence of man.[3]

Said differently, it is *through* man that the word becomes incarnate. Word made flesh—or, better yet, word made *hand*—is the essence of man, an essence that man holds in his hands. As Costica Bradatan notes, "[L]ike language, the hand is what makes our life properly *human*.... [It] distinguishes us decisively from animals."[4] (Returning, for a moment, to our previous discussion of the Adamic narrative, we now note two striking elements: first, what man *is*—the breath (word) of life breathed into the flesh of the world [Genesis 2:7]; second, what he *does*—he names [2:19] and he works the earth with his hands [2:15].)[5]

If a word is spoken but not felt, if it does not touch us, move us, call us to action, then it does not register, does not connect. It remains as self-inclosed, as meaningless, indeed as mute, as if it were not spoken at all. More so. For, as our dialogue with Derrida has shown, even words left unsaid can be interpreted and understood. But a fleshless word, like a fleshless soul, is a dead thing. It is literally non-sense, that which cannot be sensed. It may be pure, but its purity is born of its refusal to associate with the messiness of the world—a refusal which, as we have said, amounts to a denial of life itself. *Actions*, so the saying goes, *speak louder than words*. Actions speak? How can an action speak if it is not first and foremost a word? Actions speak louder than words—they speak with more force, with more meaning—because they are words incarnate, words made manifest in the mouths and hands of those who live them into existence.

The soul that touches, or self-knowledge at a price

In *De Anima*, Aristotle tells us that "the soul ... acts like a hand."[6] Unlike unthinking sensation, which receives the external world as "wax receives the impression of the signet-ring,"[7] the soul does not merely receive knowledge passively but reaches out and touches "the objects of thought" which "reside in sensible forms."[8] (Interestingly, Augustine too speaks of the "mental hand" and of how "remembered items ... come to hand easily ... as soon as they are summoned.")[9] It is for this reason, Rosen argues, that "it is not sight but touch, which is the most philosophical of the senses ... [W]e grasp the forms of the things which are, and thereby know them.... Knowing is touching."[10] Yet, as Manoussakis rightly observes, "It is not ... *any* kind of touching that exemplifies knowledge but *grasping*. The soul stretches out toward the things, like a hand ready to feel and hold them in its grip."[11] Indeed, common language betrays the connection: we attempt to *grasp* difficult ideas, to *get a hold* of them, to *handle* them, we *latch on to* their meanings.

This relation between the head and the hand, the rational soul and the sensing body—as Kant says, the hand is "the window on to the mind"[12]—is, Heidegger insists, the essence of man. Manoussakis, commenting on Heidegger, asks, "Dare we say that without his hands man would have been unable to think?"[13] For him, "man began thinking, and still thinks, with his hands, that is, according to a fundamental structure implied by the paradigms of touch."[14] Indeed, it is not until the hand has become a hand—not until it has learned to hold, handle, and manipulate its other—that man has become man, the creature capable of rational thought.

The origin of humanity, as both historians and anthropologists agree, is to be traced back to the invention of tools.... Thus, the hand became emancipated from being used only as a tool—it now manipulates the tools it had itself produced. With much of its duties transferred to tools, the hand became free—it became creative. In fact, the two moments must have coincided: the creation of the first tool by the hand marks the moment when the hand ceases to be a tool. It is now recognized as that which it has always been, but only now can I become aware of it: *my body*. The awareness of my body and consequently … my self-awareness as a subject have always been dependent upon this dialectical relation between the grasping hand and its tool. The tool always refers back to the hand, for the one is meaningful only in relation to the other. The tool is precisely what is graspable: our first concept (*Begriff*).[15]

That Manoussakis locates the birth of the thinking subject in the advent of the body—the recognition of *self as body*, "I am a body"—and grounds the advent of the body in the emancipation of the hand—the freedom of the hand to grasp and manipulate the world around it—points to the fundamentally corporeal nature of the human psyche. As Aristotle says, "[N]o one could ever learn or understand anything without the exercise of perception," without the use of one's hands.[16] But perception, we have said, is that which receives the impression made upon it by the outside world. Thus it is in this connection between the hand that touches and the soul that knows that we begin to see the dependence of the self on its other. Unlike the purely receptive sense organs, the soul is both passive and active—extending itself beyond itself in order to receive that which exists independently of it. As Freud's celebrated posthumous fragment states: *Psyche ist ausgedehnt*. Or, as Chrétien argues, the "soul is the act of touch."[17]

Yet the act of touch always implies duplicity: the soul that touches, in touching, is touched.[18] "Hence the reciprocity of the haptic phenomenon: there cannot be touch that is not 'touched' back—to touch already means to make oneself tangible."[19] And that which exists independently of the soul is that which confronts the soul with itself.

> For in 'touching' the things it seeks to know, the soul-hand is also 'touched' back by the world. As 'touched,' in the act of comprehending, the soul becomes aware of itself. It becomes aware of itself as a soul that 'touches' the world.[20]

Thus we only ever

> sense ourselves … *obliquely*, in the sensing of the other. "Tactile experiencing of the other is simultaneously *self*-experiencing, since otherwise I would not be the one experiencing." But without the other made available to me by my body there would have been no self-experience or self-awareness at all. … "I feel myself only by a favor of the other. It is the other who gives me to myself."[21]

Is this encounter with the self by means of the (soul-)hand's touch upon the other—be it another human being or the otherness of the outside world—an example of the erotic unity for which we have been searching? No. For, if the other brings me to myself, this "favor" of the other is not offered but taken— and, if necessary, taken by force: "It is by virtue of the violence of the hand (its grasping, seizing, and killing the Other) that I first become aware of myself as a separate and distinct self."[22] After all, the soul is like the hand and "[t]he hand brings about the 'work' of destruction."[23] In order to know the self by means of the other, one must first "know" (i.e. grasp) the other. But to know the other is to objectify the other, to make of the other a *thing* to be known. And to know the self by means of the other is to *use*—and, consequently, to abuse—the other as a tool for self-knowledge.

Manoussakis tells us that "One presupposes … things-to-be-thought as things-to-be-grasped, things that, in the grasp of mental comprehension, are to be turned into 'tools.'" "You know something," he insists, only "once you know how to use it. Knowledge amounts to instrumentality."[24] But if "things become known to us by their usage *qua* 'tools,'" how much more do we "know" the other only by the ways in which he presents himself as useful or not, fulfilling or failing to fulfill the role we have ascribed to him? (Think, for instance, of Sartre's famous analysis of the expectations placed upon the tradesman—the waiter, the grocer, the auctioneer, the tailor—by society: "A grocer who dreams is offensive to the buyer, because such a grocer is not wholly a grocer. Society demands that he limit himself to his function as a grocer.")[25]

For Manoussakis, "We never quite know a thing in itself; we know only its function, that is, its instrumentality."[26] Again, if this can be said of objects, how much more can it be said of persons? Is there anything more impenetrable than the soul of another human being? Can it not be said that the "human body directly constitutes the monstrance of what is invisible,"[27] what is most hidden— the other's secret transcendence?[28] But if we only know the other as object, as tool to be grasped and manipulated at will, how then does our knowledge of the other lead us to an understanding of the self?

> The Other is the Other because he or she appears as a tool for me in a way that my body cannot present itself.… The Other's accessibility or resistance to my touch (mental or sensory) furnishes me with a sense of myself *qua myself*. I *am* myself because I can grasp, hold, or seize the Other—who, precisely because of my capability to handle him or her, is not I. The notion of the I cannot come before or independently of the Other. The soul cannot touch (i.e., know) itself but in touching the Other. Self-consciousness is a by-product excreted by the process of sensing the Other.[29]

Self-consciousness as the result of *excretion*, the wasteful by-product of the attempt to grasp, objectify, and violate the other. It is not a happy image. But when we recall the conclusion of our last chapter, the fact that it is by means of the concept

(*Begriff*) that philosophers usher in the death of God—"these honorable idolaters of concepts [*diese Herren Begriffs-Götzendiener*] ... threaten the life of everything they worship"[30]—and when we recognize that, in order to "know" the other, one must first make the other knowable, graspable, a tool—"The tool is precisely what is graspable: our first concept (*Begriff*)"[31]—then we begin to comprehend the monstrous price at which self-knowledge is bought, the cost of being a self, of being human.[32]

The caressing hand, or the impossibility of desire

"A thing," Manoussakis writes, "cannot be loved ... it can only be used."[33] This insight, coupled with the belief that one cannot *not* treat the other as a thing, is perhaps the root cause of Ivan Karamazov's rebellion against "the whole world of knowledge," his insistence that no amount of knowledge is worth the suffering we humans inflict upon one another.[34] Love, he says, is impossible.[35] One can only "love one's neighbor abstractly,"[36] that is, not as a person but as an idea (*Begriff*), *my idea*, that which I can grasp, pin down, objectify. For Ivan, we are incapable of loving real, flesh-and-blood human beings. "If we're to come to love a man, the man himself should stay hidden, because as soon as he shows his face—love vanishes." It is the face of the other—that is, his physicality, *his body*—that makes him so unlovable. It is because he has "a bad smell, or a foolish face, or once stepped on [my] foot" that I find him so revolting.[37]

Yet as Levinas has so convincingly argued, the face of the other is precisely that which "resists possession, resists my powers."[38] (Perhaps this is why Ivan [each of us?] finds the face so unlovable?) "The face presents itself, and demands justice."[39] It "speaks to me and thereby invites me to a relation incommensurate with a power exercised, be it enjoyment or knowledge."[40] According to Levinas, the face is the "total resistance to the grasp,"[41] that which "overflows images which are always immanent to my thought, as though they came from me."[42] My attempt to enslave and objectify the other with the grasp of my soul-hand falls in upon itself. The face represents a "refusal to be contained.... it cannot be comprehended, that is, encompassed."[43] It cannot be known. It must be loved.

But if the grasp fails precisely at its point of departure, if "[t]he Other as Other evades my grasp, slips through my fingers [and] what I am left with is only the outer skin, an empty garment,"[44] how then can I enter into a relation with the other, a relation to which the face of the other invites me? How can I love without insisting that the other stay hidden, without hiding him beneath my attempt to know/grasp him? How can I allow him to reveal himself from himself, to show himself as he who can never be reduced to my concept, my knowledge, the projection of my image onto the body of a man?

The grasp, we have said, brings self-knowledge by means of oppression: "the privilege of touch consists" in giving me "the knowledge of my body through the body of the Other ... '[whose] body appears to me originally as ... an *instrument* which I can utilize with other instruments.'"[45] According to Manoussakis, the subjective realization that "I am a body" is brought about "by the act of grasp-ing," by my objectification of the other who has fallen into my hands.[46] Thus to refuse to grasp, to relinquish power, the power that I exercise over the other, is to renounce my subjectivity, to make myself graspable, an object, a thing to be cared for or condemned, consecrated or cursed. One cannot love a thing. One can only love a person. Thus if I am to be a lover, if I am to love another and not simply a projection of myself, I must first forgo my desire to possess the object of my love. I must instead become for my beloved a gift, an offering which when given may be accepted or rejected, received with gratitude or denounced and disowned. The lover does not grasp. He does not use force. The lover presents himself as an object, weak and vulnerable, so that the subjectivity of the beloved may emerge. He touches in order to offer himself as touchable. He denies his desire so that the desire of the beloved may be realized through the renunciation of his own.

How might this be accomplished? What becomes of the grasping hand when it loosens its grip, when it lets go of all it has known? "The domestication of the grasping hand," Manoussakis writes, "has given rise to the caress."[47] "Whereas the grasping hand sought to establish distance by affirming dominance over the Other (a subjugated human being, a hunted animal, a seized object), the caress is nothing else than the continuous annihilation of the distance that separates me from the Other."[48] The caress, Sartre insists, is primarily concerned with the other as other. It is a desire for the otherness of the other, "an attempt to *incar-nate* the Other's body,"[49] "to impregnate the Other's body with consciousness and freedom."[50] "The caress is not a simple stroking; it is a *shaping*. In caressing the Other I cause her flesh to be born beneath my caress, under my fingers."[51] According to Sartre, the lover desires the other as "pure flesh"—that is, he desires her as "the *pure contingency of presence*," that which is not concealed behind "move-ments," "action," "situation," or "possibilities."[52]

> By flesh we do not mean a *part* of the body such as the dermis, the con-nective tissues or, specifically, epidermis.... But the caress reveals the flesh by stripping the body of its action, by cutting it off from the possibilities which surround it; the caress is designed to uncover the web of inertia beneath the action—i.e., the pure 'being-there'—which sustains it.[53]

In caressing the other, the lover desires the beloved as a person, not an object or actor. He desires her as "touched passivity," that is, the pure being-there of a body which has been stripped of all of its accidents and has become what it truly is—a body "made flesh." But in order to approach the flesh of the other, the lover must himself become flesh, must forsake the grasp of the hand and instead offer himself as a passivity which, in touching, is touched:

> To take hold of the Other reveals to her her inertia and her passivity ... but this is not to caress her. In the caress it is not only my body as a synthetic

form in action which caresses the Other; it is my body as flesh which causes the Other's flesh to be born. The caress is designed to cause the Other's body to be born, through pleasure, for the Other—and for myself—as *touched* passivity in such a way that my body is made flesh in order to touch the Other's body with its own passivity; that is, by caressing itself with the Other's body rather than by caressing hers.[54]

For Sartre, "it is not a question so much of taking hold of a part of the Other's body as of placing one's own body against the Other's body. Not so much to push or touch in an active sense but to place against."[55] Thus the *activity* of the grasping hand—the hand that reaches out and manipulates its object at will—is relinquished. The lover, for the sake of the beloved, adopts a *passivity* which, in touching itself with the flesh of the beloved, causes "her flesh to be born beneath [his] caress, under [his] fingers."[56]

And yet, his "fingers which [he] run[s] over her arm are inert at the end of [his] hand"[57]—the lover refuses to violate the beloved, to turn her into an object, a tool for self-knowledge. Instead, he makes of himself an offering, a gift of flesh which, through pleasure, brings the beloved to herself (and him along with her).

> Thus the revelation of the Other's flesh is made through my own flesh; in desire and in the caress which expresses desire, I incarnate myself in order to realize the incarnation of the Other. The caress by *realizing* the Other's incarnation reveals to me my own incarnation; that is, I make myself flesh in order to impel the Other to realize *for-herself* and *for me* her own flesh, and my caresses cause my flesh to be born for me in so far as it is for the Other *flesh causing her to be born as flesh.* I make her enjoy my flesh through her flesh in order to compel her to feel herself flesh.... Thus in desire there is an attempt at the incarnation of consciousness ... in order to realize the incarnation of the Other.[58]

The caress, it would seem, is the unmaking of the grasp, the renunciation of the self out of love for the other.

> Each stroke of my hand assures the Other of my resignation from violence, of the relinquishing of my power to grasp, seize, or kill him. Each stroke of my hand abdicates my authority as a subject to whom the Other is forced to be subjected.[59]

Rather, it is *I* who have become an object for the sake of the other, I who am now subjected to the other's will:

> in order to allow the Other's subjectivity to manifest itself as such, I have to resign from mine. I have to undertake or undergo a self-willed *kenosis.* I let

myself become an object for the Other. I make myself open and vulnerable to the Other's touch.[60]

In doing so, the experience of *myself as body*—the "I am a body" of subjectivity—is "abandoned" and the possibility of experiencing myself as *having a body*—that is, being an object for the other—arises.[61]

Manoussakis is unambiguous on this point:

> In the caress the Other is not any more the Object of my grasp but the intangible Subject of my touch.... My caress offers recognition to the Other's subjectivity, witness to the Other's transcendence, a transcendence beyond the realm of the things palpable by my hand—*for it would be meaningless for me to caress an object or a thing*. In caressing the Other, I have already recognized the Other as Other and not as a thing to be felt or known. Under my caress the Other is not a 'tool' assigned with a given function ... the caress seeks the infinite but an infinite mysteriously immanent, that is, embodied in the body of the Other.[62]

In caressing the other, in touching her flesh with the passivity of my flesh, I seek to annihilate the distance that separates us. My hand passes over the warmth of her body; she freely accepts my touch, my fingers in her hair, her mouth, on her skin; there is excitation and rapid breathing, pleasure—hers and mine—I can no longer tell where hers ends and mine begins. Who is touching whom? I am lost in the dizzying proximity of flesh on flesh, warm on warm, she and I achieving an intimacy, a nearness, a reciprocity of desire and of touch that neither could have experienced alone—

And yet ... "Such is the impossible ideal of desire: to possess the Other's transcendence as pure transcendence and at the same time as body."[63] But this ideal is impossible, this desire futile, because "[t]he Other's free subjectivity is precisely that which cannot be touched,"[64] that which can never be penetrated or possessed, that which I cannot enter, will never fully know. According to Manoussakis, "[T]he caress only 'veils' distance as its very condition.... The caress is not the contact of flesh with flesh, but rather the *approach* of a body toward another."[65] And this approach which veils distance, this attraction of one body to another, "amounts to a forgetfulness of the violence of touch," a forgetfulness which conceals from the lover and the beloved the hideous truth that "the caressing hand is nothing else than the grasping hand that forgets or resigns from its violence."[66]

The caressing hand *is* the grasping hand. It is the grasping that forgets (deceives itself into forgetting?) its own violence, the essence of its being. But is not such a hand—the hand that conceals its pitiless, objectifying grasp—doomed, sooner or later, to become what it already is? Is not such a hand secretly working to achieve its unspoken desire, its thirst for power, domination, destruction, and death? Is there not, ever at work, a pernicious and pervasive compulsion to repeat?

The chiasmus of the kiss, or a possible way forward

Beyond the subject/object distinction revealed by contrasting the grasp with the caress is, according to Manoussakis, the unity or chiasmus of the kiss. "The 'I am a body,' yielded by the act of grasping, and the 'I have a body,' revealed to me through the caress" are not "merely two different phenomena of *one* and the same reality (essence or nature), but rather two distinct manifestations that are brought to unity by a chiastic 'kiss.'"[67] For Manoussakis, the kiss symbolizes man's (erotic) striving for "perfect unity." It is for this reason that "the kiss resists conceptualization," that no "concepts, paradigms, or metaphors could be employed in order to think the kiss."[68]

> Our thought suffers primarily from the lack of concepts by which to think the kiss—for the kiss itself is a *symbol* (in the literary sense of *symballein*: to put together two halves) and is thus unable to be represented with anything other than itself.[69]

> The metaphor comes from the ancient practice of two people breaking between them a piece of pottery, a coin, or a seal with each keeping one fragment of it, as a reminder and future evidence of the kinship or friendship between them. When the holders of each half meet again they would put together (συμβάλλειν) the two pieces and thus affirm (or prove) their relationship with each other. For that reason, each fragment of the divided coin or seal was called a "*symbolon*." It is easy to see how the union of lips, the two mouths brought together in kissing, stands as a symbol of this practice of *symballein*. As if my mouth were one of two matching tallies, to be "fitted" on the Other's mouth, like two pieces of a puzzle fit together. The kiss is a symbol of this symbol, a symbolism of an intimacy that affirms itself as it strives to achieve perfect unity.[70]

Symbolically, the kiss reveals to us "our longing for union with our 'other half.'"[71] (The reader will, no doubt, recognize the resonance not only with Plato's *Symposium* but also with our opening comments on *Beyond the Pleasure Principle*.) But the kiss also brings unity to the "two fragmentary views of my body," the *I am* and *I have* discussed above.[72]

How does the kiss bridge the gap between these "two different ways of affirming myself"?[73] According to Manoussakis, the kiss, like the caress, represents a kind self-willed *kenosis* in which the lover renounces his will for the sake of the beloved. "The mouth or, more precisely, the possibilities of the mouth reveal the implied intentions of the hand: the grasping of an object implies biting while the caressing of the Other implies kissing."[74] If in the caress I offer myself as an object to my beloved—if I give myself to her as the toucher who in touching is made touchable—then in the kiss I find her response. In the kiss, I find the gift of her reception of my self-gift. The caress is my incarnate word's declaration, "Here I am."[75] It is my self-offering *kenosis* to my beloved for her pleasure and my own.

The kiss is her reception of my kenotic self-emptying. It is her response, her "may it be done to me according to your word" (Luke 1:38), which constitutes a thanksgiving (*eucharistia*) which empties itself in order to receive my "Here I am." And by emptying herself in thanksgiving—an act as selfless and unreserved as my original self-emptying—she offers herself back to me as self-giving, self-receiving gift. The "I am a body" of subjectivity and the "I have a body" of objectivity "crisscross each other in the double manifestation of my body that is united in the chiasmus of the kiss."[76]

Like the caress, the kiss finds the lover freely giving himself to the beloved. But unlike the caress, the kiss allows the beloved to respond and reciprocate. In the kiss, the beloved responds to the self-giving of the lover by receiving his self-gift and by, in the very act of receiving, giving both her reception and herself back to the lover as a eucharistic thanksgiving. In the kiss, the one who is kissed is never simply kissed but also kisser. She not only receives but also gives. And she gives far more than she receives. For, the kisser gives only his kiss, only himself. But the one kissed gives her kiss—herself—and infinitely more. She gives the kisser his very being. For, if she so chooses, she can reject the kisser's kiss and thus deny him his being as kisser. Her acceptance of his kiss affirms him as kisser and thus makes him who he is. Without her reception, he is neither who he is nor who he wants to be. With her reception, he is himself and more than he could have ever dreamed to be.

The beloved's reception of the lover's kiss allows the lover to become not only kisser but also kissed. He is no longer simply himself as the one who offers his kiss but is now transformed into both the one who kisses and the one who is kissed. And at the very moment that he becomes both kisser and kissed, he also receives the power to transform the beloved into both who she is as the one kissed and more than who she is as kisser. The kiss, then, constitutes for the lover (1) his gift-of-self to the beloved, (2) her reception of his self-gift in the kiss, and (3) the transformation brought about by her reception of him into him as both kisser (affirming who he is) and kissed (affirming who he could not have been). And the kiss constitutes for the beloved (1) her reception of the gift given to her by the lover, (2) her reception's transformation of the lover into both kisser and kissed and (3) his transformation's transformation of her into both the one who is kissed (affirming who she is) and kisser (affirming who she could not have been). Thanks to these transformations (and the unity of self/other, subject/object, lover/beloved that they occasion), "the 'I' of the 'I have' fully overlaps and is at last identified with the 'I' of the 'I am'"[77] and I become for the first time what I have always been yet could never be: myself and not myself, myself as the other, in the other, revealed through the other, a self conceived by and for the sake of love.

Betraying Eros with a kiss, or biting the bread of life

Yet ... have not the pretenses of language and the forgetfulness of the hand taught us to be wary of any phenomenon that promises to deliver such marvels?

Ought not the corrupting influence of Thanatos—which, we have said, is only a false Eros, a wolf in erotic clothes—to give us pause, especially before so seductive a symbol? Can it truly be that the kiss represents the eschatological end of the erotic drive, the "perfect unity" of lover and beloved? Does the kiss really unify my fragmented psyche, save my splintered soul? *How now?* When Manoussakis himself points out the natural link between kissing and biting?[78] When it is he who reminds us that "the kiss of betrayal" is among "the different types" of kisses?[79] (Careful philosophers, lest you hear repeated to you that most dreadful utterance: "Are you betraying the Son of Man with a kiss?")

According to Manoussakis, "The mouth is the arbiter of touch."

> It has been often observed that as soon as babies are able to grasp their toys, they bring them to their mouth. In that gesture, the infant reenacts a 'natural' move: from the hand to the mouth. ... The mouth provides the context within which the hand's activity becomes meaningful."[80]

For Freud, however, the exact inverse is true. "Infants," he writes, "perform actions which have no purpose other than obtaining pleasure;"[81] and their earliest experience of pleasure comes in "connection with taking nourishment," that is, in the "excitation of the areas of the mouth and lips."[82] Soon, infants learn to separate the experience of pleasure from the need for food and thus develop "the pleasure derived from sucking"—a pleasure which Freud describes as "a sexual one."

> Sucking at the mother's breast is the starting-point of the whole sexual life, the unmatched prototype of every later sexual satisfaction.... This sucking involves making the mother's breast the first object of the sexual instinct.... at first the infant, in his sucking activity, gives up this object and replaces it by a part of his own body. He begins to suck his thumbs or own tongue. In this way he makes himself independent of the consent of the external world as regards gaining pleasure.[83]

From the mouth to the hand is for Freud the natural progression. And from the hand onward: "it is ... an important experience when the infant ... discovers, in the course of feeling around, the specially excitable regions afforded by his genitals and so finds his way from sucking to masturbation."[84]

But infantile masturbation is not the only behavior born of sensual sucking. According to Freud, the whole sexual life—healthy and perverse—finds its origin in the mouth.[85] "Behind the sadistic-anal phase of libidinal development we get a glimpse of a still earlier and more primitive stage of organization in which the erotogenic zone of the mouth plays the chief role. As you will guess, the sexual activity of sensual sucking belongs to it."[86] Far from providing us with an inverted hierarchy of the senses which allows touch—and thus "the arbiter of touch," the mouth[87]—to "occupy the highest and most exalted place,"[88] as

Manoussakis is wont to do, Freud finds in the mouth the root cause of perversion.[89] "For Freud ... the kiss is the first perversion. It is the prelude to all other perversions, since it is a use of erogenous zones with the aim of pure pleasure, separated from the goal of reproduction."[90]

In the kiss, Freud sees not a symbol of "perfect unity" but an example of how "[n]o healthy person ... can fail to make some addition that might be called perverse to the normal sexual aim."[91] Consider the following "somewhat puritanical"[92] passage from Freud's twenty-first lecture in the *Introductory Lectures on Psychoanalysis*:

> However infamous they may be, however sharply they may be contrasted with normal sexual activity, quiet consideration will show that some perverse trait or other is seldom absent from the sexual life of normal people. Even a kiss can claim to be described as a perverse act, since it consists in the bringing together of two oral erotogenic zones instead of the two genitals. Yet no one rejects it as perverse; on the contrary, it is permitted in theatrical performances as a softened hint at the sexual act. But precisely kissing can easily turn into complete perversion—if, that is to say, it becomes so intense that a genital discharge and orgasm follow upon it directly, an event that is far from rare.[93]

The literary critic J. Hillis Miller detects "a faint disgust" in Freud's views on kissing.[94] And when we consider another passage from Freud found in a related essay, we begin to understand why:

> But even in the most normal sexual process we may detect rudiments which, if they had developed, would have led to the deviations described as "perversions." ... the kiss, one particular contact of this kind, between the mucous membrane of the lips of the two people concerned, is held in high sexual esteem among many nations (including the most highly civilized ones), in spite of the fact that the parts of the body involved do not form part of the sexual apparatus but constitute the entrance to the digestive tract. Here, then, are factors which provide a point of contact between the perversions and normal sexual life and which can also serve as a basis for their classification.[95]

Miller remarks, "Who, when kissing one's beloved, would want to remember that her or his lips are no more than the entrance to the stomach and intestines?"[96]

Yet if we share Dr. Miller's disgust with such realizations, if we find the thought that erotic "Love has pitched his mansion in/ The place of excrement" as revolting as Miller clearly does,[97] perhaps it is because the kiss, for us, remains symbolic—and nothing more. Perhaps we prefer the kiss to be metaphorical, an image of perfect unity, the unity of the self which, when achieved, leaves little room for the other. (It is telling that Manoussakis, as

Augustinian a thinker as there is, allows just a hint of that old Gnostic belief in self-divinization to enter his work precisely when speaking of that which is meant to be most carnal; the kiss, he tells us, brings unity to the "two different ways of affirming myself.")[98]

It is true that kissing is related to biting, that "[t]he lips are a boundary … portals where the inside is exposed to the outside, where the breath of life passes in and out, where food is taken in and speech is breathed forth."[99] To kiss, then, is to do more than press the entrance of one's digestive tract to that of the other's. It is to open oneself to the other, to expose one's insides, what is deepest and most concealed, one's guts, one's bowels, one's soul (*psyche* literally means "breath"). It is to take the other into oneself, to receive the other as one receives his daily bread, to ingest him, to scarf him down. The nearness of kissing and biting— sometimes kissing involves biting—reveals the desire to consume the other, to devour him, to bring him into myself and make him what I am.

For Manoussakis—and here, he renounces any Gnostic tendencies once and for all—the task of Christianity "is not to spiritualize the flesh, but to incarnate the spirit, and in this regard the verticality of the Greek schema (Platonic and Neo-Platonic) of ascents and descents has to be abandoned for the sake of a communion between exteriority and interiority."[100] That which is outside of me, which is other than me, must enter into me, must become me, must be made my flesh and blood, the marrow of my bones. But that is not all. I too must vacate myself, must offer myself, must pour myself forth. I must enter into that which is not me, that which transcends me, the wholly other.

This communion between inside and outside, self and other, Manoussakis tells us, is made manifest every time we eat a meal:

> Eating is not only a way for recognizing our dependency to each other and to the world … but by eating we assimilate the world to ourselves, we turn that which is outside inside…. Ultimately, distance comes down to this opposition between an inside (that I identify with myself) and everything else that is outside me. In eating, however, this wall of separation collapses—when I am hungry I am really hungry for the Other (following Sartre and Levinas)—and eating is one of the ways we have in overcoming our isolation that is the result of being scattered beings.[101]

When I eat, I declare "my dependence on the world, on the cows which provide me with their meat, but also on the grass that fed the cows, on the water that fertilized the soil on which that grass grew, and so on."[102] (Does this dependence upon the other negate the independence from "the consent of the external world as regards gaining pleasure" that I seized for myself as an infant through the autoerotism of "sexual sucking"?)[103] When I eat, I take into myself the entire world, all that exists beyond me.[104] And, more importantly, I take in the other—the farmer who worked the land, the butcher who slaughtered the cow, the cook who prepared the meal, the waiter who brought it to my table. "No meal is ever solitary—even if I eat alone in the seclusion of my room—every meal is a public and communal event. A community established and referred to by every bite."[105]

But not only does the world enter into me when it passes through my lips, the portals where inside is exposed and outside enters in. Eating also has the power to take me out of myself and unite me with that which transcends me.

> It is our body that abridges the distance that keeps separating us from others, but it is our body that allows us to be united with God—it is not accidental that we *eat* the Eucharist and that the liturgy takes the form of a meal.[106]

> Every time one partakes of communion he or she does not change the host into their body but it changes them—in an inverse digestion indicative and exemplary of inverse intentionality—into Christ's body. As Augustine was told: "I am the food of the mature; grow then, and you will eat me. You will not change me into yourself like bodily food: you will be changed into me" (VII. 10.16, 173). The Church is turning the world into Christ a mass at a time.[107]

Here, in the eucharistic meal, the communion between exteriority and interiority is accomplished. Here, the incarnation of the word is achieved.

Yet it is important to note that this glimpse of the eschaton, this taste of the end toward which man's erotic drive is striving, is not brought about by ascending away from the carnality of the kiss. (Receiving the Eucharist unites my body with the body of Christ, his *Corpus*, his flesh and blood; as a communicant, I am not seeking to unify myself or the conflicting ways of "affirming myself.") Nor does it simply do away with the violence of the mouth. In the Eucharist, the lips that kiss and the mouth that bites are understood to be one and the same mouth, sanctified and vulgar, sacredly profane. These lips that would be "kissed with the kiss of truth, for Truth has revealed Himself as a person (John 14:6),"[108] are instead invited to gnaw on his body, to bite it, to betray it, to gnash it between the teeth. (The formulation of the prayer for the consecration of the host in the Canon of the Mass is insightful: "Take this all of you and eat it [*Accipite et manducate*, literally "take and chew"]. This is my body [*Corpus*], which will be given up for you [*quod pro vobis tradetur*, which is betrayed for you].")

Even the kiss of betrayal can be sanctified. (It is worth pondering how, in receiving the Eucharist, each of us is invited into the role of betrayer, placing the kiss of death upon the bread of life; we must never forget our relation to Judas who was invited to receive the first Eucharist at the last supper.) And at the eschaton, when the incarnate word reconciles all things to himself (Colossians 1:20) and makes "all things new" (Revelation 21:5), then the communion between exteriority and interiority, self and other, will be fully realized—made manifest in the loving embrace of husband and wife (cf. Ephesians 5:32).

Notes

1 Manoussakis, *The Ethics of Time*, 106.
2 Julia Kristeva, in her recent work on St. Teresa, notes the influence that the Jesuits had on Teresa's prayer life. According to Kristeva, they taught her to "pray through the excitation of the senses" and to identify with the suffering Christ by employing

> a quasi-infantile nonexistent language that regresses toward and drowns itself in the sensible. Here we find a language that is not language, the dismantling of language itself, the investment of the sensorial body in the identification of the different stages of Christ's crucifixion.
>
> *(Kristeva, "Mysticism and Anatheism," 78)*

3 Heidegger, *Parmenides*, as quoted in Manoussakis, *God After Metaphysics*, 125.
4 Bradatan, *Dying for Ideas*, 50.
5 See:

> It would be difficult to overestimate the role of the hand in the human history and ontology. Much of what we are—not only anatomically, but also in terms of our cognitive capacities—is due to it. We use the hand to act upon the world, to position ourselves in relation to it, as well as to make sense of the world—to "grasp" it.
>
> *(Ibid., 49)*

6 Aristotle, *On the Soul*, (III. viii, p. 181).
7 Ibid., (II, xii, p. 137).
8 Ibid., (III. viii, p. 181).
9 See, Augustine, *Confessions*, (10.8.12).
10 SH Rosen, as quoted in Manoussakis, *God After Metaphysics*, 126.
11 Manoussakis, *God After Metaphysics*, 126.
12 As quoted in Bradatan, *Dying for Ideas*, 49.
13 Manoussakis, *God After Metaphysics*, 126.
14 Ibid.
15 Ibid., 125.
16 Aristotle, *On the Soul*, (III. viii, p. 181).
17 Chrétien, *The Call and the Response*, 108.
18 Cf.

> The touched and touching body—touched because it touches, touching because it is touched, always having elsewhere the sufficient reason of its bodily being— this body organizes itself around itself, that is, around this contact of bodies that has no end other than itself.
>
> *(Nancy, Corpus II, 96)*

19 Manoussakis, *God After Metaphysics*, 132.
20 Ibid., 127.
21 Ibid., 128.
22 Ibid., 124.
23 Heidegger, *Parmenides*, as quoted in ibid., 125.
24 Ibid., 126.
25 Sartre, *Being and Nothingness*, 102.
26 Manoussakis, *God After Metaphysics*, 126–127.
27 Chrétien, *The Call and the Response*, 83.
28 Cf. "The Other remains infinitely transcendent, infinitely foreign." Levinas, *Totality and Infinity*, 194.

29 Manoussakis, *God After Metaphysics*, 128.
30 Nietzsche, *Twilight of the Idols*, as quoted in Manoussakis, "The Philosopher-Priest,"
    1.
31 Manoussakis, *God After Metaphysics*, 125.
32 See,

> The man who makes the first tool is not anymore an animal. The man who hunts
> and eats his kill with his own hands is not any more an animal.... I become more
> than an animal. I become a human. Other humans ... have no indemnity against
> being treated as animals. The other human, once fallen to my *hands*, loses its
> human status and assumes that of an animal.... Wars imitate tribal huntings and
> reenact the game of killing. Slaves were counted together with other animals as
> part of one's livestock, and they were to be treated as such. Arrest and imprison-
> ment are institutions that spring from the practices of catching and caging wild
> animals. The Other, whom I can manipulate according to my will and whims,
> has taken the place of the animal.
>
> *(Ibid., 124–125)*

33 Ibid., 141.
34 Dostoevsky, *The Brothers Karamazov*, 242.
35 See, "'I must make an admission,' Ivan began. 'I never could understand how it's
    possible to love one's neighbor. In my opinion, it is precisely one's neighbors that
    one cannot possibly love.'" Ibid., 236.
36 Ibid., 237.
37 Ibid.
38 Levinas, *Totality and Infinity*, 197.
39 Ibid., 294.
40 Ibid., 198.
41 Ibid., 197.
42 Ibid., 297.
43 Ibid., 194.
44 Manoussakis, *God After Metaphysics*, 130.
45 Ibid., 128.
46 Ibid., 138.
47 Ibid., 129.
48 Ibid., 130.
49 Sartre, *Being and Nothingness*, 506.
50 Ibid., 516.
51 Ibid., 506–507.
52 Ibid.
53 Ibid., 507.
54 Ibid.
55 Ibid., 507–508.
56 Ibid., 507.
57 Ibid., 508.
58 Ibid.
59 Manoussakis, *God After Metaphysics*, 132.
60 Ibid.
61 "The Other's touch has caused me to *have* a body (incarnation), which is still the
    body that I am, but now posited as another's." Ibid., 132.
62 Ibid., 131.
63 Sartre, *Being and Nothingness*, 512.
64 Manoussakis, *God After Metaphysics*, 131.
65 Ibid., 130.

66 Ibid., 130.
67 Ibid., 138.
68 Ibid., 137.
69 Ibid.
70 Ibid., 137–138.
71 Ibid., 137.
72 Ibid., 138.
73 Ibid.
74 Ibid., 137.
75 Here, I make use of the scriptural language (cf. Genesis 22:1) employed by Marion to describe the "oath" made by the lover to the beloved. According to Marion, "Here I am" represents the lover's self-presentation, his self-offering which dares "to claim to give itself without holding back, without return—forever." Marion, however, would hardly agree with my appropriating his language to refer to the caress, which he calls "superficial in every sense." "The eroticization that gives rise to the flesh does not result from a touch that is simply less possessive, groping, or predatory than another." See Marion, *The Erotic Phenomenon*, 104 and 119 respectively.
76 Manoussakis, *God After Metaphysics*, 139.
77 Ibid.
78 In addition to the passage from *God After Metaphysics* quoted above, cf. also Manoussakis's recent commentary on Oscar Wilde's banned play *Salome* which tells the story of the beheading of John the Baptist by Herod at the behest of his stepdaughter:

> The macabre object of her [Salome's] desire is served to her on a silver platter: the decapitated head of St. John the Baptist (Iokanaan). What could she possibly want to do with a dead head? ... Isn't it the desire of every woman to kiss the decapitated head? As soon as the head of the Prophet emerges from the underground cistern, Salome seizes it and addresses him in these words: "Ah! thou wouldst not suffer me to kiss thy mouth, Iokanaan. Well! I will kiss it now. I will bite it with my teeth as one bites a ripe fruit. Yes, I will kiss thy mouth, Iokanaan. I said it; did I not say it?" ... Like a praying mantis, Salome wants to eat the head of St. John's decapitated body.
>
> *(Manoussakis, "Dying to Desire," 132)*

79 Manoussakis, *God After Metaphysics*, 137.
80 Ibid.
81 Freud, *Introductory Lectures on Psychoanalysis*, 313–314.
82 Ibid., 314.
83 Ibid.
84 Ibid.
85 "Both perverse and normal sexuality have arisen out of infantile sexuality." Ibid., 323.
86 Ibid., 327.
87 Manoussakis, *God After Metaphysics*, 137.
88 Ibid., 147.
89 For Freud,

> The abandonment of the reproductive function is the common feature of all perversions. We actually describe a sexual activity as perverse if it has given up the aim of reproduction and pursues the attainment of pleasure as an aim independent of it.
>
> *(Introductory Lectures on Psychoanalysis, 316)*

90 Miller, *Literature as Conduct*, 33.
91 Freud, *Three Essays on Sexuality*, 160.
92 Miller, *Literature as Conduct*, 33.
93 Freud, *Introductory Lectures on Psychoanalysis*, 322.
94 Miller, *Literature as Conduct*, 34.
95 Freud, *Three Essays on Sexuality*, 149–150.
96 Miller, *Literature as Conduct*, 34.
97 WB Yeats, "Crazy Jane Talks with the Bishop," as quoted in ibid., 35.
98 Manoussakis, *God After Metaphysics*, 138.
99 Miller, *Literature as Conduct*, 35.
100 Manoussakis, *The Ethics of Time*, 103–104.
101 Ibid., 104.
102 Ibid.
103 Freud, *Introductory Lectures on Psychoanalysis*, 314.
104 See,

> In eating, I make the world my flesh and my blood, *not* my spirit, but I incarnate or rather I incorporate—the original and literal meaning of incorporation—the world which, otherwise, would have remained an abstraction in spite of its cows, its grass, and its soil.
>
> *(Manoussakis,* The Ethics of Time, *105)*

105 Ibid., 104.
106 Ibid., 104.
107 Ibid., 105.
108 Manoussakis, *God After Metaphysics*, 142.

Bibliography

Aristotle, *On the Soul. Parva Naturalia. On Breath*, trans. WS Hett, Loeb Classical Library No. 288 (Cambridge: Harvard University Press, 1957).

Augustine, *Confessions*, trans. Maria Boulding (New York: Vintage, 1998).

Bradatan, Costica, *Dying for Ideas: The Dangerous Lives of the Philosophers* (London: Bloomsbury, 2015).

Chrétien, Jean-Louis, *The Call and the Response*, trans. Anne Davenport (New York: Fordham University Press, 2004).

Dostoevsky, Fyodor, *The Brothers Karamazov*, trans. Richard Pevear and Larissa Volokhonsky (New York: Farrar, Straus and Giroux, 2002).

Freud, Sigmund, *Three Essays on Sexuality*, in *The Standard Edition of the Complete Psychological Works of Sigmund Freud*, trans. James Strachey, vol. VII (London: Hogarth, 1953).

Freud, Sigmund, *Introductory Lectures on Psychoanalysis*, trans. James Strachey (New York: WW Norton, 1977).

Kristeva, Julia, "Mysticism and Anatheism: The Case of Teresa," in *Richard Kearney's Anatheistic Wager: Philosophy, Theology, Poetics*, eds. Chris Doude van Troostwijk and Matthew Clemente (Bloomington: Indiana University Press, 2018), 68–87.

Levinas, Emmanuel, *Totality and Infinity: An Essay on Exteriority*, trans. Alphonso Lingis (Pittsburg: Duquesne University Press, 1969).

Manoussakis, John, *God After Metaphysics: A Theological Aesthetic* (Bloomington: Indiana University Press, 2007).

Manoussakis, John, "The Philosopher-Priest and the Mythology of Reason," in *Analecta Hermeneutica*, vol. 4 (2012), 1–18.

Manoussakis, John, *The Ethics of Time* (London: Bloomsbury, 2017).

Manoussakis, John, "Dying to Desire: Soma, Sema, Sarx, and Sex," in *Somatic Desire: Rethinking Corporeality in Contemporary Thought*, eds. Sarah Horton, et al. (London: Lexington Books, 2019), 117–137.

Marion, Jean-Luc, *The Erotic Phenomenon*, trans. Stephen E Lewis (Chicago: University of Chicago, 2007).

Miller, J Hillis, *Literature as Conduct*: *Speech Acts in Henry James* (New York: Fordham University Press, 2005).

Nancy, Jean-Luc, *Corpus II: Writings on Sexuality*, trans. Anne O'Byrne (New York: Fordham University Press, 2013).

Sartre, Jean-Paul, *Being and Nothingness: An Essay on Phenomenological Ontology*, trans. Hazel Bames (New York: Simon and Schuster, 1992).

4

ESCHATON

Sex as contradiction

Toward the end of our last chapter we noted that, according to Freud, "No healthy person ... can fail to make some addition that might be called perverse to the normal sexual aim."[1] Indeed, for him the fact that "unusual kinds of sexual satisfaction ... are ... quite common and widespread phenomena"[2] is attributable to the psychoanalytic hypothesis that

> all these inclinations to perversion had their roots in childhood, that children have a predisposition to all of them and carry them out to an extent corresponding to their immaturity—in short, that perverse sexuality is nothing else than a magnified infantile sexuality split up into separate impulses.[3]

Accordingly, Freud concludes that

> people who are normal to-day have passed along a path of development that has led through the perversions and object-cathexes of the Oedipus complex, that that is the path of normal development and that neurotics merely exhibit to us in a magnified and coarsened form what the analysis of dreams reveals to us in healthy people as well.[4]

The assertion that we honest, God-fearing citizens closely resemble the pervert, that we share his devious predisposition and have *already* (as children, no less!) carried out his revolting crimes, is unsettling to say the least. (It is for this reason, Freud contends, that "sexual perversions are subject to a quite special ban."

> It is as though no one could forget that they are not only something disgusting but also something monstrous and dangerous—as though people felt them as seductive, and had at bottom to fight down a secret envy of those who were enjoying them.)[5]

Yet, in spite of his fear that we, his listeners, "have been waiting for a long time to interrupt and exclaim: 'Enough of these atrocities!'"[6] Freud's assessment, upon further consideration, is perhaps less contentious than he would have us believe. (We will not go so far as to call it prosaic.) Was it not, after all, a 5th century bishop who found it necessary to confess "whatever sins I did not commit, for what would I not have been capable of, I who could be enamored even of a wanton crime"?[7] Was it not he who openly admitted to having satisfied his "carnal desire" by masturbating in a church during mass?[8] (And let us not forget this pious saint's extended discourse on the sinfulness of infants.) No, that the human heart is more perverse than anything—"beyond remedy," the prophet insists (Jeremiah 17:9)—is not so startling a claim; it is, rather, one of the first discoveries made by any man who honestly examines himself.

"The strongest saints and the strongest sceptics," GK Chesterton once remarked, "took positive evil as the starting-point of their argument."

> If it be true (as it certainly is) that a man can feel exquisite happiness in skinning a cat, then the religious philosopher can only draw one of two deductions. He must either deny the existence of God, as all atheists do; or he must deny the present union between God and man, as all Christians do.[9]

That we find so much overlap between Freud and Augustine, the psychoanalyst and the orthodox Christian—especially on the topic of perversion—ought not to surprise us. (Lacan goes so far as to assert that "Saint Augustine … foreshadowed psychoanalysis.")[10] After all, both attempt to offer an image of the phenomena of life by plumbing the depths of the human soul. And it is by doing so, by examining the perpetual struggle which wars in the heart of man and the "violent contradictions"[11] that manifest themselves in sexuality—make no mistake, the two are connected[12]—that we begin to unearth a deeper, more arresting paradox; one which will inevitably lead us beyond the considerations that have concerned us thus far. But more on that in the pages to come.

The omnipotence of love: Sex as the highest and the lowest

If we are ready to agree with Freud that "normal people too can substitute a perversion … for the normal sexual aim"[13] and that "[i]n the sphere of sexual life we are brought up against peculiar and, indeed, insoluble difficulties as soon as we try to draw a sharp line to distinguish mere variations within the range of what is physiological from pathological symptoms,"[14] then we will be forced not only to admit that "the universality of this finding is in itself enough to show how inappropriate it is to use the word perversion as a term of reproach"[15] but will also have to take seriously Freud's more shocking claim: "It is perhaps in connection precisely with the most repulsive perversions" that the beauty and mystery of human sexuality—"the omnipotence of love"—shines through.[16] Certain perversions, Freud writes, "are so far removed from the normal in their content that we cannot avoid pronouncing them 'pathological.'"[17] Among these pathologies, he lists "cases of licking excrement [and] of intercourse with dead bodies," cases where "the sexual instinct goes to astonishing lengths in successfully overriding the resistances of shame, disgust, horror or pain."[18]

That such perversions exist is hardly newsworthy. Sexual depravity has been around as long as we featherless bipeds have populated the earth. That they somehow reveal the heights of man's erotic love is, however, a more contestable claim. And yet, that is precisely what Freud argues:

> It is impossible to deny that in [such] case[s] a piece of mental work has been performed which, in spite of its horrifying result, is the equivalent of an idealization of the instinct. The omnipotence of love is perhaps never more strongly proved than in such of its aberrations as these. The highest and the lowest are always closest to each other in the sphere of sexuality: 'vom Himmel durch die Welt zur Hölle.'[19]

"The first two facts which a healthy boy or girl feels about sex," Chesterton writes, "are these: first that it is beautiful and then that it is dangerous."[20] True enough. But is it really the case that the beauty of sex is most palpably felt when the danger is most monstrously realized? Chesterton, it seems, will not follow Freud down this rabbit hole.[21] Will we?

In *The Ethics of Time*, Manoussakis notes that "Freud's *Beyond the Pleasure Principle* ... offers thematically a close resemblance to the *Confessions*."[22] And indeed, the influence of Freud—particularly with regards to topics that have been psychology's patrimony: memory, temporality, and desire—can be found throughout Manoussakis's work.[23] Yet it is Freud's introduction of the competing drives Eros and Thanatos that allows Manoussakis to begin to approach the mysterious connection Augustine draws between carnal desire and spiritual love. (For instance, Manoussakis notes that for Augustine the *restlessness* [*inquietum*] of the heart is somehow related to the *restless* [*inquieta*] time of pubescence.)[24]

This paradox, emphasized by Freud's bold assertion that "The highest and the lowest are always closest to each other in the sphere of sexuality," finds an odd resonance in the Epistles of St. Paul. In his First Letter to the Corinthians, Paul warns that those who sleep with prostitutes will be joined to them as "one flesh" (1 Corinthians 6:16), a formula reserved elsewhere in scripture for the sacramental unity brought about by God's transformation of man and woman into husband and wife (cf. Genesis 2:24; Matthew 19:5; Mark 10:8; Ephesians 5:31). Thus the unitive power of God—dare we call it *grace*?—is manifest even in the most perverse acts of one who "sins against his own body" (1 Corinthians 6:18) and, in so doing, sins against the Lord (cf. 1 Corinthians 6:13).

That the sexual act implies both perversion and perfection, that it brings together the lowest and the highest, man's baseness and his beatitude, and that this is *always* the case, that no sexual act—no matter how loving, no matter how depraved—can ever be free from the heights and depths of human existence is a riddle to which the Catholic theologian Hans Urs von Balthasar gestures when he makes the shocking assertion that "sexual desire and the passions might be considered a 'sacrament of sin'"[25]—(the sacraments being, for Catholics, the highest: tangible manifestations of God's grace; sin being the lowest: man's self-willed alienation from the love of God). Indeed, according to Balthasar's reading of Maximus the Confessor, "The built-in sadness of sexual desire is nothing else than the dark contradiction one senses in sexuality,"[26] the contradiction that weds "sensual desire and death."[27]

> "Fear of death" is the hidden thorn that drives us to try to make our nature eternal by procreation; from this source, however, only another victim of death can be produced.... Between "fear of death" and "slavery to sensual desire through love of life", the circle is inescapably closed; the perpetuation of life, for which man strives, is in fact a perpetuation of death.... the circling wheel of births and deaths is a tragedy, in itself beyond redemption.[28]

And yet, Balthasar insists, "The role of sexuality ... is not exclusively this somewhat negative one."[29] Rather, "Desire itself ... is a beneficial force."[30] It brings about "a positive mode of union," the union of man and woman, which represents "the tender love a comrade in mortality" and provides "a distant, weak echo of the love of God."[31] "The sexual synthesis is the first level of the progressive syntheses by which the world is unified and brought to its perfection in the unity of God"[32]—a staggering assertion to say the least.

This "adhesion of sexuality to sin," as Balthasar calls it, is on full display in Dostoevsky's *The Brothers Karamazov*. To be a Karamazov, we are told, is to be both "a sensualist" and "a holy fool":

> You, Alyosha, are the quiet type, you're a saint, I admit; you're the quiet type, but the devil knows what hasn't gone through your head, the devil knows what you don't know already! A virgin, and you're already dug so deep.... You are a Karamazov yourself, a full-fledged Karamazov.... You're a sensualist after your father, and after your mother—a holy fool.[33]

During Dmitri's trial, Ippolit Kirillovich, the prosecutor, makes the following assertion about the defendant and the family into which he was born:

> It is usually in life that when there are two opposites one must look for truth in the middle; in the present case it is literally not so.... Why? Precisely because we are [dealing with] a broad, Karamazovian nature ... capable of containing all possible opposites and of contemplating both abysses at once, the abyss above us, an abyss of lofty ideals, and the abyss beneath us, an abyss of the lowest and foulest degradation.... the whole Karamazov family ... needs this unnatural mixture, constantly and ceaselessly.[34]

If sexuality is always bound up with the highest and the lowest, sanctity and degradation, if it is that which weds these "two abysses," the "unnatural mixture" that brings together "a lofty nobility" with that which is "so repugnant,"[35] then Freudian psychoanalytic theory—which posits two drives, Eros (sexual desire) and Thanatos (the desire for death)—cannot but inform our understanding of the mystery of sex. And indeed Manoussakis, who is quick to acknowledge his own indebtedness to Balthasar[36] and Dostoevsky,[37] devotes much of his recent work to drawing out the implications that Freud's dualistic drive theory has for Christian theology.

Theater of cruelty: Sex as the mysticism of perversion

In his recent essay, "Cracked: The Black Theology of Anatheism," Manoussakis discusses the relation between Eros and Thanatos as it concerns artistic creation. Following Sartre, he notes that "every act of human creation presupposes destruction."[38] "The creative forces of Eros emerge from the deep waters of a self at odds with itself, of a cracked self that exists by negating itself (Thanatos)."[39]

> For us humans … the creative Eros is never free but always purchased at the cost of destruction (Thanatos), inasmuch as human creation, be it artistic or *ex nihilo*, but conditioned by the givenness of the world which, precisely as given, human creation cannot but alter, refigure, and thus, in some sense, negate. Human Eros could never escape Thanatos altogether.… [F]or man creation is negation—man can create *because* man can destroy.[40]

This connection between creation and destruction, this grounding of man's creativity in his ability to destroy, is reminiscent not only of Freud, but also of Nietzsche's *The Birth of Tragedy* where the ordered beauty of the Apollonian finds it "roots" in the chaotic terror of the Dionysian, the "substratum" of all life.[41] Indeed, Manoussakis acknowledges the influence of "the prophet of Sils-Maria."[42] Quoting from some of the more challenging passages of *On the Genealogy of Morals*, he writes,

> If this theater of human cruelty [i.e. the world in which we live] … is pleasing to the gods—and make no mistake, "without cruelty there is no festival"—that's because the meaning of pain is pleasure. "To see others suffer does one good, to make others suffer even more."[43]

(According to Deleuze, these passages from Nietzsche offer "the only fitting answer" to the "essentially religious problem of the meaning of pain": "if pain and suffering have any meaning, it must be that they are enjoyable to someone.")[44]

The notion that pleasure is derived from pain, that one can only make sense of pain if it is first and foremost seen as something to be enjoyed, leads Manoussakis to a discussion of sadomasochism. We will return to that discussion momentarily. But before we do, let us consider once more Freud's *Three Essays on Sexuality*. In the section that precedes his analysis of sadism and masochism, Freud discusses how the "pleasure of looking [scopophilia] becomes a perversion."[45] For him, "seeing" is "an activity that is ultimately derived from touching."[46] Yet at times, seeing becomes a movement away from, a replacement for, touching—as in the case of voyeurism or when looking is no longer seen as preparation for the normal sexual aim but instead has supplanted it.[47] This ascending away from touch, away from the body, toward the "idealization of the instinct," as Freud calls it, these perversions "which are directed towards looking and being looked at," share remarkable similarities with sadism and masochism.[48] And for Manoussakis, this makes sense. "Vision," he tells us, "presupposes distance and it is rightly regarded as the most philosophical of senses.... Yet Augustine in the course of the *Confessions* becomes increasingly suspicious of the *concupiscentia oculorum*, the lust of the eyes, in its double desire to see and to know, especially of what ought not to be seen and of that which cannot be known."[49]

According to Manoussakis, the lust of the eyes can manifest itself in different ways:

a) In the desire and enjoyment of watching the suffering of others [sadism];
b) In the desire and enjoyment of watching the suffering of oneself [masochism];
c) In the desire to know or to see what is off-limits (in which case one sees or knows with a relative impunity for one is not seen back, or, alternatively in order to gain access to a secret one can offer a sacrifice, a small animal or oneself).

Here, we are told, "the panorama of vision encompasses the whole theater of human sinfulness"[50] (and we ought, I think, to hear resonances with the passage quoted above from "Cracked" in which Manoussakis discusses the "theater of human cruelty"). In both sadism and masochism—in perversion, cruelty, and sinfulness in general—we are presented with the *disincarnation* of man. "The more spiritualized a desire is, the more serious or 'sinful' it becomes."[51] Thus, we see that for Manoussakis, following Augustine, the root of all evil is the flight away from the flesh.[52] (Indeed, even the pride of the philosophers—who, "in claiming to be wise ... have become stupid"[53]—is, as Nietzsche says, attributable to "the spiritualization of *cruelty*": "in all desire to know there is a drop of cruelty.")[54]

This spiritualization is nothing other than the "idealization of the instinct" which, as we noted earlier, Freud aligns with "the most repulsive perversions."[55] (Here, one might justly object that Freud sees the idealization of the instinct as precisely what is *highest* in man—his ability to initiate a "transformation of the sexual instinct" which, "in spite of its horrifying result," overcomes "the resistances of shame, disgust, horror or pain" in the service of love[56]—whereas Manoussakis sees man's ability to spiritualize, his power to turn "something carnal into what it is not," as that which is *lowest* in man, that which constitutes sin and perversion.[57] Yet, we must be careful not to miss one of Manoussakis's subtler yet more startling points: "perversion or, to use a theological term, sin is man's exclusive privilege."[58] Or, to borrow a line of thinking made famous by Kierkegaard, the possibility of sin is what makes man great, the actualization of that possibility is what makes him wretched.) Thus, both the sadist and the masochist—the masochist, of course, being only a sadist whose destructive impulses "cannot find employment in actual life" and have thus turned inward on himself, yet himself posited as another[59]—are able to find pleasure in pain only because they can watch it from a safe distance.

Returning now to Manoussakis's discussion of sadism and masochism, we find this point made explicit:

> Between the sadist and his victim there is a distance incommensurable with geographical space. It is the distance between a subject's super-ego and its objects. Since the other's pain could never reach him, thanks to the distance solidified by the very difference between the other's pain and his pleasure, the sadist enjoys the theater of cruelty from a god-like distance and with a god-like impunity. The sadist's pleasure is the desire to be like God.[60]

And yet, Manoussakis goes on, "pleasure as defined here is a perversion of a human being who is not and cannot be God."[61] It is for that reason that Freud notes in *Civilization and Its Discontents* that the more "godlike" man becomes, the less happy he is. The spiritualization of the flesh, the self-deification of man, the disincarnation of sin, is the destruction of man. It is the perversion of man's Thanatonic drive toward his own annihilation.

In sex, this perverse desire to be like God, this idolatry of the self which makes of the self a false God, a substitute God, is on full display. Manoussakis, like Freud, identifies in human sexuality the destructive "spiritualized pleasure" of the compulsion to repeat.

> Andy Warhol's observation that "sex is nostalgia for sex" betrays the connection between temporality and embodiment insofar as nostalgia is the desire to return, to go back to an idealized past that never was … to one's childhood and, ultimately, to the mother's womb. It is, therefore, our desperate effort to escape the burden of existence, to refuse the presence of the present and to cancel out the promise of the future.[62]

This denial of the present that *is*, this attempt to go back to some illusory past, some wholeness, some *oceanic* oneness that never was, is for Manoussakis, sin itself:

> Evil is … nothing more than the denial of life's trauma and as such, the nostalgia for non-existence, that is, the nostalgia for a timeless existence,

which, since it was never given or experienced, means nothing else but the nostalgia for nothing itself.[63]

If "[b]eneath the sound and fury of sadism and masochism the terrible force of repetition is at work," that is because the repetition of sex "affords the finite human being a semblance of eternity" satisfying, at least for a time, man's nostalgia for a "timeless existence," his desire to be like God.[64] (Marion calls the tendency of the erotic drive to become "obsessed with the haunting memory of the same" a "hell on earth.")[65] Here, again, we see the influence of Freud on Manoussakis's work. The compulsion to repeat, Freud tells us, seeks to return man to "an old state, an initial state"—the inanimate, inorganic, nonexistence out of which life unexpectedly emerged.[66] Thus for Freud, and for Manoussakis, the death-drive is primary: in sex, man exhausts himself in pursuing without attaining an impossible return, a return to the womb that ultimately represents a return—to the tomb.

Sacred onanism: Sex as self-transcendence

The dangers implicit in a spiritualized sexuality are, in many ways, on full display in Jean-Luc Nancy's analysis of what he calls "the body of pleasure"—that is, the body of sexual pleasure—in *Corpus II: Writings on Sexuality*. Such a body, Nancy tells us, "is not turned toward the world, not even toward the other with whom—since we're talking about sexual pleasure—it is engaged in an exchange."[67] "It is a body detached from the schemas of perception and operation. It is no longer available to sight, or to sensation in general, in any of the usual ways of its functional, active, relational life."[68] This lack of "relational life" is, for Nancy, a crucial designation of what it means to be a body swept up in sexual pleasure, a body overcome by the "blurring of all the distinctions, roles, or operations connected to the functions, actions and representations of daily life."[69] (Indeed, as he will say in a later essay included in the same book, "the sexual relation represents the unaccomplishment of relation. Or, put a better way, it could be said that *the sexual in all relation* (linguistic, social, affective, aesthetic) resides in the dimension of unaccomplishment.")[70]

For the body of pleasure, "There is no longer an 'other' in the ordinary sense of the word, just as there is no self-sameness or fusion." Rather, when a body finds itself caught up in sexual pleasure, it finds itself "caught up in a mingling that is not just a mingling of these different bodies but at the same time the blurring" of everything experienced in life, "whether daily or not."[71] Nancy compares the experience to that of an athlete on the field or an actor on the stage: the body that burns with sexual pleasure loses the outside world, so enraptured is it by its own performance.

> It is a body mingled with itself and organized by this mingling. It is mingled with itself and with another (or others), with self *as* other. It becomes

a stranger to itself in order to relate to itself as another or even itself as the other who encroaches upon it and besieges it, in order to enjoy it [*jouir de lui*] and also rejoice in itself [*ré-jouir lui-même*].[72]

For Nancy, this "mingling" that the body undergoes in sexual pleasure is a profound affirmation of life (the resonances with Nietzsche are as obvious as they are abundant.) The sexual body "invents itself, recomposes and replays itself."[73] But it does more than this. It overcomes itself, transcends itself, "affirms itself" as

a capacity for transforming itself, reforming itself, or, perhaps, informing or even *exforming* itself, passing from conformation, even conformity regulated by a collection of social, cultural, and technological practices, to a form that is itself always in the process of formation.[74]

Said differently, in perhaps a more familiar, Nietzschean language, the body of pleasure frees itself from the (social, cultural, technological) restraints of the herd and becomes for itself what it truly is—a constant self-overcoming, a self ever-transcending itself in order to affirm itself as itself. "It reaches its limit, it passes its limit, it makes itself limitless."[75] And it does so "for itself only."[76] It alone exists.[77]

How does this body of pleasure transcend itself toward the becoming that it alone truly is? "It reforms itself and almost ex-forms itself, indeed de-forms itself in such a way that it is now nothing more than this exposition of self."[78] That is, it spiritualizes itself by stripping itself of all that informs it—all "the functions, actions and representations of daily life"—and by exposing itself as ex-formed, stark naked, without structure or configuration. Indeed, this is precisely what it means to be a body of pleasure. "The body of pleasure tends toward limitlessness, as if it were no longer body at all but pure soul."[79]

Here, then, we begin to see the grave danger of a spiritualized sexuality. For, this "pure soul" which exposes itself through the body of pleasure is indeed a "de-formed" thing. It has been robbed of all that would make it identifiable as a self. It has no history (no "daily life"), no personality (it is "a stranger to itself"), no other (no "relational life"), indeed, no body (no "perception," "operation," or "sensation"). As such, it is no-body. That is, it is no one's body—no one in particular. It is "the dismantling of the self"[80] which leaves us with the same fleshless, purified spirit that we connected at the end of Chapter 2 with the nothingness of death.

To be sure, Nancy insists that the "pure soul" of sexual pleasure is born of the body, born of "mouth, eye, ear, nostril, sex, anus, skin, skin indefinitely reclaimed and all its pores reopened."[81] (So too do all Platonic thinkers begin their ascent away from the body with the body in order to move beyond it.) And to his credit, Nancy does resist the temptation of fusion or identification—which often goes under the guise of "unity"—and instead maintains the pathos of distance.[82] But even if the "pure soul" of sexuality bursts forth from a pleasure so intense that "[a] body ... would arise completely from a breast, a palm, a belly," still Nancy's insistence that "[i]n sex, bodies testify to a vocation for infinitizing oneself beyond all secondary determinations of a given order" remains problematic.[83] First, because it is a spiritualization of the highest degree, one which threatens to eliminate from the sexual act the actual living, feeling, loving persons who alone are capable of experiencing the pleasure of sex. Second, and worse still, because if the body of pleasure "illimits the body," if "[i]t is transcendence,"[84] then the body that relates itself to itself in order to "rejoice in itself," to invent itself, affirm itself, transcend itself, has lost both itself and its other. Such a body is no longer a self capable of enjoying the other, of loving her, rejoicing in her, presenting itself to her as an offering or gift. No, we can't even say that in sex conceived as such the self *uses* the other. Strictly speaking, there is no self and no other. There is no sex. Only the purely masturbatory pleasure of a self seeking to rid itself of itself, to expel itself from itself so as to no longer be the self that it is.

We need not rely upon any technical philosophical argument to understand that the (illusory) pleasure of ridding oneself of oneself, reducing oneself to nothing, is a sterile perversion, a sign of profound despair (though Kierkegaard's *The Sickness Unto Death*, for instance, provides such an exposition). We need only to recall the example of Augustine who confesses above (see n. 8) that the onanistic desire for self-affirmation bears no fruit and yields only a harvest of death.

Secret onanism: Sex as that which conceals perversion

If our tone in the previous section has made it seem that we somehow disagree with Nancy's analysis, that we take his views to be deficient or perverse, then we must clarify and insist that we largely agree with the picture of sex provided therein. The spiritualization of the flesh, the desire to lose oneself and the other, the masturbatory drive for self-affirmation, self-transcendence, which amounts to nothing more than a veiled thirst for power, destruction, and death, is indeed central to our understanding of human sexuality. We have called it the death-drive, Thanatos, perversion, sin. What we do take issue with (if we take issue at all) is the enthusiastic, almost celebratory tone with which Nancy describes what we see to be the cause of man's profound despair. That perversion is a fact of human existence is a tautology. That it is therefore something to revel in, something to exalt, is a fallacy. And at the bottom of Nancy's "body of pleasure" we find once more the sadist's pleasure, the desire to be God—which, we have said, is "a perversion of a human being who is not and cannot be God."[85]

It goes without saying—or at least, by now, it ought to—that when we speak of perversion, of *sin*, we do not speak in moral terms. Indeed, it would be impossible to understand this present text without first grasping the veritable abyss that exists between sin and immorality. (So crucial is the distinction that it might be considered the first principle upon which everything we have said and will say stands or falls). The picture of sexuality painted by Nancy is perverse. But we find no fault with its painter for that. For, it is an accurate picture; one which (perhaps unconsciously) identifies the dark forces at work beneath the surface of man's erotic life.

Freud tells us that masturbation, especially during puberty, is unavoidable. He speaks of it as "masturbation by necessity" [*Notonanie*].[86] That sex conceals this onanistic impulse—this autoerotic drive that aims at making me independent of the external world, the author of my own pleasure, the author of myself—is a realization that has been brought to light by Nancy's reading of the body of pleasure; and for that, we owe him a debt of gratitude. Is this hidden attempt to purchase independence at the expense of the other a perversion? Without question it is. (As we have said, the "pure soul" sought by such solipsistic advances represents nothing more than the death of the self, the destruction of the body, the desire for nothingness.) Is it therefore immoral? The answer could only be provided by moral philosophers, which we make no pretenses to be.

But if we feel uncomfortable calling such desires "perverse," if we no longer like the word "sin" and, following the suggestion of Nietzsche, use instead sickness[87]—are we any better off? Is the pervasiveness of this sickness, the universality of this worm in the heart, the way that it infects and pollutes every man's erotic life, any less grotesque because we now see "how inappropriate it is to use the word perversion as a term of reproach"?[88] No, to "eliminate the concept *sin* from the world"[89] will not do away with sin. (And here, Nietzsche's thought suffers from his inability to separate sin from immorality.) If anything, it will only exacerbate the problem. For, each of us hides within himself this sadistic desire to be God. We have inherited it through our common ancestry. And to deny that is not only to conceal sin but to allow sin to fester.

"*Original* sin," Manoussakis writes, "means simply that sin is just that: original, prior and antecedent. That is, inescapable."[90] For him, "sin precedes freedom" and thus the ability to say "no" to sin "remains humanly impossible."[91] "I cannot not sin."[92] And yet, it is this realization—"revealed only in and through time; for example, through the repetition of sin"—that constitutes the undoing of sin itself. "A sin that is aware of itself as sin is already beyond sinfulness, an evil that judges itself as evil cannot do this but in the name of the good, by becoming good."[93] Can we say, then, that the compulsion to repeat, the nostalgia of sex for sex, the obsession with "the haunting memory of the same" which turns sex into a "hell on earth"[94] may in fact provide the necessary grounds for the self-deconstruction of sex and thereby constitute its transcendence toward something higher? The danger should be immediately apparent. Indeed, it is the danger that has dogged us from the start: the flight from the flesh, from this world, Plato's erotic ascent. Let us leave off, then, with this line of questioning and instead take up another. If man's erotic drive is always already perverted by the desire for death, how then does Eros emerge at all?

Cracked: Sex as an image of God

We said earlier that for both Manoussakis and Freud, Thanatos is primary. (Manoussakis goes so far as to say that sin is "original," "antecedent," "inescapable.") But the two differ greatly in their understandings of Eros. Whereas Freud offers only the unsatisfying, if honest, admission that for him life was awakened in nonliving matter "through the influence of a completely inconceivable force,"[95] Manoussakis asserts that when man perverts himself by playing at God, he does so by denying that he is already like God. Thus, he imitates in a false way that which he, in truth, already resembles. "All pleasure ... is sadistic as all human creation is destructive. Yet, as all human creation is an imitation of the Creator (theopoetics), similarly all pleasure is an imitation of God (theoerotics)."[96]

How do we resemble the Creator who we, in our perverse ways, always try to imitate? "God," Manoussakis proclaims, "is cracked."[97] God is "a God who takes a distance from God," "a God who is free to exist because he *ek-sists*, that is, because He 'exits' and 'stands beyond' himself," a God of the perichoretic *khora*, of the "gap within divinity."[98] "The Logos of God is always a *dialogue* within God. And a dialogue presupposes a trinity: the two interlocutors and the space (*khora*) which distinguishes them while uniting them precisely as the common ground of their dialogical possibility."[99] It is out of that space, that ground, that gap within the Godhead, that man is born.

"I wonder," Manoussakis muses,

> whether this sabbatical crack within God finds its reflection in the invisible crack that runs through us and splits us asunder? "In man," Lacan writes, "there's already a crack, a profound perturbation of the regulation of life." Perhaps we could come to recognize in this crack the *imago dei*, the birthmark of our creation[100]

—a birthmark that each of us bears and one that serves as the wellspring from which our own erotic drive toward life, love, and unity bursts forth. For, just as "it is thanks to this 'sabbatical crack or fracture' [in God] that 'the life-drive of eros' emerges in the act of divine creation, so it is with the crack in each one of us."[101] It is out of "our continuous and inevitable self-division," the "splitting that we are," that our artistic, intellectual, and erotic creations arise.[102]

Yet this life-drive, this creative Eros at the heart of God which is mirrored in the heart of man, is not and cannot be understood as some disincarnate, spiritual life-force. For, it is the gap of *perichoresis*—the split that God himself is—that gives rise to otherness and the desire for the other. And that desire is fulfilled and overflows when "[t]he self-emptying God becomes what He is *not*, non-God, the *sarx* [flesh] of the incarnation, by exteriorizing in history the difference within God."[103] Thus Manoussakis insists that spiritualizing or sublimating offers no solution to the problem of sin. Rather, "The resolution is to be found in and effected by a descent into the bodily."[104] "It is our body," he writes in stark contrast to the Platonic prejudices we have been battling all along, "that allows us to be united with God."[105] (One can understand why Paul calls the carnality of the crucifixion "foolishness" for philosophers [1 Corinthians 1:23].) Here, in this body, in the carnality of this flesh, *my* flesh, I can experience the incredible heights of human sexuality. If it is true that the sphere of sexuality is always already tainted by perversion, if no sexual act is ever entirely pure, so too does man's Eros always strive for, reach toward, *touch* the divine. "Christ's revelation offers something radically new: it offers Himself in flesh. The divine Word is not anymore only to be heard but also to be touched."[106] "God is no longer reserved and inaccessible, but He has come into contact with our nature on account of the human body that He assumed in the Incarnation. His is a body available to our touch and willing to touch us."[107]

Indeed, it is by "entering through our senses [that] He makes Himself manifest."[108] But this manifestation takes place not only in those rare, mystical encounters with Christ, as when one meets him face to face and experiences him in all of "His physicality, His corporeality that is indispensable to Him."[109] It happens also in a mediated way through the encounter with the other. (It is telling that Levinas, when asked what he thinks of when he imagines of the face of the other, answered "I think of Christ.")[110] "The desire for God is not independent from the desire for the other human.… One who has not felt the latter rarely and with difficulty would seek the former."[111]

It is the body's capacity for sex, Manoussakis writes quoting Ricoeur, "that enables us to exist 'with no distance between us and ourself, in an experience of completeness exactly contrary to the incompleteness of perception and spoken communication.'"[112] Unlike the distance and fragmentation presupposed and furthered by vision and language, touch brings unity. Flesh fulfills. My sexuality makes me whole. Or at least it has the potential to. The descent into the bodily, into the flesh, *my flesh*, is always something "desired but never completely achieved—the impossibility of desire, the impossibility of 'existing as body, and nothing but body' is due to the inescapable fact that desire … is never simply the desire for the Other but the desire for the Other's desire, the demand 'Desire me!'"[113]

In sex, I never offer myself fully without desiring something in return. I want to give myself, yes. But I also want to receive. And I want that which I receive to be given as freely and as generously as I have given. More so. (One need not invoke specific perversions to illustrate this point. Anyone who has had bad sex—and anyone who has had sex has had bad sex—knows that the pain and frustration of bad sex is born of the creeping suspicion, whether warranted or not, that the other has held something back, that she has not given herself fully or has not received fully the offering of myself, or, conversely, that I have held myself back and not given as generously as I have desired to give.) And because I desire something *from* the other—that is, her desire—I must of necessity objectify her. She must become for me an object capable of fulfilling my desire. Indeed, the object of my desire. A subject will not do. If she is to fulfill my desire, she must be a thing, a tool, an instrument which I can manipulate at will. (It is no accident that Freud speaks of sexuality in the terms of "object relations.") But if the other has become a thing, she has become a dead thing—as, indeed, is true of every object. My desire, then, is a desire for nothing, for no living thing, for a lifeless corpse, for death itself. Thanatos rears its ugly head once more. My masturbatory impulse to affirm myself at the expense of the other remains ever-present. "Eros is never free but always purchased at the cost of destruction."[114]

Eschaton: One flesh, or the time is now

If, as Manoussakis asserts, the precondition for authentically giving oneself to the other (*kenosis*) is to exist "as body and nothing but body," if that is the sincerest form of Eros, untainted by the destructive impulse to reduce the other to a thing, and if it is impossible for man to ever be free of that impulse, if we can never manifest our sexuality fully, lovingly, generously, authentically, that is because none of us is capable of living like

> him who becomes fully and entirely flesh (John 1:14) and who is one with the utterance "this is my body"—only for him who is his body and nothing but his body, the descent to the bodily has not only become possible but actual in a desire that is not any longer desired but lived.[115]

And yet—one might push back—if we believe that we are "one body in Christ" (Romans 12:5) and if Christ is "him who becomes fully and entirely flesh," then can we really speak of the impossibility of desire, the preordained failure of sex to reach the most carnal of heights? Ought we not rather to say that "[f]or human beings this is impossible, but for God all things are possible" (Matthew 19:26)? Ought we not to insist that "[t]he kenosis of the anachorite God does not stop with the flesh of the incarnation; it reaches out to the farthest limits of creation, it encompasses every aspect of materiality, it reverberates through every word and action"—including sexual love?[116] Who was it, after all, that assured us that in sex man experiences the wedding of two separate human bodies into one inseparable flesh? Who was it that joined those two in nuptial unity? Whose oneness brought them together (cf. Mark 10:9)?

Contrary to the onanistic attempts at self-spiritualization that we have seen at work just beneath the surface of human sexuality, Eros himself does not illimit the body by turning it into "pure soul." Rather, he initiates a descent into the bodily by which soul becomes "body and nothing but body." Further, he reveals himself as the one who fashioned our bodies—who made us in his image and likeness—when his own body is lifted up (John 8:28); that is, when he has become so bodily that he is no longer recognizable as a human being (Isaiah 52:14)—when he has become instead Eros crucified.

That the self-willed *kenosis* of Eros on the cross opened for us the possibility of manifesting our bodies as he so lovingly offered his is gestured at even by Manoussakis. "The distance that splits our consciousness," he writes, "is overcome at the moment of orgasm or prayer." "Thus, for a moment, *Psyche ist ausgedehnt*—not any more."[117] To offer one's body as body to the other and to receive the other's body unconditionally and unreservedly is to be wedded together as one body; that is, one flesh. This, Manoussakis tells us, occurs first and foremost at the Eucharistic table, in the Mass, where the phrase "this is my body"—"an erotic declaration" in its own right—is repeated and the eschatological Wedding Feast of the Lamb is made present here and now.[118]

> The invitation to "take, eat, this is my body" does not inform but it performs: it offers unconditionally and unreservedly the Other's body at a moment—and it could only be for a moment—where the torturous stretching of the soul on the rack of time is closed over a body infinitely condensed because it condenses infinity in a body.[119]

Does this self-willed *kenosis* by which the lover (Christ) allows himself to become fully vulnerable and thus fully present to the other (us) cease the moment we turn our backs to the altar and exit the church? Or might we say that "it reverberates through every word and action," that it is played out and made manifest again and again every time a lover offers his body to his beloved?

In *The Erotic Phenomenon*, Jean-Luc Marion grapples with this very question. The problem for lovers—as, indeed, has been intimated above ("it could only be for a moment")—is *time*.

> In order to continue the same erotic reduction, it is necessary for us to start all over again from the beginning, unceasingly. We only love one another at the price of continued re-creation, a continuous quasi-creation, without end or rest.[120]

The repetitive nature of sex, as we have seen, only serves to underscore its failure. "I find myself, as lover, taken up again in time; we, the lovers, find ourselves subjected to a repetition, exposed to the danger of being able to lose our [love] at any moment—thus obliged to assure it each time once again. The amorous phenomenon thus imposes its repetition in order to hope to save itself."[121]

If, as scripture tells us, the lovers, by joining their bodies, are mysteriously joined together as "one flesh" (Mark 10:9), whence comes this failure of love? Whence the compulsion to join bodies again and again *ad infinitum*? Why this tedious obsession with "the haunting memory of the same"? According to Marion, although the desire for sex is nostalgic—that is, it longs to repeat what in actuality can never be repeated: a singular event—sex itself has about it not this desire to recapture an idealized past but rather the expectancy, the promise even, of a future made manifest here and now.

> At the moment of loving, the lover can only believe what he or she says and does under a certain aspect of eternity. The lover just as much as the beloved needs the possible conviction that he or she loves this time forever, irreversibly, once and for all. For the lover, making love implies irreversibility by definition (just as in metaphysics the essence of God implies his existence).[122]

The moment of lovemaking does indeed have the power to overcome "the tor-turous stretching of the soul on the rack of time," as Manoussakis puts it. It does so by individualizing for me a single moment as unrepeatable, utterly unique.

> In time, I have marked, if only for a time, an eternal moment, which belongs to me, which came about only through and for me, and, thus, which individualizes me once and for all. Once and for all—to have said it is sufficient to wound me with a wound that marks me forever and delivers me to myself.[123]

But I am not the only one irrevocably marked by the wounding of this eternal moment. My beloved too is marked. And, to speak more accurately, it is she who marks me, as I mark her, with the moment we have given one another.

> Since we have made love one time, we have made it always and forever, because what was made cannot not have been made.... Once a lover, I remain so always, for it no longer depends upon me not to have loved—the other will always testify, even if I deny her, that I made myself her lover.[124]

(Hence the warning of Paul, noted above, to avoid copulating with prostitutes, cf. 1 Corinthians 6:16.) When we lovers offer each other our bodies—wounded, vulnerable, bare—we set one another as seals upon each other's hearts (Song of Songs 8:6), we wound one another eternally by our shared woundedness, we share with one another the woundedness that each of us individually is. Does this moment of shared woundedness constitute an erotic unity? Have the two truly been bonded together as one flesh? Is the offering of one's fragile, broken body enough?

For Marion, the threat that "the next instant can sink into the insignificance of dissipation, and thus repetition" cannot be overstated;[125] for, the realization of that threat would mean the end of love. But that very real and devastating pos-sibility does not exclude another: the "eschatological" possibility to "love this instant as if you no longer had any other in which to love, ever."[126] That is, to experience this moment not as a *mere* moment—but as eternity. To do so, Marion says, is "to assert as my definitive lover's status the erotic situation in which that instant finds and fixes me."[127] It is to fix the moment of love in the forever of eternity by being willing "(and this depends only upon me) to love at each instant for eternity."[128]

> The point is to transform one instant among others—a simple insignificant *item* of repetition—into a final instance, or put another way, to render it eschatological by setting it up as the third party, which will witness forever [our love], since no other will ever succeed it. And this can be accom-plished, provided that I decide to assume the instant just to come not only

as a decisive event, but as the event of the final instance—as the advent of the final instance. Which can be done, provided that I resolve myself, in this instant, to love as I would want to find myself loving (and loved) on the last day and forever, if this instant had to remain without another, and freeze my lover's face.[129]

The lover who does this "accomplishes the promises of eternity without waiting, in the present instant"; he does not "promise" the beloved eternity but "provokes" it and gives it to her "starting now."[130]

As lover, I must, we must, love as if the next instant decided, in the final instance, everything. To love requires loving without being able or willing to wait any longer to love perfectly, definitively, forever. Loving demands that the first time already coincide with the last time.... Thus we have only one single instant at our disposal, one single atom of an instant, and it is now.... [W]e must love now, now or never, now and forever.[131]

Notes

1 Freud, *Three Essays on Sexuality*, 160.
2 Freud, *Introductory Lectures on Psychoanalysis*, 306–307.
3 Ibid., 311.
4 Ibid., 338.
5 Ibid., 321.
6 Ibid., 315.
7 Augustine, *Confessions*, (2.7.15).
8 "Even within the walls of your church, during the celebration of your sacred mysteries, I once made bold to indulge in carnal desire and conduct that could yield only a harvest of death." Ibid., (3.3.5).
9 Chesterton, *Orthodoxy*, 8.
10 Lacan, *Ecrits*, 93.
11 Freud, *Introductory Lectures on Psychoanalysis*, 320.
12 Cf. "The degree and kind of a man's sexuality reach up into the ultimate pinnacle of his spirit." Nietzsche, *Beyond Good and Evil*, (§75).
13 Freud, *Three Essays on Sexuality*, 160.
14 Ibid., 160–161.
15 Ibid., 160.
16 Ibid., 162.
17 Ibid., 161
18 Ibid.
19 Ibid, 161–162.
20 Chesterton, *Collected Works vol. 28*, 251.
21 Cf.:

Mankind declares this with one deafening voice: that sex may be ecstatic so long as it is also restricted. It is not necessary even that the restriction should be reasonable; it is necessary that it should restrict. That is the beginning of all purity; and purity is the beginning of all passion. In other words, the creation of conditions for love, or even for flirting, is the first common-sense of Society.

(Ibid., 251–252)

22 Manoussakis, *The Ethics of Time*, 101.
23 That Manoussakis, writing as a phenomenologist, borrows freely from a field—psychoanalysis—that he believes to be strikingly conversant with his own ought not to surprise us. In fact, we can credit him for having encouraged us to do the same:

> To … translate psychoanalysis to phenomenology and phenomenology to psychoanalysis is an admirable task of which I am fully supportive. Without question, it is the ability of a synthetic mind and of a good scholar to recognize family resemblances between one's own field and that of others, to be "multilingual" when it comes to the language games by which specific schools of thought articulate themselves, and to refuse the confinement to one's epistemic home.
>
> *(Manoussakis, "The Place of Das Ding")*

24 Manoussakis, *The Ethics of Time*, 105.
25 Balthasar, *Cosmic Liturgy*, 199.
26 Ibid., 198.
27 Ibid., 197.
28 Ibid., 198.
29 Ibid., 199.
30 Ibid., 200.
31 Ibid., 199–200.
32 Ibid., 199.
33 Dostoevsky, *The Brothers Karamazov*, 80.
34 Ibid., 699.
35 Ibid.
36 Manoussakis, *God After Metaphysics*, 2.
37 Manoussakis, *The Ethics of Time*, 159–161.
38 Manoussakis, "Cracked," 56.
39 Ibid.
40 Ibid, 57.
41 Nietzsche, *The Birth of Tragedy*, (§4).
42 Manoussakis, "Cracked," 56.
43 Ibid.
44 As quoted on ibid., 59.
45 Freud, *Three Essays on Sexuality*, 157.
46 Ibid., 156.
47 Ibid., 157.
48 Ibid.
49 Manoussakis, *The Ethics of Time*, 98.
50 Ibid.
51 Ibid., 102.
52 Cf.:

> Reviewing our foregoing discussion, we seem to reach the following conclusion: *superbia vitae* (pride) is the sublimated form of *concupiscentia oculorum* and *concupiscentia oculorum* is the result of a frustrated *concupiscentia carnis*. What the subtler and loftier temptations seek in their respective spiritualized objects is the satisfaction that has failed to satisfy the flesh.
>
> *(Ibid., 102–103)*

53 Augustine, *Confessions*, (7.9.15).
54 Nietzsche, *Beyond Good and Evil*, (§229).
55 Freud, *Three Essays on Sexuality*, 161.
56 Ibid.

57 Manoussakis, "Cracked," 60.

58 Ibid., 61.

59 Freud, *Three Essays on Sexuality*, 158 n. 2.

60 Manoussakis, "Cracked," 60.

61 Ibid.

62 Manoussakis, *The Ethics of Time*, 108.

63 Ibid., 77.

64 Manoussakis, "Cracked," 60–61.

65 Marion, *The Erotic Phenomenon*, 207.

66 Freud, *Beyond the Pleasure Principle*, 45–46.

67 Nancy, *Corpus II*, 93.

68 Ibid.

69 Ibid.

70 Ibid., 101.

71 Ibid., 93.

72 Ibid., 93–94.

73 Ibid., 94.

74 Ibid.

75 Ibid.

76 Ibid.

77 According to Nancy, that which is "outside" the living being—though it does indeed act as "an exterior agent" which touches, excites, and calls for a response—is nothing more than "the empty outside of a non-world" which is itself "nothing." Ibid. And again, "outside does not exist.... There is no outside." Ibid., 95.

78 Ibid., 94.

79 Ibid.

80 Ibid., 95.

81 Ibid., 96.

82 See,

> Nor is there an erosion of the difference between self and other. The body mingled with itself and with an other (or others), with itself as with the other, does not enter into identification or confusion, but rather into a proximity that is troubling because pleasure consists in tasting the always uncertain, unstable, and trembling measure of proximity, the approach of a certain distinction and renewal, repetition and revival of distance.
>
> *(Ibid., 95)*

83 Ibid., 96.

84 Ibid.

85 Manoussakis, "Cracked," 60.

86 Freud, *Introductory Lectures on Psychoanalysis*, 317.

87 Nietzsche, *The Dawn of the Day*, (§202).

88 Freud, *Three Essays on Sexuality*, 160.

89 Nietzsche, *The Dawn of the Day*, (§202).

90 Manoussakis, *The Ethics of Time*, 76.

91 Ibid.

92 Ibid.

93 Ibid.

94 Marion, *The Erotic Phenomenon*, 207.

95 Freud, *Beyond the Pleasure Principle*, 46.

96 Manoussakis, "Cracked," 60.

97 Ibid., 50. This bold assertion is but one of the many examples of how Manoussakis gives new life to old dogmas by articulating Christian orthodoxy in challenging and unorthodox ways.

98 Ibid., 52.
99 Ibid., 50–51.
100 Ibid., 51.
101 Ibid.
102 Ibid., 53.
103 Ibid.
104 Manoussakis, *The Ethics of Time*, 102.
105 Ibid., 104.
106 Manoussakis, *God After Metaphysics*, 145.
107 Ibid., 144.
108 Ibid., 150.
109 Ibid., 148.
110 Kearney, *Debates in Continental Philosophy*, 236–237.
111 Manoussakis, *The Ethics of Time*, 105.
112 Ibid., 107.
113 Ibid., 108.
114 Manoussakis, "Cracked," 57.
115 Manoussakis, *The Ethics of Time*, 108–109.
116 Manoussakis, "Cracked," 53.
117 Manoussakis, *The Ethics of Time*, 109.
118 Cf. Emmanuel Falque's aptly titled *The Wedding Feast of the Lamb: Eros, the Body, and the Eucharist*.
119 Manoussakis, *The Ethics of Time*, 109.
120 Marion, *The Erotic Phenomenon*, 195.
121 Ibid., 207.
122 Ibid., 109.
123 Ibid., 110.
124 Ibid., 212.
125 Ibid., 208.
126 Ibid.
127 Ibid.
128 Ibid., 209.
129 Ibid., 208.
130 Ibid., 209.
131 Ibid., 211.

Bibliography

Augustine, *Confessions*, trans. Maria Boulding (New York: Vintage, 1998).

Balthasar, Hans Urs von, *Cosmic Liturgy: The Universe According to Maximus the Confessor*, trans. Brian E Daley, SJ (San Francisco: Communio, Ignatius, 2003).

Chesterton, GK, *Collected Works, vol. 28: Illustrated London News, 1908–1910* (San Francisco: Ignatius, 1987).

Dostoevsky, Fyodor, *The Brothers Karamazov*, trans. Richard Pevear and Larissa Volokhonsky (New York: Farrar, Straus and Giroux, 2002).

Falque, Emmanuel, *The Wedding Feast of the Lamb: Eros, the Body, and the Eucharist*, trans. George Hughes (New York: Fordham University Press, 2016).

Freud, Sigmund, *Three Essays on Sexuality*, in *The Standard Edition of the Complete Psychological Works of Sigmund Freud*, trans. James Strachey, vol. VII (London: Hogarth, 1953).

Freud, Sigmund, *Introductory Lectures on Psychoanalysis*, trans. James Strachey (New York: WW Norton, 1977).

Freud, Sigmund, *Beyond the Pleasure Principle*, trans. Gregory C Richter, ed. Todd Dufresne (Peterborough, ON: Broadview Editions, 2011).

Kearney, Richard, *Debates in Continental Philosophy: Conversations with Contemporary Thinkers* (New York: Fordham University Press, 2004).

Lacan, Jacques, *Ecrits: The First Complete Edition in English*, trans. Bruce Fink (New York: WW Norton, 2007).

Manoussakis, John, *God After Metaphysics: A Theological Aesthetic* (Bloomington: Indiana University Press, 2007).

Manoussakis, John, "Cracked: The Black Theology of Anatheism," in *The Art of Anatheism*, eds. Richard Kearney and Matthew Clemente (London: Rowman & Littlefield, 2017a), 49–66.

Manoussakis, John, *The Ethics of Time* (London: Bloomsbury, 2017b).

Manoussakis, John, "The Place of Das Ding: Psychoanalysis, Phenomenology, Religion," in *Religious Theory: The Online Edition of The Journal for Cultural and Religious Theory* (February, 2017c).

Marion, Jean-Luc, *The Erotic Phenomenon*, trans. Stephen E. Lewis (Chicago: University of Chicago, 2007).

Nancy, Jean-Luc, *Corpus II: Writings on Sexuality*, trans. Anne O'Byrne (New York: Fordham University Press, 2013).

Nietzsche, Friedrich, *The Birth of Tragedy*, trans. Walter Kaufmann (New York: Vintage, 1967a).

Nietzsche, Friedrich, *The Dawn of Day*, trans. John McFarland Kennedy (Scotts Valley, CA: CreateSpace, 1967b).

Nietzsche, Friedrich, *Beyond Good and Evil*, trans. Walter Kaufmann (New York: Vintage, 1989).

PART II

Incarnation: A theological dramatic

For my lover

Through earth and air the angel glides
With flames for hair and fallen eyes
From silent lips, ecstatic cries
My Lover has been crucified!

With leaf and fig our fruits we hide
Beneath the tree where shadows lie
No spoken word, just muffled sighs
My Lover has been crucified!

In dirt and dark we poor abide
With breaking bones and broken pride
Our brows are damp, our mouths are dry
My Lover has been crucified!

Eyes cast down but hands inside
While trumpet blasts resound on high
Mother weeps. Child dies.
My Lover has been crucified!

O lay me down within the stone
Where ash is ash and dust is bone
And I will build a wedding bed
For toes and teeth and hands and head.

O lay me down within the rock
No breaking day, no waking cock
And next to you I will reside
My Love, my Sweet, my Crucified.

5

THE HERMENEUTICS OF DESIRE

On the Song of Songs

In his essay "The Nuptial Metaphor," Ricoeur objects to the narrow readings of the Song of Songs—a book which, with its abundant use of erotic language and sexually evocative imagery, dramatically differs from the rest of the bible— offered by both modern Judeo-Christian commentators and "naturalistic" or erotic interpreters alike. While the former tend to trade in the carnality of the text for an overly spiritualized, allegorical reading, the latter reduce the Song to "nothing more than an epithalamium, a carnal love song in dialogue form."[1] Both readings, Ricoeur argues, "claim to tell us the true meaning that was intended by the author,"[2] but both fall flat. While the strictly allegorical ascends away from the body and thus loses the Eros of the flesh, the reductively erotic eliminates the transcendent and thus confines Eros to the biological. Neither reading is sufficient. Neither can account for the other. And ironically, both are rooted in the same false premise, the belief that "there exists one true meaning of the text namely, the one that was intended by its author, authors, or the last redactor, who are held to have somehow inscribed this meaning in the text, from which exegesis has subsequently to extract it, and, if possible, restore it to its originary meaning."[3]

Echoing Augustine's realization in Book XII of the *Confessions* that "[a] great variety of interpretations, many of them legitimate, confronts our exploring minds as we search among the words" of scripture,[4] Ricoeur rejects the notion that "commentary ... consists in identifying this overall true, intended, and orig- inal meaning."[5] Like TS Eliot—who reminds us that "[n]o poet, no artist of any art, has his complete meaning alone"[6] and goes on, in a proto-Barthesian vein (*La mort de l'auteur*), to insist that "[t]o divert interest from the poet to the poetry is a laudable aim"[7]—Ricoeur argues that, even if it were possible to identify the author's "intended meaning" (a dubious prospect in its own right, especially since "[w]e have to admit that we never know with certitude who is speaking, to whom, or where"),[8] still, the Song would not be reducible to any one reading. Rather, it is precisely because we never know who is speaking that the Song—which is, after all, *a song*; that is, a poem, a work of art—is "open to a plurality of interpretations."[9] As Kearney, a former-student of Ricoeur's, argues,

> the primacy of the indeterminately fluid 'movements of love' over the specific identities of the lover and the beloved guards the open door.... This guarding of the Song as an open text of multiple readings and double entendres—divine and human, eschatological and carnal—provokes a hermeneutic play of constant 'demetaphorizing and remetaphorizing,' which never allows the Song to end.[10]

According to Eliot, "Poetry ... is not the expression of personality, but an escape from personality."[11] That is, a true work of art is not the unpacking of the artist's personal life but the creation of "a new art emotion,"[12] one which engenders an ongoing need for interpretation. That the "movements of love" found in the Song of Songs give voice not merely to the "personal emotions" of the lover and beloved, but represent an expression of the fluidity, complexity, and irreducibility of desire means that the Song must be interpreted and reinterpreted anew.

> The Song of Songs confronts us with a desire that desires beneath desire and beyond desire while remaining desire. It is a desire that spills out beyond the limits of the Song itself, sending innumerable ripples throughout the many readings.[13]

If, as Bonaventure contends, *bonum est diffusivum sui* (goodness pours itself out), then we must insist without hesitation that each new reading of the Song of Songs has the potential to further illuminate a text which already overflows with meaning. Thus, in the pages that follow, we will not only consider the manifold interpretations that have come before, but will venture to offer our own—one which seeks neither to exclude past readings nor to minimize the import of the one being offered, but rather to remain open to the plurality of interpretations (Ricoeur) while also attempting to bring "conformity between the old and the new" (Eliot).

God, the husband of Israel

In his essay "The Shulammite's Song: Divine Eros, Ascending and Descending," Kearney examines the many readings of the Song of Songs handed down through the centuries. Noting that the Song "offers no single, stable perspective" from which it speaks, he writes, "The sustained ambiguities of identity and fluid reversals of erotic roles have made this text fertile ground for conceiving and reconceiving the mysteries of desire, in particular the mysteries of divine desire."[14] Like Ricoeur, who views the Song as opening the space for an on-going play of hermeneutic interpretation, Kearney asks, "Does the Song celebrate God's desire for us? Our desire for God? Or both?"[15] and ultimately concludes that the rich-ness of the text lies in that fact that "We are kept guessing."[16]

Kearney begins his survey of the plurality of interpretations with some of the earliest commentaries found in the Talmudic and Kabbalistic traditions. Such readings, he notes, interpret the Song as referring to "the love between God and Israel."[17] In spite of the fact that God is never explicitly mentioned in the text—one commentator, however, asserts that the presence of the divine can be found in the "all-consuming blaze" of Song 8:6[18]—nevertheless, God is here inter-preted as playing the role of Solomon, the Song's bridegroom. Kearney quotes Elliot Wolfson:

> A number of aphoristic comments scattered throughout Talmudic and midrashic literature, including the critical exegetical remark that every Solomon mentioned in the Song is holy, for the name refers to God, the 'one to whom peace belongs' (li-mi she-ha-shalom shelo), indicate the alle-gorical interpretation of the Song for some rabbis seems to have been predicated on a theosophical conception that attributed gender and sexual images to God.[19]

This reading, which finds echoes throughout the Hebrew bible, posits God as the lover, the husband of Israel. "You shall call me 'My husband,'" declares the Lord through the prophet Hosea (Hosea 2:18). "Your husband is your Maker," says Isaiah, "the Lord of hosts is his name, your redeemer, the Holy One of Israel, called God of all the earth" (Isaiah 54:5).

This interpretation has theological implications. The distinctively Judaic emphasis on divine transcendence can be traced to the analogy employed here. God is the bridegroom who approaches the beloved from without. Creation does not emanate from and return to some Plotinian oneness. There is a dis-tance, a space, a gap. Like a husband to his bride, God resists identification, remains other, unique. (Žižek, in a fascinating passage, sees this as that which establishes

> the intimate link between Judaism and psychoanalysis: in both cases, the focus is on the traumatic encounter with the abyss of the desiring Other—the Jewish people's encounter with their God whose impenetrable Call derails the routine of daily existence; the child's encounter with the enigma of the Other's jouissance.)[20]

What is more, this reading begins to shine light upon an idea gestured to but not fully unpacked in Part I of this present work: the connection between sex and sin. We said above that for Balthasar there is an "adhesion of sexuality to sin."[21]

An impartial consideration of the prophets' continuous rebuking of Israel for her adulterous ways reveals as much. As Anna Silvas notes,

> In the pagan religions surrounding Israel, licentiousness became, in the most literal and physical sense, coterminous with religious worship.... The idea was imitative magic: cultic forms of sexual intercourse were practiced in order to secure agricultural fertility. It was the burden of the prophets to recall Israel and Judah from this seductive brew of religious and sexual promiscuity.[22]

That Deleuze identifies "a kind of mysticism in perversion ... [comparable] to a 'black' theology" ought not to surprise us.[23] For, not only did we identify above a drive for self-affirmation which amounts to a veiled thirst for power and death hidden at the heart of sex, but from the beginning of biblical history it has been clear that "idolatry is implicated quite literally in sexual sin, and conversely sexual sin is idolatry."[24] (Is it any wonder that Augustine begins Book II of his *Confessions*—the Book in which he famously probes the perplexing nature of sin—with considerations of his "sexual awakening" and "adolescent lust"?)

> Every one of Israel's foes, each of the hostile nations or tribes, is traced back to some sexual sin leading to a rupture in the family and to social ruin. The sins of parents in the sexual realm affect the lives of their children, and their children's children, and so on. In fact, there is scarcely a major figure in Genesis untouched by sexual sin. As a result, even the great patriarchal families are all in one way or another "dysfunctional." What is depicted in Genesis continues throughout the Old Testament. Scarcely a hero of salvation history is uncompromised in his own behavior and that of his own family.[25]

It is for this reason that, whenever Israel wanders away from God and into idolatry, she is compared to an adulterous wife. Sexual sin is idolatry and idolatry is adultery—that is, sexual sin.

Yet saying this does not mean that we must conclude with Kierkegaard that sin and sexuality are "inseparable," that "without sin, there is no sexuality."[26] Perhaps no sexuality as we know it, sexuality in which Eros is always bound up with Thanatos, "purchased at the cost of destruction."[27] But, as Genesis makes clear, "the first consequence of Adam and Eve's sin is that their sexuality was affected"—they clothed themselves to hide their nakedness (cf. Genesis 3:7).[28] And if their sexuality was affected, that is because it was already an essential aspect of their being. (To take a tangent, for a moment, to a topic not wholly unrelated—one might ask why it is that man wears clothes even when there is no need for him to do so; for instance, when he is alone in the comfort of his own home. The answer, I think, is rooted in this idea that the fall affected man's sexuality. If we accept Nietzsche's observation that "The degree and kind of a man's sexuality reach up into the ultimate pinnacle of his spirit,"[29] then we must conclude that the concealing of one's sexual organs is an attempt to conceal that which is most intimate, one's secret interiority. But conceal it from whom? There can be no doubt. For, it was not from Eve that Adam tried to hide himself:

> When they heard the sound of the Lord God walking about in the garden … the man and his wife hid themselves from the Lord God among the trees of the garden. The Lord God then called to the man and asked him: Where are you? He answered, "I heard you in the garden; but I was afraid, because I was naked, so I hid."[30]
>
> *(See Genesis 3:8–10)*

And yet, what can be hidden from God? What can man conceal? One may wonder why God made circumcision the sign of his "everlasting covenant" (Genesis 17:13). A secret sign, hidden from sight. Yet what does the lover desire if not that which is most intimate: the flesh, the clandestine interiority, the ultimate pinnacle of the beloved's spirit? The beloved's nakedness is not for all to see. Such intimacy is reserved for lovers.)

The Song, read in this light, is a song of divine longing. The bride has been unfaithful, adulterous, untrue. But still her bridegroom waits. No, not *waits*: wants, beckons, calls, pursues. "The sound of my lover! here he comes springing across the mountains, leaping across the hills" (Song of Songs 2:8). "The Lord calls you back, like a wife forsaken and grieved in spirit, a wife married in youth and then cast off, says your God. For a brief moment I abandoned you, but with great tenderness I will take you back. In an outburst of wrath, for a moment I hid my face from you; but with enduring love I take pity on you, says the Lord, your redeemer" (Isaiah 54:6–8). Kearney notes that

> this reading finds support in the famous view of R. Aqiva that if all of Scripture is holy, the Song is the holy of holies, for it suggests that the Song captures, *in nuce*, the entire matrimonial and erotic charge of the divine revelation of Torah to the people.[31]

It cries out for the eschatological wedding of God and his chosen ones: "the lover longing for his 'promised bride' anticipates the promised kingdom."[32]

Christ, the bridegroom of the church

If the traumatic encounter with the other's desire is, as Žižek says, that which distinguishes the Jewish-psychoanalytic "paradigm" from other worldviews (Platonic, Gnostic, Hindu, etc.), it is also that which both aligns it with and differentiates it from the Christian. On the one hand, Žižek notes, both Judaism and Christianity share the "notion of an *external* traumatic encounter."[33] On the other, he asks, "does the latter not 'overcome' the Otherness of the Jewish God through the principle of Love, the reconciliation/unification of God and Man in the becoming-man of God?"[34] That God's desire for man is an inherent part of the Judaic tradition has been evidenced by the interpretations of the Song of Songs examined above. Yet there can be no doubt that—if, as Kearney says, such readings "anticipate the promised kingdom"—the Christian interpreters who follow are wont to take matters one step further and declare that "the kingdom of heaven is at hand" (Matthew 4:17). The adulterous wife of the Hebrew bible has—through the incarnation, death, and resurrection of her bridegroom—been made new (see Revelation 21:5).

That "[i]n Jesus of Nazareth, the Bridegroom of Israel so long proclaimed by the prophets and in the Song of Songs has come in the flesh"[35] is asserted by Paul in the oft-misrepresented Chapter 5 of his Letter to the Ephesians. The passage is worth quoting in its entirety:

> Be subordinate to one another out of reverence for Christ. Wives should be subordinate to their husbands as to the Lord. For the husband is head of his wife just as Christ is head of the church, he himself the savior of the body. As the church is subordinate to Christ, so wives should be subordinate to their husbands in everything. Husbands, love your wives, even as Christ loved the church and handed himself over for her to sanctify her, cleansing her by the bath of water with the word, that he might present to himself the church in splendor, without spot or wrinkle or any such thing, that she might be holy and without blemish. So [also] husbands should love their wives as their own bodies. He who loves his wife loves himself. For no one hates his own flesh but rather nourishes and cherishes it, even as Christ does the church, because we are members of his body. "For this reason a man shall leave [his] father and [his] mother and be joined to his wife, and the two shall become one flesh." This is a great mystery, but I speak in reference to Christ and the church. In any case, each one of you should love his wife as himself, and the wife should respect her husband.
>
> *(Ephesians 5:21–33)*

There is much to comment on here. Our first observation is one that young couples are not likely to receive in their Pre-Cana classes: marriage represents a lifelong crucifixion, an unfolding of Christ's passion over not three days but three or more decades. Husbands are told to love their wives—and here's the kicker—"even as Christ loved the church and handed himself over for her" (5:25). Wives are instructed to be "subordinate to their husbands;" and who could fail to hear the resonances with Philippians 2:5–8?[36] Yes, according to this Pauline injunction, "The path that *eros* must tread is the path that any love, if it is to be true, must eventually walk: the path of crucifixion with Christ."[37] Yet it is only by walking such a narrow and harrowing path that spouses can be awakened to a profound mystery: the "intimate connection between the body and love."[38]

Paul insists that "husbands should love their wives as their own bodies" (5:28); they should nourish and cherish their wives as they do their own flesh. And he goes on to say that in doing so husbands resemble Christ and his love for the church (5:29). By identifying wives with both the body and the church, Paul resists two dangerous errors—ones which, ironically, Christians throughout the ages have used this very passage to justify. The first is the subjugation of women. The second is the spiritualization of the flesh. And the two, as this text makes clear, are not unrelated. Hatred of one's wife is here likened to hatred of one's own flesh. And the same can be said in reverse because to hate one's flesh is to hate the flesh that is a member of Christ's body, the church—that is, to hate one's flesh *as wife*, as bride of Christ. Any movement away from the body, away from its needs, wants, and desires, is not only a movement that seeks power and control,[39] but is also an attempt to defeminize the essentially feminine role of man in relation to Christ.

In a stunning reversal, Paul tells us that it is not the husband but the wife who takes the privileged place. For, the bride is the *embodiment* of Christ. If we take Paul's assertion that "the husband is head of his wife just as Christ is head of the church" to be an exaltation of the husband, that is only because we have failed to understand the radical revaluation introduced by the Christian paradigm. For the Platonist, the head is indeed the privileged position. Christianity, however, tells us that "the first shall be last" (Matthew 20:16). It is not the head but "the flesh," as Tertullian insists, that provides "the very condition on which salvation hinges."[40] The wife, then, is the necessary condition for the salvation of her husband—think Monica and Patricius—just as the flesh prepares the way for the salvation of the soul.[41] If we push this analogy further and consider it in light of Augustine's claim that "it was not the corruptible flesh that made the soul sinful; it was the sinful soul that made the flesh corruptible,"[42] then we must—contrary to the misreadings of Genesis that would pin the fall on Eve—say that the husband is actually the corruptor of his spouse. (Did we not argue in Chapter 1 that, when the serpent tempted Eve, he was actually giving voice to Adam's internal struggle?)

And yet, matters are more complicated still—this is no mere reversal of classical binaries—for, husbands are also commanded to act as Christ, "the savior of the body" (5:23). Neither spouse, then, is capable of saving him- or herself. Each depends upon, *needs*, the other. (Are we willing to extend the metaphor back to the relation between Christ and church as, say, Eckhart is want to do?)[43] This mutual dependence amounts to a mutual subservience, a continuous struggle between the spouses to see who can lower him- or herself more, who can make the greatest sacrifice, who can raise the other higher, outdo the other in praise. It is "a dynamic of giving and receiving, identity and difference, otherness and relationship, a kind of mutual subordination—in short, of Love."[44] Does it offend our contemporary sensibilities to hear that "[a]s the church is subordinate to Christ, so wives should be subordinate to their husbands in everything" (5:24)? But what does it mean to be subordinate as the church is subordinate to Christ— that is, to the one who made himself subordinate to all? The reversals and double meanings abound. As is the case with the Song itself, "Throughout this passage Paul weaves so closely between human marriage and the metaphor of the Christ/ Church union that at times it is almost difficult to distinguish which dimension he is referencing."[45]

Pornographic puritanism: Allegorical (mis)readings

Both the Judaic and Christian interpretations of the Song of Songs considered above hinge upon a sort of *this-worldliness* that enables them to attend to the transcendent God's concern for creaturely matters. The God of Israel is a God entangled with his people. He is a jealous God who cannot stand the thought of his bride having any lover but him (Exodus 20:5). Christ is a God who weeps (John 35:11); a God who has been pierced, wounded by this life. And yet, the temptation—especially for the philosophically inclined—is to leave this world behind, to escape into the purity of ideas. Thus countless commentators in both the Jewish and Christian traditions have chosen to vacate the carnality of the Song and replace it with reductively allegorical readings.

Kearney explores such interpretations at length. "Maimonides," he notes, "like many of the Christian medieval commentators indebted to Neoplatonic and Aristotelian sources, takes the amorous symbolism as code for the contempla-tive ideal of union between the rational soul (the bride) and the Active Intellect (bridegroom)."[46] Such readings seek a "final overcoming of carnal desire" by enacting a "certain transformation of the original heterosexual language of the poem into a spiritualized homoeroticism that is itself predicated upon an ascetic renunciation of physical, carnal desire."[47] The erotic relationship referred to in the Song is no longer read as existing between a man and a woman but "between the soul and God, engendered respectively as feminine and masculine."[48] (Again we see that the spiritualization of the flesh leads to the marginalization of women. It is worth noting here that Plato's erotic ascent also excludes women. Indeed, they are literally banished, cast out of the party [cf. *Symposium* 176e].)

The irony of turning the carnal aspects of the Song—for example the kiss found in its opening lines—into a type allegory for "intellectual communion with the lights of the divine Intellect predicated on the emancipation of the human mind from the lures of physical pleasure"[49] is that such readings are, con-trary to their intended purposes, hyper-carnal. As Augustine notes,

> anyone who exalts the soul as the Supreme Good, and censures the nature of the flesh as something evil, is in fact carnal alike in his cult of the soul and in his revulsion from the flesh, since this attitude is prompted by human folly, not by divine truth.[50]

That is, asserting that the flesh is more sinful than the soul is a mistake of reason made by those who live under the law of the flesh rather than in the freedom of spirit (cf. Galatians 5.13–26).

Like Ricoeur, Kearney worries about this attempt to spiritualize the Song and thus lose the incarnate Eros of bodily desire. He notes that, by means of this more philosophical reading, "sex is taken out of the Song" and laments the fact that

> [g]ender becomes a matter of supra-physical symbolism and sublimation. The bride's appeal to the kiss of the mouth … has little to do with love between real lovers and everything to do with … the return journey of the lower spirit to the higher Spirit from which it originated.[51]

This "ascetic renunciation of the flesh," however, is not confined to the work of Maimonides. Kearney highlights narrow Christian readings which eliminate Paul's insistence on the import of the body in spiritual as well as nuptial love and reduce the Song to nothing more than the "symbolic relationship between Church and God or soul and Christ."[52]

In Origen's *Homily on the Song of Songs*, for instance,

> The right use of love … is [said to be] in the service of a higher truth and wisdom, far removed from the embodied love of flesh and blood. Only those who are spiritually detached from their physical desire can raise themselves up to this intellectual form of love.[53]

For Kearney, this allegorical interpretation constitutes an "anti-carnal" reading of desire: "It takes the threat out of the sexual imagery by disembodying and depersonalizing the actual lovers in favor of more abstract movements of love."[54] These abstractions aim to "subordinate desire to wisdom."[55] Like the more philosophical reading offered by Maimonides, Origen's account attempts to exchange the carnal Eros of the body for the spiritual Eros of the soul. For Origen, "All references to the body, the senses, flowers, animals, landscapes, nature are no more than ciphers for higher spiritual truths."[56] And the Song's celebrated bride is merely "a thinly disguised emblem of the soul or Church" searching for the immaterial, transcendent God.[57]

Contrary to what one might assume, the puritanical impulse that motivates this kind of overly-spiritualized, allegorical reading shares much in common with the reductive view that sex is "just sex"—a purely biological or naturalistic reality. In his essay on the connection between bodily love and the love of God, Conor Sweeney writes:

> [T]here would seem to be a straight line from thinking of love and marriage as purely natural or human realities to the radical secularization and deconstruction of sexuality, marriage, and love in general…. To trap this truly mysterious reality in the realm of "nature," reductively understood, is thus to secularize love itself. And the secularization of human love has the undesirable consequence that our hearts and desires begin to lose their receptivity to divine love.[58]

The risk is real. (Think, for instance, of Marie Bonaparte's attempt to reduce the mystical experience of Teresa of Avila to a "violent venereal orgasm.")[59] But to conclude, therefore, that "[t]he intuition behind the nuptial mystery is that the human experience of love is actually a primer for ultimate fulfillment in Trinitarian love"[60] because "[t]he love experienced by human persons ... can never fully satisfy"[61] is to run the same risk in the opposite direction—to reduce sex and the body to mere steppingstones on the path to transcendence, vestiges of a fallen world which, once overcome, can be left behind and forgotten. As Žižek, in his reading of the Song of Songs, rightly points out:

> [T]he most perspicacious Bible scholars themselves are the first to empha-size the limits of such a metaphorical reading that dismisses the sexual content as "only a simile": it is precisely such a "symbolic" reading that is "purely human," that is to say, that persists in the external opposition of the symbol and its meaning, clumsily attaching a "deeper meaning" to the explosive sexual content. The literal reading (say, of the Song of Songs as almost pornographic eroticism) and the allegorical reading are two sides of the same operation: what they share is the common presupposition that "real" sexuality is "purely human," with no discernible divine dimension.[62]

Echoing Žižek's unexpected coupling, Kearney notes that "pornography is, paradoxically, a twin of Puritanism. Both display an alienation from flesh—one replacing it with the virtuous, the other with the virtual. Each is out of touch with the body."[63] With the body—and perhaps with the darker side of desire as well. For, while the puritanical interpretation of Eros longs to leave behind the dangers of the flesh and ascend toward purity and light, the pornographic watches from a safe and sterile distance, unaffected and uninvolved. In reality, the assertions that the Form of Beauty is the ultimate aim of Eros (cf. *Symposium* 209e–212a) and that sex is "just sex," an animal activity, are one and the same. Neither is willing to descend into a "love as strong as death" (Song of Songs 8:6). Neither is capable of embodying a desire as fierce and as frightful "as Sheol" (8:6).[64]

Love like death: Mysticism and the void

It is impossible to read an account of a mystical experience without recogniz-ing the mystic's encounter as something at once awesome and awful. It is beau-tiful and unbearable. The sweetest pleasure. The bitterest pain. The mystic is wounded by a love so overwhelming that she both gasps for relief and pants with delight. Everything in her wants the intensity to subside. Everything wants it to intensify. It is a spiritual ecstasy that pains the body. It is life so abundant that it is as overwhelming as death.

> In his hands I saw a long golden spear and at the end of the iron tip I seemed to see a point of fire. With this he seemed to pierce my heart several

times so that it penetrated my entrails. When he drew it out I thought he was drawing them out with it and he left me completely afire with a great love for God. The pain was so sharp that it made me utter several moans; and so excessive was the sweetness caused me by this intense pain that one can never wish to lose it, nor will one's soul be content with anything less than God. It is not bodily pain, but spiritual, though the body has a share in it—indeed, a great share. So sweet are the colloquies of love which pass between the soul and God that if anyone thinks I am lying I beseech God, in His goodness, to give him the same experience.[65]

Here, Teresa joins the choir of saints and mystics who have sung in unison, even when they have sung in a plurality of voices. She echoes her friend John of the Cross's ecstatic exclamation, "May the vision of your beauty be my death!"[66]

Speaking of the connection between Teresa's writings and the experiences recounted by other mystics, Kristeva notes that the mystic's relation to God—who is viewed as both "an ideal father from a psychoanalytic point of view" and also "a beaten father who is tortured and crucified"—is "resexualized" such that an intense "suffering is also aggravated in the mystical experience."[67] "This suffering is experienced as pleasure alongside death and vulnerability and the castration of the father. He is ideal, but he is suffering and he is a source of ultimate pleasure and ultimate suffering."[68] It ought not to surprise us, then, to find John of the Cross speaking on the one hand "of a superabundance of love … where the soul may 'taste a splendid spiritual sweetness'" and on the other of "terror and fear before the very force of mystical ecstasy. The soul is compelled to beg the beloved to 'withdraw the eyes I have desired'; it is clearly too much for either the senses or mind to endure."[69]

For the mystic, the experience of God is "sensorial and quite disturbing sexually in the sense that some mystics—male mystics, for instance—experience themselves as women being penetrated by God."[70] Pleasure and pain, joy and sorrow, life and death, good and evil collide and become one in this moment of unspeakable ecstasy. John, who is remembered as both a mystic and a stigmatic, opens his *Spiritual Canticle* with the image of the poem's speaker being wounded by a divine stag. "He has already been shot through with 'the thrust of the lance,' which now leaves him 'moaning' and disoriented—sick with love. And yet this wounding, which leaves him in such destitute loss, is also, he avows, something blissful and benign."[71] One is reminded of St. Francis of Assisi's reception of the stigmata which Dante, echoing the language of Song 8:6, calls the "final seal" received by the mystic from Christ (*Paradiso*, XI, 107).[72] As Francis's first biographer Thomas of Celano notes, during that mystical experience Francis felt "sad and happy, joy and grief alternating in him."[73] His wounds ignited his ecstasy. From the depth of his suffering, his bliss sprang forth.

According Bataille, the experiences recounted by these mystics share a direct link with the Song of Songs. In the second volume of *The Accursed Share*, he includes a subsection titled "From the *Song of Songs* to the Formless and Modeless

God of the Mystics" in which he rejects any interpretation of the Song that attempts to reduce its mystical language to a "transposition of sexual states."[74] "The whole thrust of my book is contrary to these simplifications. It seems no more legitimate to reduce mysticism to sexual eroticism than to reduce the latter, as people do, even without saying it, to animal sexuality."[75] Yet even if the burning desire expressed by the mystics is not reducible to the passion of sexual eroticism, still the two are analogous to one another and Bataille is not afraid to explore the unsettling power that connects them. It is in this context that he offers a reading of the Song of Songs darker and more troubling than any of the reductive interpreters would dare.

In sex and in God, Bataille sees death. Like Nietzsche, who finds "a womanly tenderness and lust" at the heart of the mystic's pursuit of a "*unio mystica et physica*,"[76] Bataille identifies "a fundamental connection between religious ecstasy and eroticism."[77] (Indeed, contrary to the distinction insisted upon above, he— in his book *On Nietzsche*—goes so far as to assert: "There is no wall between eroticism and mysticism!")[78] And like Nietzsche, who insists that "the desire for a *unio mystica* with God is the desire of the Buddhist for nothingness ... and no more,"[79] Bataille is ready admit "the identity of these perfect contraries, divine ecstasy and its opposite, extreme horror,"[80] the abyss of "*religious eroticism*" and the nothingness of death.

> [A]nguish, which lays us open to annihilation and death, is always linked to eroticism; our sexual activity finally rivets us to the distressing image of death, and the knowledge of death deepens the abyss of eroticism. The curse of decay constantly recoils on sexuality, which it tends to eroticize: in sexual anguish there is a sadness of death, an apprehension of death which is rather vague but which we will never be able to shake off.[81]

Sexuality's "fragrance of death," Bataille writes, "ensures all its power."[82] A power at once destructive and divine. For, it is "in the darkness of eroticism," in the encounter with "horror, anguish, death," that "the experience of God is kept alive."[83] "What the mystic glimpses in the laceration of his knees is a God dying on the Cross, the horror of death and suffering—a vision granted him to the very degree that his strength gives way."[84]

The mystic, like the lover, loses himself in the anguish of this horrific/beatific vision. He is overcome by the "desire to blissfully and sublimely dissolve into limitless fusion ... [into] nothingness, death, indifferentiation."[85] "Only eroticism is capable, in silence and transgression, of admitting the lovers into that void where even the mumbling is stopped, where no speech is conceivable, where it is no longer just the other but rather the bottomlessness and boundlessness of the universe that is designated by the embrace."[86] For Bataille, this mystical eroticism represents a dark assent to life lived to the point of death, "the desire to fall headlong,"[87] "to live while ceasing to live, or to die without ceasing to live,"[88] "to fall, to fail, and to squander all one's reserves until there is no firm ground beneath one's feet."[89] It is "the desire of an extreme state that Saint Teresa has perhaps been the only one to depict strongly enough in words: 'I die because I cannot die,'"[90] "the complete destruction of the world of common reality, the passage from the perfect Being of positive theology to that formless and modeless God of 'theopathy' akin to the 'apathy' of Sade."[91]

In Umberto Eco's *The Name of the Rose*, Adso of Melk—a Benedictine novice who serves as the novel's narrator—recounts the details of his first and only sexual encounter. Like Bataille's lovers, Adso finds that his experience of eroticism leaves him "bereft of any expression, because my tongue and my mind had not been instructed in how to name sensations of that sort."[92] Overwhelmed by "joy in that moment"—which, we should note, is a carnal joy born of intimacy with a "human reality" and "not a vision"[93]—Adso recalls "other words, heard in another time and in other places, spoken certainly for other ends, but which seemed wondrously in keeping with my joy ... as if they had been born consubstantially to express it."[94] "Suddenly the girl appeared to me as the black but comely virgin of whom the Song of Songs speaks."[95]

In the pages that follow, Adso's reflections seem to confirm not only Bataille's reading of the Song but also the connection he draws between mysticism, eroticism, and death. Noting that there is nothing "more sweet and terrible" than sexuality's "invitation of [the] whole spirit to lose all memory in bliss," "as if one no longer existed, not feeling one's identity at all, or feeling lowered, almost annihilated,"[96] Adso writes:

> As a little drop of water added to a quantity of wine is completely dispersed and takes on the color and taste of wine, as red-hot iron becomes like molten fire losing its original form, as air when it is inundated with the sun's light is transformed into total splendor and clarity so that it no longer seems illuminated but, rather, seems to be light itself, so I felt myself die of tender liquefaction, and I had only the strength left to murmur the words of the psalm: "Behold my bosom is like new wine, sealed, which bursts new vessels." ... Then I understood the abyss, and the deeper abysses that it conjured up.[97]

To his surprise and horror, Adso soon realizes that "to describe my wicked ecstasy of that instant I have used the same words that I used ... to describe the fire that burned the martyred body of the Fraticello Michael."[98] "Why," he asks,

> did I ... depict the ecstasy of death that had impressed me in the martyr Michael in the words the saint had used for the ecstasy of (divine) life, and yet I could not refrain from depicting in the same words the ecstasy (culpable and fleeting) of earthly pleasure, which immediately afterward had spontaneously appeared to me as a sensation of death and annihilation? ...
>
> What was similar in Michael's desire for death, in the transport I felt at the sight of the flame consuming him, in the desire for carnal union I felt

with the girl, in the mystic shame with which I translated it allegorically, and in the desire for joyous annihilation that moved the saint to die in his own love in order to live longer and eternally?[99]

For Bataille and for Nietzsche, the answer to these questions is clear: without the "fragrance of death," sexuality "would not be erotic"[100] nor would God be divine.[101]

A reading "more dark and awful"

In his consideration of the mystical theology of Meister Eckhart, Žižek criticizes Eckhart's "refusal (or inability) to endorse Christ's full humanity," his reducing of "Christ to an ethereal being foreign to earthly reality."[102] "Eckhart avoids the *monstrosity* of Christ's Incarnation, he is unable to accept Christ's full humanity: 'When Eckhart speaks of Christ, he almost always stresses his divinity at the expense of his humanity. Even in the scriptural texts clearly describing the humanity of Jesus, he still finds ways of reading his divine nature.'"[103] That Eckhart's mysticism is predicated upon a desire to return to "the abyss of Godhead, the Nothingness of the Ungod"[104]—which, for him, precedes the existence of God who only comes into being through man[105]—is a direct consequence of his minimizing the import of the incarnation.

> When Eckhart writes that anyone who wants to receive Jesus must become as free of all representations "as he was when he was not yet," before his birth on earth, he is, of course, referring to Plato, to the Platonic notion of the soul prior to its bodily dwelling; however, in contrast to Plato, this preexistence does not involve a soul which, uncontaminated by the images of sensory things, beholds eternal ideas, but one which purifies itself of all "things," ideas included (and including God himself as a Thing)—more a kind of *tabula rasa*, an empty receptacle.[106]

For Eckhart, "God is not a person."[107] In fact, "God is nothing outside man."[108] He is "[n]othing itself, Godhead as the abyss of *Unding*."[109] But "this nothing is not a mere nothing;" it is "the abyss of Godhead prior to God"—an abyss into which the mystic longs to descend, a formless and modeless abyss in which "all opposition is effaced" and "the very difference between God and man is annihilated-obliterated."[110]

If this exposition of Eckhartian mysticism seems to confirm Nietzsche's critique that "the desire for a *unio mystica* with God is the desire of the Buddhist for nothingness, Nirvana"[111]—that is, the nihilistic desire for death—that is because it does. And herein lies the problem. "Eckhart in effect misses the central feature of the Judeo-Christian tradition, in which man's encounter with divinity is not the result of withdrawal into the depths of my inner Self" but "the shock of the external encounter."[112] It is the encounter with the "unfathomable otherness" of the other, the refusal to seek deliverance by means of "the 'inner journey' of spiritual self-purification, the return to one's true Inner Self, the self's 'rediscovery,'" that for Žižek rescues the Jewish-Christian paradigm from the accusation of nihilism levelled above.[113]

Quoting Laplanche—"the otherness of the other is [one's] response to his unconscious, that is to say, to his otherness to himself"—Žižek goes on to make a startling theological claim (one which resonates with Manoussakis's notion of the "cracked God" examined in Chapter 4):

> Is it not crucial to accomplish this move also apropos of the notion of *Dieu obscur*, of the elusive, impenetrable God: this God has to be impenetrable also to himself, he has to have a dark side, an otherness in himself, something that is in himself more than himself? Perhaps this accounts for the shift from Judaism to Christianity: Judaism remains at the level of the enigma *of* God, while Christianity moves to the enigma *in* God himself.... it is precisely because God is an enigma also *in and for himself*, because he has an unfathomable Otherness in himself, that Christ had to emerge to reveal God not only to humanity, but *to God himself*—it is only through Christ that God fully actualizes himself as God.[114]

The implications of this assertion are far-reaching. For one, it means that, as Chesterton says, "omnipotence made God incomplete.... God, to be wholly God, must have been a rebel as well as a king."[115] But a rebel in rebellion against what? His own kingship? Here we begin to touch upon "a matter more dark and awful than it is easy to discuss"[116]—the notion that an "antagonism [is] inscribed into the very heart of God," "a contradiction tearing apart the very unity of the All."[117] And it is one short step from this claim to the appalling assertion that "God is not primary Reconciliation but the infinite pain of self-tearing-apart."[118] (Is this, one might ask, the Christian God or the god of Nietzsche: "the suffering Dionysus of the Mysteries," "the original and primal cause of all suffering," "a dismembered god" who has been "torn to pieces" and "possesses the dual nature of a cruel, barbarized demon and a mild, gentle ruler"?)[119]

What does this have to do with our reading of the Song of Songs? A love song? A song which so passionately celebrates life? As we make our way through the scriptural text, we cannot help but be struck by an unexpected repetition. The repetition of a color. Not the green of springtime: the vegetation, the gardens, the fields, and the fruits. No, another color. A violent color. The deep red of the rose of Sharon. The darkness of the rose, as black as blood. The dark night of abandonment. A bride, forlorn. Lost and alone. Left to search the streets for her missing lover (Song of Songs 3). She is wounded, beaten, her mantle is torn (5:7). Her lover is gone. He has left her and cannot be found (5:6).

The bride is the rose—comely and dark (1:5), trampled underfoot. In contradistinction to the Song's green and vibrant setting, she fixes herself at the center of the poem. But who is this rose? Why has she been wounded? Forsaken by the one that she loves? Žižek quotes Chesterton:

> When the world shook and the sun was wiped out of heaven, it was not at the crucifixion, but at the cry from the cross: the cry which confessed that God was forsaken of God. And now let the revolutionists choose a creed from all the creeds and a god from all the gods of the world, carefully weighing all the gods of inevitable recurrence and of unalterable power. They will not find another god who has himself been in revolt. Nay, (the matter grows too difficult for human speech) but let the atheists themselves choose a god. They will find only one divinity who ever uttered their isolation; only one religion in which God seemed for an instant to be an atheist.[120]

This dark insight is, for Žižek, "the central mystery of Christianity."[121] "In the standard form of atheism, God dies for men who stop believing in him; in Christianity, God dies *for himself*."[122] "In his 'Father, why have you forsaken me?', Christ himself commits what is for a Christian the ultimate sin: he wavers in his Faith. While, in all other religions, there are people who do not believe in God, only in Christianity does God not believe in himself."[123]

St. Bernard of Clairvaux, in his reading of the Song, tells us that from the opening line—"O that you would kiss me with the kisses of your mouth!" (1:1)—we find ourselves in the presence the Trinity: "The Father kisses. The Son is kissed. The Holy Spirit is the kiss."[124] Who, then, is the rose of Sharon, the Song's abandoned bride? Can there be any doubt? She is "Christ, the ultimate divine Fool, deprived of all majesty and dignity."[125] Her bridegroom, the Father, has hidden his face. He has left her "sick with love" (5:8), sick with the Spirit who is her longing for her missing lover.[126] This bride is the revelation of her bridegroom's "name" (John 17:6); it is through her suffering that his name becomes "oil poured out" (Song of Songs 1:3). She is "a lily" and "a rose" (2:1)—spotless and crucified. She is "a lily among brambles" (2:2), sent like a sheep in the midst of wolves (Matthew 10:16). From the cross, she seeks her lover; but she finds him not. "I called him, but he gave no answer" (Song of Songs 5:6). She must lower herself (Philippians 2:8), must descend "from the lairs of lions, from the leopards' heights" in order to meet her lost lover in his hidden dwelling place (Song of Songs 4:8). Where does her bridegroom dwell? Where does he make his abode? "In the clefts of the rock, in the secret recesses of the cliff" (2:14)—that is, a tomb cut out of the rock (Mark 15:46), the secrecy of the grave.

This, then, is the meaning of that terrible phrase "love is strong as death, longing is fierce as Sheol" (8:6). Only a love which descends to the depths—to sin, death, godlessness itself—can be the love of God. If, as Origen says, one cannot "be blamed if he calls God *eros*, just as John called him *agape*,"[127] then we must proclaim along with Ignatius of Antioch that "Eros has been crucified."[128] And we must insist that there can be no greater love than this. Indeed, in this love—a love which is death itself, a death as "meaningless" as any other[129] and yet "[m]ore profound than … ordinary human death" in that it represents the full "'realization' of all Godlessness, of all the sins of the world, now experienced as agony and a sinking down into the 'second death' or 'second chaos,' outside the world"[130]—in *this* love, all other loves are grounded and contained. (As Balthasar says, "Everything temporal takes place within the embrace of the eternal action and as its consequence;"[131] and "the Father's self-surrender to the Son and their relationship in the Spirit" "grounds everything.")[132]

How horrible, then, is this God of love? How monstrous? How strange? Marion's pious assertion, "God precedes and transcends us, but first and above all in the fact that he loves us infinitely better than we love, than we love him. God surpasses us as the best lover,"[133] takes on a terrible new tone and tenor when considered in light of what that love means, what it costs. In a startling and paradoxical move, Eros reveals himself to be both Eros and Thanatos.[134] He is an Eros who descends into Thanatos, who is literally "made to be sin" (2 Corinthians 5:21).[135] He is not a God who brings unity, reconciliation, but—the sword: "God is … the infinite pain of self-tearing-apart." How is man to relate to this God, this apish God who is love itself? Žižek does not mince words: "[H]umiliation and pain are the only transcendental feelings: it is preposterous to think that I can identify myself with the divine bliss—only when I experience the infinite pain of separation from God do I share an experience with God Himself (Christ on the Cross)."[136]

Notes

1 Ricoeur, "The Nuptial Metaphor," 265.
2 Ibid., 276.
3 Ibid., 266.
4 Augustine, *Confessions*, (12.24.33).
5 Ricoeur, "The Nuptial Metaphor," 266.
6 Eliot, "Tradition and the Individual Talent," 28.
7 Ibid., 33.
8 Ricoeur, "The Nuptial Metaphor," 269.
9 Ibid., 267.
10 Kearney, "The Shulammite's Song," 339.
11 Eliot, "Tradition and the Individual Talent," 33.
12 Ibid., 32.
13 Kearney, "The Shulammite's Song," 339.
14 Ibid., 306.
15 Ibid.
16 Ibid., 339.
17 Ibid., 312.
18 Kearney quotes Todd Linafelt: "-*yah*, the last syllable of the last word of the verse, is a shortened form of Israel's personal name for God, Yahweh, and serves grammatically as an intensifying particle." Ibid., 308.
19 Ibid., 312.
20 Žižek, "The Fear of Four Words," 37.
21 Balthasar, *Cosmic Liturgy*, 199.
22 Silvas, "Communion with God," 68.
23 Deleuze as quoted in Manoussakis, "Cracked," 61.
24 Silvas, "Communion with God," 68.

25 Ibid., 66.
26 Kierkegaard, *The Concept of Anxiety*, 49.
27 Manoussakis, "Cracked," 57.
28 Silvas, "Communion with God,"64.
29 Nietzsche, *Beyond Good and Evil*, (§75).
30 Brian Becker offers another reading of this passage which is merits our consideration:

> Defecation, more so even than nakedness, is the great source of shame. We are fully ready to have another see us naked before ever, if ever, being seen to defecate. Genesis notes Adam and Eve's shame of their nakedness. However, we may now wonder if this was perhaps a tactful euphemism for the far more primordial indignity of defecating in the presence of the Other. At the same time, this withholding would have allowed Adam and Eve to retain the digested remnants of the forbidden fruit from the tree of knowledge. This withholding is our entry into the logic of economy, which will subsequently manifest its most characteristic forms of possessiveness: envy, jealousy, greed, and, through reaction formation, various forms of incontinence.
>
> (Becker, *"The Cost of* das Ding," 70–71)

31 Kearney, "The Shulammite's Song," 312.
32 Ibid., 311.
33 Žižek, "The Fear of Four Words," 37.
34 Ibid.
35 Silvas, "God and Communion," 73.
36 These verses read:

> Have among yourselves the same attitude that is also yours in Christ Jesus, who, though he was in the form of God, did not regard equality with God something to be grasped. Rather, he emptied himself, taking the form of a slave, coming in human likeness; and found human in appearance, he humbled himself, becoming obedient to death, even death on a cross.

37 Cooper, "The Story of God and *Eros*," 102.
38 Sweeney, "Bodily Love and the *Imago Trinitatis*," 108.
39 There is no shortage of examples in the history of philosophy of thinkers arguing that distancing oneself from the body leads to an increase of power. Boethius, to offer just one, tells us that we must "despise every earthly affair" and be "freed from the earthly prison" in order to achieve "true and perfect happiness ... which makes a man self-sufficient, strong, worthy of respect, glorious and joyful." "Self-sufficiency and power," he writes, "are of one and the same nature." Boethius, *The Consolation of Philosophy*, (II, VII; III, IX).
40 Tertullian, *De Resurrectione Carnis*, <www.vatican.va/spirit/documents/spirit_2 0000908_tertulliano_en.html>.
41 See,

> Since the soul is, in consequence of its salvation, chosen for the service of God, it is the flesh which actually renders it capable of such service. The flesh, indeed, is washed, in order that the soul may be cleansed; the flesh is anointed, that the soul may be consecrated; the flesh is signed (with the cross), that the soul too may be fortified; the flesh is shadowed with the imposition of hands, that the soul also may be illuminated by the Spirit; the flesh feeds on the body and blood of Christ, that the soul likewise may fatten on its God. They cannot then be separated in their recompense, when they are united in their service.
>
> (Ibid.)

42 Augustine, *City of God*, (XIV, 3).
43 Cf. "See how dearly God loves us, how he implores us.... God has such a need to seek us out—exactly as if all his Godhead depended on it." Eckhart, "Sermon: 'Woman, the Hour is Coming,'" 56.
44 Sweeney, "Bodily Love and the *Imago Trinitatis*," 117.
45 Silvas, "God and Communion," 84.
46 Kearney, "The Shulammite's Song," 312.
47 Ibid., 312–313.
48 Ibid., 313.
49 Ibid., 312.
50 Augustine, *City of God*, (XIV, 5).
51 Kearney, "The Shulammite's Song," 313.
52 Ibid., 317.
53 Ibid.
54 Ibid., 317–318.
55 Ibid., 318.
56 Ibid.
57 Ibid.
58 Sweeney, "Bodily Love and the *Imago Trinitatis*," 120–121.
59 As quoted in Bataille, *Erotism*, 225. Bataille calls "the hypothesis that all mystical experience is nothing but transposed sexuality and hence neurotic behavior" "unlikely."
60 Sweeney, "Bodily Love and the *Imago Trinitatis*," 121.
61 Ibid., 116.
62 Žižek, *The Puppet and the Dwarf*, 123.
63 Kearney, "Losing Our Touch."
64 See,

> What, however, if the Song of Songs is to be read *not* as an allegory but, much more literally, as the description of purely sensual erotic play? What if the 'deeper' spiritual dimension is already operative in the passionate sexual interaction itself? The true task is thus not to reduce sexuality to mere allegory, but to unearth the inherent 'spiritual' dimension that forever separates human sexuality from animal coupling.
> *(Žižek, The Puppet and the Dwarf, 123)*

> What is that spiritual dimension? Bataille makes it clear: "sexuality's fragrance of death ensures all its power. This is the meaning of anguish, without which sexuality would be only an animal activity, and would not be erotic."
> *(Bataille, The Accursed Share, 100)*

65 Teresa of Avila as quoted in Bataille, *Erotism*, 224.
66 John of the Cross, *Selected Writings*, 233.
67 Kristeva, "Mysticism and Anatheism," 70.
68 Ibid., 71.
69 Kearney, "The Shulammite's Song," 325.
70 Kristeva, "Mysticism and Anatheism," 70.
71 Kearney, "The Shulammite's Song," 324.
72 Marion also picks up the language of being "sealed" by one's beloved. "As lover, I allow myself to be struck by the seal of that which comes upon me, to the point that, in receiving it as the mark of the other, I also receive myself." Marion, *The Erotic Phenomenon*, 110.
73 Thomas of Celano, *First and Second Lives of St. Francis*. <sourcebooks.fordham.edu/source/stfran-lives.asp>

74 Bataille, *The Accursed Share*, 170.

75 Ibid.

76 Nietzsche, *Beyond Good and Evil*, (§50).

77 Bataille, *The Tears of Eros*, 206.

78 Bataille, *On Nietzsche*, 131.

79 Nietzsche, *On the Genealogy of Morals*, (1, §6).

80 Bataille, *The Tears of Eros*, 207.

81 Bataille, *The Accursed Share*, 84.

82 Ibid., 100.

83 Ibid., 169.

84 Ibid., 170.

85 Kearney, "The Shulammite's Song," 336.

86 Bataille, *The Accursed Share*, 168.

87 Bataille, *Erotism*, 243.

88 Kearney, "The Shulammite's Song," 337.

89 Ibid.

90 Ibid.

91 Bataille, *The Accursed Share*, 171.

92 Eco, *The Name of the Rose*, 277.

93 Ibid., 276.

94 Ibid., 277.

95 Ibid.

96 Ibid., 282–283.

97 Ibid., 280.

98 Ibid., 280–281.

99 Ibid., 281.

100 Bataille, *The Accursed Share*, 100.

101 Nietzsche calls the Christian God "nothingness deified, the will to nothingness sanctified." See, Nietzsche, *Anti-Christ*, (§18).

102 Žižek, "The Fear of Four Words," 33.

103 Ibid., 40.

104 Ibid., 36.

105 "[For Eckhart] it is not just that God gives birth to—creates—man, it is also not merely that only through and in man, God becomes fully God; much more radically, it is man himself who gives birth to God." Ibid., 33.

106 Ibid., 36.

107 Ibid., 35.

108 Ibid., 33.

109 Ibid., 35.

110 Ibid., 33.

111 Nietzsche, *On the Genealogy of Morals*, (1, §6).

112 Žižek, "The Fear of Four Words," 37.

113 Ibid.

114 Ibid., 38.

115 As quoted in ibid., 48.

116 Ibid.

117 Ibid., 49.

118 Ibid., 50 n. 71.

119 Nietzsche, *The Birth of Tragedy*, (§10). For more on the connection between the "unknown God" of Nietzsche and Christ see, Clemente, "Disciple of a Still Unknown God," 163–165.

120 Chesterton, as quoted in Žižek, "The Fear of Four Words," 48.

121 Ibid.

122 Ibid.

123 Ibid., 48–49.

124 Bernard of Clairvaux, *Talks on the Song of Songs*, 14.
125 Žižek, *The Puppet and the Dwarf*, 90–91.
126 Cf. "[T]he Holy Spirit is the Love between Father and Son, a pure and generous overflow." Eckhart, as quoted in Balthasar, *The Glory of the Lord, vol. 5*, 32.
127 As quoted in Cooper, "The Story of God and *Eros*," 94.
128 See, Dionysius, *The Divine Names*, (IV.12.709B).
129 Žižek, *The Puppet and the Dwarf*, 125.
130 Balthasar, *Mysterium Paschale*, 51–52.
131 Balthasar, *Theo-drama, vol. 4*, 327.
132 Ibid., 328.
133 Marion, *The Erotic Phenomenon*, 222.
134 Žižek, in his reading of Chesterton's metaphysical detective novel *The Man Who Was Thursday*, observes that

> the very final twist … in which 'Sunday,' the arch-criminal, the anarchists' all-powerful leader, is revealed to be the mysterious chief of the super-secret police unit who mobilizes … the fight against the anarchists … [and] is [also] none other than God himself

reveals the "unity of opposites" that exists in God: "it means that 'God' is a mask (a travesty) of 'Devil,' that the difference between Good and Evil is internal to Evil" (Žižek, "The Fear of Four Words," 45–50). What Žižek misses, however, is the relation between Sunday and Syme's love interest Rosamond ("the rose of the world"). Of her, Chesterton writes:

> In the wild events which were to follow this girl had no part at all; [Syme] never saw her again until all his tale was over. And yet, in some indescribable way, she kept recurring like a motive in music through all his mad adventures afterwards, and the glory of her strange hair ran like a red thread through those dark and ill-drawn tapestries of the night.
>
> *(Chesterton, Collected Works, vol. 6, 482–483)*

That the "red thread" is an allusion to Christ—who is often referred to as the red thread running through the whole of scripture, from Genesis to Revelation—raises the question: is Sunday—"the suffering God" whose emergence at the end of the novel "resolves this tension of God's two faces" (Žižek, "The Fear of Four Words," 53)—also Syme's beloved? Or, said differently, to what degree is every "beloved" a mask (a travesty) of the lover, Eros crucified?
135 Cf. "Jesus has to experience from within every sin and ungodly doing that has estranged mankind, without distancing himself from it, so that, as Paul says, he is literally made 'sin' for us (2 Cor 5:21)." Balthasar, *Life Out of Death*, 37.
136 Žižek, *The Puppet and the Dwarf*, 91.

Bibliography

Augustine, *Confessions*, trans. Maria Boulding (New York: Vintage, 1998).

Augustine, *City of God*, trans. Henry Bettenson (New York: Penguin, 2003).

Balthasar, Hans Urs von, *Theo-Drama: Theological Dramatic Theory*, trans. Graham Harrison, vols. 1–5 (San Francisco: Ignatius, 1988–1998).

Balthasar, Hans Urs von, *Mysterium Paschale: The Mystery of Easter*, trans. Aidan Nichols (Edinburgh, Scotland: T&T Clark, 1990).

Balthasar, Hans Urs von, *The Glory of the Lord, vol. 5: The Realm of Metaphysics in the Modern Age*, trans. Oliver Davies, et al. (Edinburgh, Scotland: T&T Clark, 1991).

Balthasar, Hans Urs von, *Cosmic Liturgy: The Universe According to Maximus the Confessor*, trans. Brian E Daley, SJ (San Francisco: Communio, Ignatius, 2003).

Balthasar, Hans Urs von, *Life Out of Death: Meditations on the Paschal Mystery*, trans. Martina Stockl (San Francisco: Ignatius, 2012).

Bataille, Georges, *Erotism: Death and Sensuality*, trans. Mary Dalwood (San Francisco: City Lights Books, 1986).

Bataille, Georges, *The Tears of Eros*, trans. Peter Connor (San Francisco: City Lights Books, 1989).

Bataille, Georges, *The Accursed Share: An Essay on General Economy, vol. 2: The History of Eroticism*, trans. Robert Hurley (New York: Zone Books, 1991).

Bataille, Georges, *On Nietzsche*, trans. Bruce Boone (New York: Paragon House, 1992).

Becker, Brian, "The Cost of *das Ding*: A Response to Manoussakis' 'The Place of *das Ding*'," in *Unconscious Incarnations: Psychoanalytic and Philosophical Perspectives on the Body*, eds. Brian Becker, John Manoussakis, and David Goodman (Abingdon, UK: Routledge, 2018), 66–75.

Bernard of Clairvaux, *Talks on the Song of Songs*, ed. Bernard Bangley (Brewster, MA: Paraclete, 2002).

Boethius, *The Consolation of Philosophy*, trans. Victor Watts (New York: Penguin, 1999).

Chesterton, GK, *Collected Works, vol. 6: The Man Who Was Thursday, The Club of Queer Trades, Napoleon of Notting Hill, Ball and the Cross* (San Francisco: Ignatius, 1991).

Clemente, M Saverio and Bryan J Cocchiara (eds.), *misReading Nietzsche* (Eugene, OR: Pickwick Publications, 2018).

Cooper, Adam, "The Story of God and *Eros*," in *God and Eros*, eds. Colin Patterson and Conor Sweeney (Eugene, OR: Cascade Books, 2015), 91–103.

Dionysius the Areopagite, *Divine Names in Pseudo-Dionysius: The Complete Works*, trans. Colm Luibhéid, ed. Paul Rorem (New York: Paulist, 1987).

Eckhart, Meister, "Sermon: 'Woman, the Hour is Coming'," in *Wandering Joy: Meister Eckhart's Mystical Philosophy*, trans. Reiner Schürmann (Barrington, MA: Steiner Books, 2001).

Eco, Umberto, *The Name of the Rose*, trans. William Weaver (New York: Everyman's Library, 2006).

Eliot, TS, "Tradition and the Individual Talent," in *The Sacred Wood and Major Early Essays* (Mineola, NY: Dover Publications, 1997).

John of the Cross, *John of the Cross: Selected Writings*, ed. Kieran Kavanaugh (New York: Paulist, 1987).

Kearney, Richard, "The Shulammite's Song: Desire Descending and Ascending," in *Toward a Theology of Eros: Transfiguring Passion at the Limits of Discipline*, eds. Virginia Burrus and Catherine Keller (New York: Fordham University Press, 2006).

Kearney, Richard, "Losing Our Touch," in *The New York Times Opinionator* (August 30, 2014). Available at: https://opinionator.blogs.nytimes.com/2014/08/30/losing-our-touch/.

Kierkegaard, Søren, *The Concept of Anxiety*, trans. Reidar Thomte (Princeton, NJ: Princeton University Press, 1980).

Kristeva, Julia, "Mysticism and Anatheism: The Case of Teresa," in *Richard Kearney's Anatheistic Wager: Philosophy, Theology, Poetics*, eds. Chris Doude van Troostwijk and Matthew Clemente (Bloomington: Indiana University Press, 2018), 68–87.

Manoussakis, John, "Cracked: The Black Theology of Anatheism," in *The Art of Anatheism*, eds. Richard Kearney and Matthew Clemente (London: Rowman & Littlefield, 2017), 49–66.

Marion, Jean-Luc, *The Erotic Phenomenon*, trans. Stephen E Lewis (Chicago: University of Chicago, 2007).

Nietzsche, Friedrich, *The Birth of Tragedy*, trans. Walter Kaufmann (New York: Vintage, 1967).

Nietzsche, Friedrich, *Beyond Good and Evil*, trans. Walter Kaufmann (New York: Vintage, 1989a).

Nietzsche, Friedrich, *On the Genealogy of Morals and Ecce Homo*, trans. Walter Kaufmann (New York: Vintage, 1989b).

Nietzsche, Friedrich, *Twilight of the Idols and The Anti-Christ*, trans. RJ Hollingdale (New York: Penguin, 1990).

Ricoeur, Paul, "The Nuptial Metaphor," in *Thinking Biblically: Exegetical and Hermeneutical Studies*, trans. David Pellauer, eds. André LaCocque and Paul Ricoeur (Chicago: University of Chicago Press, 1998).

Silvas, Anna, "Communion with God: Marriage as Metaphor in the Old Testament," in *God and Eros*, eds. Colin Patterson and Conor Sweeney (Eugene, OR: Cascade Books, 2015a), 60–72.

Silvas, Anna, "God and Communion: Marriage as Sacrament in the New Testament," in *God and Eros*, eds. Colin Patterson and Conor Sweeney (Eugene, OR: Cascade Books, 2015b), 73–90.

Sweeney, Conor, "Bodily Love and the *Imago Trinitatis*," in *God and Eros*, eds. Colin Patterson and Conor Sweeney (Eugene, OR: Cascade Books, 2015), 107–122.

Žižek, Slavoj, *The Puppet and the Dwarf* (Cambridge, MA: MIT Press, 2003).

Žižek, Slavoj, "The Fear of Four Words," in *The Monstrosity of Christ: Paradox or Dialectic?*, ed. Creston Davis (Cambridge, MA: MIT Press, 2009).

6

TRIUNE EROS

In *De Trinitate*, Augustine warns against conceiving of the love of God in human terms. Bodily images won't do. Analogies drawn from experience, from *this world*, mislead. Yet analogical reasoning, he also insists, offers insights into the things we cannot access through experience alone. It is that which allows us to live in relation to others, to love others, and ultimately to love God.[1] Thus we should take seriously Augustine's suggestion that the nuptial metaphor is an apt analogy for the inner-life of the divine, even if he insists that that analogy only represents an "imperfect image."[2] To say that God is love (1 John 4:6) presupposes an understanding of love.[3] And that is precisely what Augustine's analogy offers: "Behold, when I ... love something, then three things are found: I, what I love, and the love itself. For I do not love love, unless I love a lover, for there is no love where nothing is loved. There are, therefore, three things: the lover, the beloved, and the love."[4]

Love is, by its very nature, triune. It depends upon the trinity of lover, beloved, and the love that unites them, a pure and generous overflow. Understanding this metaphor is the key to grasping the interpretation of the Song of Songs offered in the previous chapter. For, if the bride, the "one who brings peace" (Song of Songs 8:10), is Christ, the "prince of peace" (Isaiah 9:5), and if the name of the bridegroom, Solomon, "refers to God, the 'one to whom peace belongs' (*li-mi she-ha-shalom shelo*)"[5]—that is, God the Father—then we must conclude along with Balthasar that "in Trinitarian terms ... the Father, who begets [the Son] ... appears primarily as (super-)masculine; the Son, in consenting, appears initially as (super-)feminine."[6] We must say that "in some mysteriously analogous way, the man-woman pair is the image of the *Trinitarian* God."[7]

Yet to reiterate our reading of the radical revaluation of gender relations introduced by the Christian understanding of sacramental sexuality, such an interpretation does not privilege masculinity at the expense of feminine desire (*en plus*).

Rather, as Kearney notes, the uniqueness of the Song of Songs resides in the fact that in it

> divine love finds privileged expression in the voice of a young woman. It is the Shulammite who takes most of the initiative and does most of the talking in the Song of Songs. And if the lover-king-Solomon speaks at some length in his own voice, his discourse often quotes the Shulammite and harks back to her as its source of reference.[8]

It is as if without the Son (the Word), the Father is mute; as if without the bride, the bridegroom cannot be revealed, not even to himself; as if, as Žižek contends, "it is only through Christ that God fully actualizes himself as God."[9]

Triune love

Kearney tells us that the Song of Songs is "a 'woman's song' from first to last."[10] It is a song in praise of carnal, bodily desire. One which proposes an erotic *descent* into the flesh, the world, the messiness of lived experience. We have argued that it is a song sung from Father to Son, from Son to Father, a love song which expresses the love that "grounds everything." At the end of our last chapter, we asserted that the triune love articulated in the Song of Songs makes possible every other form of love. In order to substantiate this claim, we ought now to consider what such love entails. What does it mean for divine love to find "privileged expression in the voice of a young woman"? What does it mean for Eros to no longer represent an ascent away from the corporeal, but a descent into the worldly, the bodily, the flesh that dwells among us?

In order to grapple with such questions, we must better understand the nature of triune love. Here, the novel interpretation of Trinitarian relations proposed by Balthasar is instructive. For, if Augustine identifies the nuptial metaphor as a possible analogy for the love that God himself is, Balthasar gives that analogy its clearest articulation. Considering the mysterious inner-life of the Trinity—a consideration which distinguishes him already from thinkers like Žižek who insist that "[t]he point of the Incarnation is that … the whole idea of approaching a transcendent God becomes irrelevant"[11]—Balthasar writes: "The immanent Trinity must be understood to be that eternal, absolute self-surrender whereby God is seen to be, in himself, absolute love."[12] Self-surrender thus becomes synonymous with love. It is the *kenosis* of God, the *kenosis* that he himself is, that defines triune Eros.

According to Balthasar, this absolute self-surrender occurs within the Godhead and is primarily seen in the begetting of the Son by the Father.

> The Father's self-utterance in the generation of the Son is an initial 'kenosis' within the Godhead that underpins all subsequent kenosis. For the

Father strips himself, without remainder, of his Godhead and hands it over to the Son; he 'imparts' to the Son all that is his.[13]

In response to this fully gratuitous gift-of-self, the Son offers his own surrender in return; he gives back to the Father the loving *kenosis* that he both receives and is. "The Son's answer to the gift of Godhead (of equal substance with the Father) can only be eternal thanksgiving (*eucharistia*) to the Father, the Source—a thanksgiving as selfless and unreserved as the Father's original self-surrender."[14] In his reception of the Father's kenotic self-emptying, the Son empties himself in thanksgiving and offers himself back to the Father as self-giving, self-receiving gift. Thus God reveals himself to be a "unity of omnipotence and powerlessness;" "an absolute renunciation;" a God who "will not be God for himself alone."[15]

Because "the whole divine essence" is contained "in this self-surrender," because God "*is* this movement of self-giving that holds nothing back"[16] (*jouissance*), the *love* of God which pours itself forth is as much a part of triune Eros as are the *lover* (Father) and *beloved* (Son).[17] "Proceeding from both, as their subsistent 'We,' there breathes the 'Spirit' who is common to both: as the essence of love, he maintains the infinite difference between them, seals it and, since he is the one Spirit of them both, bridges it."[18] This Spirit of divine love "does not want anything 'for himself' but, as his revelation in the world shows, wants simply to be the pure manifestation and communication of the love between Father and Son (John 14:26; 16:13–15)."[19] He is their consubstantial *We*, the cause of their union, the eternal third who binds Father to Son and Son to Father, the essence of their love. "Thus the absolute is manifest as 'We' in the identity of the gift-as-given and the gift-as-received in thanksgiving, which can only be such by attesting, maintaining and fueling the infinite distinction between Father and Son. Thus, within the distinction, the gift is not only the presupposition of an unsurpassable love: it is also the realized union of this love."[20]

This image of the divine bears a striking resemblance to the understanding of Eros we have offered from the start—an understanding which posits Eros as a unitive drive, a drive that necessitates otherness, that finds its fulfillment in communion with the other, rather than one that seeks wholeness at the expense of the other. According to Balthasar, such parallels are not accidental.

> For any world only has its place within that distinction between Father and Son that is maintained and bridged by the Holy Spirit. The drama of the Trinity lasts forever: the Father was never without the Son, nor were Father and Son ever without the Spirit. Everything temporal takes place within the embrace of the eternal action and as its consequence.[21]

Or, said differently, "*eros* is the glue that holds together both the universe and the Church."[22] Yet if this is indeed the case, if God "is the cause of *eros* in all things,"[23] how then have we ended up with an image of Eros as egocentric, solipsistic, shot through with sin? How has Thanatos been so adept at concealing itself behind an erotic mask?

Fracturing the Godhead: The unforgivable sin

In the Gospel of Mark, Christ makes a startling claim. Every sin, he tells us, every blasphemy "will be forgiven" (3:28). There is nothing that man can do that is beyond the reach of God's willingness to forgive. (Even the murder of God can be forgiven, *is* forgiven; and not at some later date, after the fact, but at the very moment that God himself bleeds to death under our knives [cf. Luke 23:34].) "But," Christ continues, "whoever blasphemes against the holy Spirit will never have forgiveness, but is guilty of an everlasting sin" (Mark 3:29). When taken seriously, these words fill one with dread. First, because they reveal that there exists something that is beyond the will of God, something with the power to resist God's desire to forgive. (If it is true that "God our savior ... wills everyone to be saved and to come to knowledge of the truth" [1 Timothy 2:4], then the possibility of committing an "everlasting sin" means the real possibility of rejecting God's will, denying him that which he desires.) Second, because it is not entirely clear what constitutes a blasphemy "against the holy Spirit." What is this sin that lasts forever?

Prior to offering this stark warning, Christ is accused of being possessed, of using the power of demons to cast out demons (Mark 3:22). His response to his accusers is illustrative:

> How can Satan drive out Satan? If a kingdom is divided against itself, that kingdom cannot stand. And if a house is divided against itself, that house will not be able to stand. And if Satan has risen up against himself and is divided, he cannot stand; that is the end of him."
>
> *(Mark 3:23–26)*

In a parallel passage found in the Gospel of Matthew, Christ adds, "Whoever is not with me is against me, and whoever does not gather with me scatters" (Matthew 12:30). "Therefore," he concludes, "every sin and blasphemy will be forgiven people, but blasphemy against the Spirit will not be forgiven" (12:31). As the context makes clear, the blasphemy of which Christ speaks is more than the sin of attributing to Satan the works of God. It is the sin of separating that which the Spirit of God has joined together, scattering that which *love* has gathered, dividing God against himself.

As we noted above, it is the *diastemic* nature of the fallen creation that separates man from God. Yet in this passage Christ tells us that the greatest blasphemy is to project that same division back into the Godhead, to put asunder the love that binds the triune God together as one. If the Spirit represents the "union" of God, if he is the "the essence of love," the one who "maintains the infinite difference between" Father and Son while also bridging that difference and uniting the two,[24] then anything that threatens to undermine the unitive nature of the Spirit is a blasphemy against him. Anything that eliminates otherness or refuses the possibility of communion with the other in love constitutes a sin against love, an unforgivable sin which denies that salvation comes from without, comes from the other.

When read together with a second passage that occurs later in Mark's Gospel, Christ's words become clearer still. In the famous prohibition against divorce, Christ asserts, "what God has joined together, no human being must separate" (Mark 10:9). And yet, the Pharisees contend, "Moses permitted [a husband] to write a bill of divorce and dismiss [his wife]" (10:4). Why then forbid it? Christ's response further supports our reading of the analogy between human and Trinitarian love:

> Because of the hardness of your hearts [Moses] wrote you this commandment. But from the beginning of creation, "God made them male and female. For this reason a man shall leave his father and mother [and be joined to his wife], and the two shall become one flesh." So they are no longer two but one flesh. Therefore what God has joined together, no human being must separate.
>
> *(Mark 10:5–9)*

(This seemingly nonsensical assertion—how can two separate persons become "one flesh"? Certainly husband and wife share no visible, physical unity—becomes comprehensible when one considers the distinction introduced by phenomenology between the objectified physical body [*Körper*] and the flesh (*Leib*), that which unifies lived-experience.)

The unity of husband and wife, like the unity of God, is a unity of two made one by virtue of a third: by the power of the Spirit who is the love that binds them. Christ's insistence that this has been the case "from the beginning" underscores the significance of the nuptial metaphor as an image of the divine. For, as Augustine reminds us, the Son

> is "the Beginning" who speaks to us. In this Beginning you [God] made heaven and earth ... You made them in your Word, your Son, your Power, your Wisdom, your Truth, wonderfully speaking and in a wondrous way creating.[25]

The Son is the beginning through whom "the world came to be" (John 1:10), the beginning through whom "God made them male and female," the beginning whose Spirit, whose love, weds two separate individuals together as "one flesh." The unitive power of Eros, Christ says, has been present from the start. Yet the hardness of our hearts will not allow us to see it. Our denial of love, our rejection of the other, our revulsion at the idea of communion—think of Sartre's famous quip: "Hell is other people"—condemns us with the wages of an everlasting sin.

Solipsism, necrophilia, and the wages of sin

"There is no other"—thus proclaims Manoussakis in his recent essay, "Dying to Desire: Soma, Sema, Sarx, and Sex." Like Nancy, who tells us that "the body of pleasure" "is not turned toward ... the other with whom—since we're talking about sexual pleasure—it is engaged in an exchange," but "is a body mingled with itself ... with self *as* other,"[26] Manoussakis refuses to allow us "to find comfort in the illusion that the beloved is an Other."[27] It is not the other himself, not the other as a *self*, he claims, that my desire desires. Rather it is "the object *in* the Other, the object *of* the Other, that very same Other whom our desire has reduced to its object."[28]

What sort of object is this objectified other? What has my desire reduced him to? Manoussakis is clear: "That object in the Other or the objectified Other is nothing other than myself as another, as othered by desire."[29] The other has become for me, as Nancy says, a means for my own self-transcendence, a way of mingling myself with myself "*as* other." By objectifying the other, my desire is able to turn my body into "a stranger to itself" so that it can "relate to itself as another or even itself as the other who encroaches upon it and besieges it, in order to enjoy it [*jouir de lui*] and also rejoice in itself [*ré-jouir lui-même*]."[30] And the body of the other? It has become a mirror which reflects back to me an image of myself: "The stigmata of eros are cyphers curved on the lover's flesh displaying to the beloved, as if on a mirror, that very desire he ignited in the first place."[31]

This depersonalization of the other at the behest of my desire confirms for Manoussakis that, following the Freudian formulation, "'the pleasure principle [Eros] seems actually to serve the death instincts' [Thanatos]"[32]—or, said differently, "desire is the desire of *Thanatos*."[33] "I don't know how to love, except by killing what I love."[34] Yet this reading of Eros as a covert manifestation of "the death drive" which "seeks my self-destruction not directly, as one may suppose, but rather obliquely, by a detour through the Other"[35] comes not primarily from Freud but from Manoussakis's reading of Plato. "Socrates," he reminds us,

> confesses that when it comes to beautiful boys he cannot tell the difference: to him they are all equally beautiful (*Charmides*, 154b). Their beauty has a blinding effect on him, for he is unable to see them *as them*, that is, as anything else other than beautiful and, with respect to their beauty, equally interchangeable.[36]

(One is perhaps reminded of the distinction introduced by CS Lewis in *The Four Loves* between *venus*—which is directed at no specific individual but merely "wants a pleasure for which [any] woman [or man] happens to be the necessary piece of apparatus"—and *eros* which "in some mysterious but quite indisputable fashion" causes the lover to desire "the Beloved herself, not the pleasure she can give.")[37]

That Socrates should express such disregard for the individuality of the beloved ought not to surprise us. (Indeed, this lack of concern for the individual is the impetus driving the *Kierkegaard contra Socrates* dialectic that is Kierkegaard's corpus.) Yet as Manoussakis shows, it is rooted in a more nefarious commitment than Socrates's espoused devotion to the Form of Beauty. In his reading of the pederastic structure of Eros laid out in the *Phaedrus*, Manoussakis writes:

> [W]hat is the lover's desire for the beloved if not the desire for himself? As the lover of his beloved, the lover has taken the place—and, in a sense, he has re-placed—his lover; that is, that lover from the time when he (the lover) was himself the beloved. For the lover was not long ago another's beloved, as this beloved now will become one day the lover of yet another beloved. Therefore, the lover's desire for the beloved is for the lover a desire for his younger self. The lover is in love with his past self or with the specter of himself, that is, with what lies now in the past, dead. Insofar as the present lover was the past beloved, his desire for the present beloved is the desire that he, as a beloved, had. Now, as the lover, he can finally satisfy his desire in the only way possible: by becoming his own lover ... in order to do now to the beloved (that is, to the image of his younger self, to himself) that which his lover did or did not do to him then. All the lover really wants is to fuck himself, his younger self, a self past and dead.[38]

That this understanding of Eros is true to the one put forth by Plato is illustrated by Manoussakis's close and careful reading of the text (with a particular focus on 255b–e). Yet whether this portrait paints an accurate picture of Eros is another question. For, if, as Manoussakis says, "Desire is ... the name of a nostalgia for a time before time, the attempt, always failing and always recommencing, 'to return to the inanimate state,' before corporeal existence" then he is right to conclude that "desire is the desire of *Thanatos*,"[39] that "we never desire the Other; we never desire the Other's body,"[40] only a corpse,[41] a dead thing, myself as dead. But if this is in fact the case, whence the discussion quoted in Chapter 4 of the "sabbatical crack" in God which accounts for the Eros in man? Whence the notion of *love*—existing "from the beginning"—which is predicated on the existence of the other?

Commenting on the "violently obsessive" character of "male desire," Žižek writes, "it is the very excessive-possessive nature of male desire which makes it destructive of its object—(male) love is murder."[42] The qualifier here is essential. Love itself is not murder. Only a particular kind of love, the kind that wants to grasp, possess, subjugate, take ownership of the other. Only male love—that is, *sadism*.[43] (As Lacan notes, "The act of love is the male's polymorphous perversion.")[44] We alluded earlier to the fact that Plato's account of Eros is based upon a pederastic structure which excludes female *jouissance*. (One wonders whether the lover would see in the beloved "his past self or the specter of himself" if the beloved was not a young man—that is, someone who resembles a younger version of himself. What happens to this scheme when the lover's beloved is a woman ten years his senior?)

If, as Manoussakis says, "the death drive is first and foremost directed toward" the object of my love, if "my desire knows of no other object than a corpse,"[45] that is perhaps because the desire being expressed here is *mimetic desire*—the perverse desire for sameness which quickly devolves into a desire for oneness, unity at the expense of the other. Such desire, as Girard so convincingly argues, cannot but lead to violence: I must destroy that which resembles me before it replaces me. And yet, this frantic attempt to destroy the copy of myself also leads to my own self-destruction. Once the other has been eliminated, my solipsism turns in upon itself, collapsing into a void of perfect identity and, subsequently, death.

Mimetic violence, rooted in my identification with the other, accounts for the fact that "in sex I always find in the other an image of myself,"[46] a self I desire to "fuck" and destroy. That this is the case with male/sadistic sexuality—which finds pleasure in power, in the perverse desire to subjugate, to be God—is obvious enough. The question is whether all human sexuality is tainted by this perversion.[47] (Have we not already established that the sexual act implies perversion and perfection, the lowest and the highest, baseness and beatitude?)

We might be tempted to dismiss Manoussakis's (and Plato's and Freud's) picture of Eros. But something tells me we would be wise not to. For, if anyone is free of the sadistic lust for power, the Adamic desire "to be like gods"—a temptation which tempted the first man and woman alike—it is only the one who, "though he was in the form of God, did not regard equality with God something to be grasped," only the one who "emptied himself, taking the form of a slave, coming in human likeness; and found human in appearance, humbled himself, becoming obedient to death, even death on a cross" (Philippians 2:6–8). If we are not ready to love with a love that forgoes power, that refuses to objectify, subjugate, grasp, if we will not instead surrender, renounce, abandon ourselves with a divine recklessness, a divine love, if we will not become vulnerable, powerless, obedient to a love as strong and as fierce as death, that is "because, unlike Christ, we are not ready to die."[48]

The idiocy of love

At the end of our last chapter we spoke of a love as strong as death, a love that descends to the depths, that resists neither sin nor death nor godlessness—the love of God which is God's very self. As we have suggested, Christ is the incarnation of that love.[49] He is the embodiment of the "tripersonal self-gift," "the exteriorisation of God" made manifest in the world of flesh and blood.[50] He is Eros crucified, the one who—by his death and resurrection—frees us from the bonds of solipsism and makes possible the union of self and other, the one-flesh communion of triune love. Thus, if we are to understand the radical metamorphosis of Eros being proposed in this text, we must look to the love who became man, who assumed our "concrete destiny with all that entails—suffering, death, hell."[51] We must consider the implications of saying that "[t]he Son of God took human nature in its fallen condition, and with it, the worm in its entrails—mortality,

fallenness, self-estrangement, death."[52] We must allow Christ to reveal "an altogether decisive turn-about in the way of seeing God. God is not, in the first
place, 'absolute power' but 'absolute love,' and his sovereignty manifests itself not
in holding on to what is its own but in its abandonment."[53] We must appreciate
the lunacy of love, the folly of the cross.[54]

To do so, we will consider "the problem of the *psychology of the redeemer*" as
examined by Nietzsche in *The Anti-Christ*.[55] That Nietzsche, in a text which
bears as its title a seeming denunciation of Christ, offers one of the most insightful depictions of the god-man ought not to surprise us. (If, as Paul suggests, the
"children of God" have been "clothed ... with Christ" [Galatians 3:26–27], who
has "put on" Christ [Ephesians 4:24] more than the man who named his autobi-
ography *Ecce Homo* and who, when he lost his mind, began identifying himself as
"The Crucified"?) No, it would be a profound misreading to see Nietzsche as an
enemy of the "free spirit" called Jesus.[56] (As for the decadent organized religion
known has as Christianity—or what Kierkegaard calls "Christendom"—that is
another story. I take it as no accident that *Der Antichrist* could just as easily be
translated *The Anti-Christian*.)

In his consideration of the psychology of the redeemer, Nietzsche approaches
Christ as a human being—that is, as someone with "an extreme capacity for suffering," someone capable of experiencing "irritation," "unbearable displeasure,"
and "the fear of pain."[57] These human, all too human characteristics are, he
insists, the grounds of Christ's love[58]—a love which overcomes all "opposites,"[59]
which "is not angry, does not censure, does not defend itself ... does not prove
itself," but "is every moment its own miracle, its own reward, its own proof,
its own 'kingdom of God.'"[60] A love that "*lives*."[61] Such love, Nietzsche tells
us, "resists formulas."[62] It is "opposed to any kind of word, formula, law, faith,
dogma"; the "*experience* 'life'" is the only thing it knows, the only thing it *feels*.[63]

Love—understood here as that mysterious surplus (*jouissance*) which Lacan
links with "the love of God (*l'amour de Dieu*)"[64]—is, in its essence, unthinkable.
It cannot be understood, cannot be conceptualized—that is, *grasped*—it must be
experienced, lived from within. Because such love "stands outside of all religion,
all conceptions of divine worship, all history, all natural science, all experience
of the world, all acquirements, all politics, all psychology, all books, all art—
[because its] 'knowledge' is precisely the *pure folly* of the fact that anything of this
kind exists"[65]—Nietzsche insists that Christ is no genius. (One is reminded of the
distinction introduced by Kierkegaard between the genius and the apostle, and
also Kierkegaard's insistence upon the unthinkablity of faith.) Rather, Nietzsche
asserts, "quite a different word" should be used to describe the redeemer: "the
word idiot."[66]

Yet, as is the case with Dostoevsky's Prince Myshkin, Christ's idiocy is not a
fault but a supreme virtue. It is the idiocy of love itself; a love which reveals the
perversity—the psychosis—that plagues the (phallic) world of culture, society,
civilization, thought.[67] For Christ, there is no enmity, no exclusion, no "distance." Every attempt at "grasping" causes him to "shrink back in horror."[68]

"He is not angry with anyone, does not disdain anyone."[69] His love longs to bring people together. It seeks communion, unity.[70]

Like Balthasar,[71] Nietzsche identifies self-surrender as the hallmark of Christ's love: "Jesus definitively claims nothing for himself alone."[72] The redeemer, he tells us, "denies any chasm between God and man, he *lives* this unity of God and man as *his* 'glad tidings.'"[73] From now on, "Everyone is a child of God,"[74] "every kind of distancing relationship between God and man is abolished."[75] Christ rejects moralism, legalism, Pharisaism of any kind.[76] His life does not vindicate "the good and the just," "the saints of Israel," "the social hierarchy."[77] Just the opposite: he is "a political criminal" who stands "against caste, privilege, the order, the social form"; a "holy anarchist who roused up the lowly, the outcasts and 'sinners.'"[78]

If, as Nietzsche contends, "Jesus is ... *misunderstood*,"[79] if "[t]he word 'Christianity' is already a misunderstanding," that is because "only Christian *practice*, a life such as he who died on the Cross *lived*, is Christian."[80] Love, understood as such, is "*[n]ot* a belief but a doing, above all a *not*-doing of many things, a different *being*."[81] Belief in the existence of God, Nietzsche suggests, is easy. It costs nothing.[82] By contrast, "The Christian acts, he is distinguished by a *different* mode of acting.... it is through the *practice* of one's life that one feels 'divine,' 'blessed,' 'evangelic,' at all times a 'child of God.'"[83]

Yet if Christ introduces "[a] new way of living, *not* a new belief,"[84] if "[w]hat he bequeathed to mankind is his *practice*"[85]—still, we resist. We reject this new life, this narrow path, and flee from the love that would free us from bondage, from the strictures of our own depravity. For, if "*evangelic practice alone* leads to God, it *is* God," and if "the life of the redeemer was nothing else than *this* practice"—so too was his death "nothing else."[86] It is "his bearing before the judges, before the guards, before the accusers and every kind of calumny and mockery— his bearing on the *Cross*"—that constitutes a life lived (and borne and suffered) in *love*.[87] It is the fact that "[h]e does not resist, he does not defend his rights, he takes no steps to avert the worst that can happen to him—more, *he provokes it*"[88]—that reveals his godliness. If we are to love with the love of Christ, we must love like Christ. We must practice his love, his life, his way of being-in-the-world. Christ "entreats, he suffers, he loves *with* those, *in* those who are doing evil to him."[89] Are we capable of such love? Would we even recognize it as love? "*Not* to defend oneself, *not* to grow angry, *not* to make responsible ... not to resist even the evil man—to *love* him"[90]—can we follow this strange and horrible example?

No, if we are to be honest, we must admit that "in reality there has been only one Christian, and he died on the Cross."[91]

Can you drink the cup?

And yet ... "Even today, *such* a life is possible, for *certain* men even necessary: genuine, primitive Christianity will be possible at all times."[92] What does such a life look like? Who is capable of loving with the love of Christ, the love of him who has been crucified for love? Would it be too provocative, too *scandalous*, to suggest that Nietzsche sees himself as the type of man who finds genuine, primitive Christianity not only possible but necessary? Who conceals the profundity of his love behind a mask? Whose "highest insights must—and should—sound like follies and sometimes like crimes when they are heard without permission by those who are not predisposed and predestined for them"?[93] Certainly he gives us reason to suspect that he would rather be misunderstood than understood,[94] that he "write[s] books precisely to conceal what [he] harbors,"[95] that his "strongest words" bury "something in silence,"[96] that his pride, his hubris, actually represents "the proper disguise" for his "shame," the "shame" of a "mystic"[97] who lives the "unity of God and man as *his* 'glad tidings.'"[98] What else are we to make of Nietzsche's odd assertion that he possesses "the prerequisite for understanding something nineteen centuries have misunderstood"—that is, the life of Christ?[99]

In a fascinating passage from *Beyond Good and Evil*, Nietzsche reveals what this prerequisite might be. Musing on the fate of "great men"—those whose image is venerated by the multitude while they themselves are lost, concealed behind their works[100]—he moves from a discussion of the love of "woman" (*jouissance*)—a love which pities the fractured souls of "these men"—to the love of Christ (*jouissance*); and he seems ready to connect the two:

> [W]oman—clairvoyant in the world of suffering and, unfortunately, also desirous far beyond her strength to help and save—... would like to believe that love can achieve *anything*—that is her characteristic *faith*. Alas, whoever knows the heart will guess how poor, stupid, helpless, arrogant, blundering, more apt to destroy than save is even the best and profoundest love! It is possible that underneath the holy fable and disguise of Jesus' life there lies concealed one of the most painful cases of the martyrdom of *knowledge about love*: the martyrdom of the most innocent and desirous heart, never sated by any human love; *demanding* love, to be loved and nothing else, with hardness, with insanity, with terrible eruptions against those who denied him love; the story of a poor fellow, unsated and insatiable in love, ... who finally, having gained knowledge about human love, ... has mercy on human love because it is so utterly wretched and unknowing. Anyone who feels that way, who *knows* this about love—seeks *death*.[101]

But one need not seek it. Death is the consequence of such love. It is the consequence of weakness, vulnerability, an extreme capacity for suffering, a *faith* that love can help and save, that one can "feel oneself 'in Heaven,' ... while in every other condition one by *no* means feels oneself 'in Heaven,'"[102] that "the 'Kingdom of Heaven' is a condition of the heart,"[103] a manifestation of the power of love, a love which one neither sees nor knows but *lives, practices, experiences* within oneself.

Balthasar tells us that "the 'recklessness' of divine love, in its self-giving, observed no limits and had no regard for itself."[104] Christ's life, from the beginning, was therefore "ordered to the Cross as its goal"[105] (as, indeed, is every life lived in love). "If one examines this mystery, one will prefer to say not that his death was a consequence of his birth, but that the birth was undertaken so that he could die."[106] Such a shameful and meaningless death—which, as Nietzsche reminds us, "was in general reserved for the *canaille* alone"[107]—represents "the (divine) extreme in loving," the fullest "revelation of love."[108] It represents love's violent confrontation with the frailty of human love—that arrogant, blundering, destructive love which is no more than death in disguise (Thanatos). It represents love's refusal to close itself off, to condemn, reject, harden its heart. True love—sacrificial love, the love of God—remains open even to the point of death. Indeed, death cannot but result from the *kenosis*, the absolute gift-of-self, the pouring forth of divine love in the face of human depravity.

That Nietzsche hopes to embody such love—to swallow the bitter cup and remain, all the while, open to the *overfullness* of life (*en plus*)—is conjecture. But it is not conjecture made without evidence. Consider, for instance, the line that immediately follows the block quote cited above: "But why pursue such painful matters? Assuming one does not have to.—"[109] Assuming, that is, that one is not already a follower of Christ, a *practitioner* of (female) love, one who lives life with openness, abandonment, a loving receptivity to everything and everyone—even the blows of fate.[110] (Again we see an overlap between Eros crucified—for whom "*[d]enial* is precisely what is totally impossible," who makes "no objection,"[111] loves his "fate" ("the Cross"),[112] and clings to it, demanding that his followers do the same [Luke 9:23]—and Nietzsche's *concept of Dionysus himself* who represents "the eternal Yes to all things, 'the tremendous, unbounded saying Yes and Amen.'—'Into all abysses I still carry the blessings of my saying Yes.'"[113])

Such a life, Nietzsche tells us, is one of profound misunderstanding, one in which even expressions of "kindness may look like malice,"[114] in which "[t]he discipline of suffering, of *great* suffering" leads the way forward.[115] "He shall be greatest who can be loneliest" is its first rule.[116] And yet, such a life—as the example of Christ has shown—is a life lived in unity with God, a life defined by love. If Christ "denies any chasm between God and man,"[117] Nietzsche is ready to follow suit: "In man *creature* and *creator* are united: in man there is material, fragment, excess, clay, dirt, nonsense, chaos; but in man there is also creator, form-giver, hammer hardness, spectator divinity, and seventh day."[118] *Seventh day*: the ability and responsibility to bring about "the coming of the Kingdom."[119] "It is telling," Kearney writes, "that the Lord did not make anything on the seventh day, leaving it free for humans to complete. The unfinished Sabbath is a gap calling for perpetual recreation—in imagination and action.... [Human beings are a] race capable of fashioning a Kingdom in the image of their God."[120] More. For, as Nietzsche emphasizes, "the kingdom of God is among you" (Luke 17:21), *within* you, it "is a condition of the heart."[121]

The Kingdom within, or the time is now

In *The Brothers Karamazov*, Father Zosima tells us to "look at the divine gifts around us: the clear sky, the fresh air, the tender grass, the birds, nature is beautiful and sinless, and we, we alone, are godless and foolish, and do not understand that life is paradise."[122] The minute we do understand, he says, or "only wish to understand," then paradise itself "will come at once in all its beauty, and we shall embrace each other and weep."[123] This strange, mystical perspective is one that Zosima received in his youth from his brother Markel, a "freethinking" atheist who, on his deathbed, underwent a radical conversion:

> Life is gladsome, joyful! … do not weep, life is paradise, and we are all in paradise, but we do not want to know it, and if we did want to know it, tomorrow there would be paradise the world over…. Yes … there was so much of God's glory around me: birds, trees, meadows, sky, and I alone lived in shame, I alone dishonored everything, and did not notice the beauty and glory of it all…. I am weeping from gladness, not from grief; I want to be guilty before [all], only I cannot explain it to you, for I do not even know how to love them. Let me be sinful before everyone, but so that everyone will forgive me, and that is paradise. Am I not in paradise now?[124]

It is only by knowing "how to love"—that is, how to make oneself weak, vulnerable, how to offer oneself, abandon oneself, efface oneself, find oneself "guilty in everything before everyone"[125]—that one experiences "paradise now," in the present instant, now and forever. As another of Zosima's confidants puts it:

> Paradise … is hidden in each of us, it is concealed within me, too, right now, and if I wish, it will come for me in reality, tomorrow even, and for the rest of my life…. And as for each man being guilty before all and for all … indeed it is true that when people understand this thought, the Kingdom of Heaven will come to them, no longer in a dream but in reality.[126]

That Nietzsche's portrait of the life of Christ echoes this understanding of the Kingdom as an inner-reality which can be experienced *here and now* is beyond dispute: "True life, eternal life is found—it is not promised, it is here, it is *within you*: as life lived in love, in love without deduction or exclusion, without distance."[127] "Blessedness is not promised, it is not tied to any conditions: it is the only *reality*."[128] For Nietzsche, Christ's example reveals that "The 'kingdom of God' is not something one waits for; it has no yesterday or tomorrow, it does not come 'in a thousand years'—it is an experience within a heart; it is everywhere, it is nowhere."[129] It is present, it is *now*.[130]

Criticizing the notion of personal immortality, Nietzsche condemns the doctrine of the resurrection which, he insists, negates the radical this-worldliness of Christ's love "for the benefit of a state *after* death!"[131] Yet what might it mean to say that the resurrection is not something that one experiences *after* death but— like Zosima's paradise—a living, breathing reality that can be manifested today, lived even in the face of a brutal world? What might it mean to ask, along with Shelley Rambo, whether resurrection "can testify to the ambiguities of living in the aftermath of trauma," "whether it can testify to divine presence" in *this* life rather than offering "a triumphalistic account of life overcoming death"?[132] Can, that is, "the resurrection story ... be a story of estrangement beyond recognition" and still be a story of love, a story of hope?[133] Can it represent "a Yes-saying without reservation, even to suffering, even to guilt, even to everything that is questionable and strange in existence"?[134]

Miguel de Unamuno opens his novella *Saint Manuel Bueno, Martyr* with a quotation from St. Paul (one which Nietzsche vehemently denounces): "If in this life only we have hope in Christ, we are all men most miserable" (1 Corinthians 15:19).[135] Yet his story follows a priest, Don Manuel, who cannot get himself to hope for anything more.[136] This inability to believe in life after death—this "unbearable," "terrible," "deadly" doubt[137]—becomes for Manuel an obsession that haunts him,[138] "an infinite, eternal sadness which the priest conceal[s] from the eyes and ears of the world with heroic saintliness."[139] It tortures him, torments him, pushes him to the brink of suicide.[140]

Yet even as this struggle dominates his interior life, still Don Manuel works to help the "poor villagers to die well."[141] Fully aware of "the black abyss of their life-weariness,"[142] he nevertheless instills in them a belief that "[t]he most important thing ... is for people to be happy; everyone must be happy just to be alive."[143] For Don Manuel, death is the greatest cruelty—and an untimely death most of all:

> it was his opinion that the old wives' saying "from the cradle to heaven" and the other one about "little angels belong in heaven" were nothing short of blasphemy. The death of a child moved him deeply. "A stillborn child, or one who dies soon after birth, are like suicides, the most terrible mystery to me.... Like a child crucified!"[144]

But if the story of Manuel Bueno reveals anything, it is that *this* life—which, as Augustine says, is "but a dying"[145]—is perhaps also "Heaven, the Heaven we can see;"[146] it is that God "is all around us, and you will see Him from here, right from here. And all of us see in Him, and He in all of us."[147] In a strange afterword, Unamuno suggests that Don Manuel's life testifies to a faith of which the priest himself is unaware, a faith which is *lived* even when it is not believed.[148]

Yet this emphasis on orthopraxy (right conduct) over orthodoxy (right belief) seems only to skim the surface of what is going on in this fantastical text. Unamuno's afterword continues:

> I am well aware of the fact that no action takes place in this narrative, this *novelistic* narrative, if you will—the novel is, after all, the most intimate, the truest history, so that I scarcely understand why some people are outraged to have the Gospels called a novel, when such a designation actually sets it above some mere chronicle or other. In short, nothing happens. But I hope that this is because everything in it remains, remains forever like the

> lakes and the mountains and the blessed simple souls, who, beyond faith
> and despair, the blessed souls who, in the lakes and the mountains, outside
> history, took refuge in a divine novel.[149]

The "simple souls" depicted in this work—*like each of us?*—"remain forever,"
not in the "mere chronicle," mere *chronology*, of history, but "outside history" in
a "divine novel." They remain forever on the page, to be read and reread again.

The real after-life, Unamuno seems to suggest, is not *after* life, but after a
certain way of experiencing life: after letting go of the belief in "life beyond the
grave" which causes one to "despise this life as a transitory thing;" after giving
up the utopian hope which "looks forward to some vague future society" at the
expense of "finding consolation" in life as it is;[150] after viewing life as "a mere
chronicle" which, CS Lewis tells us, "comes to us moment by moment," "[o]ne
moment disappears before the next comes along."[151] Perhaps the resurrection is
not an endpoint, not a goal, but a way of seeing life differently, of living it artfully, like a character in a novel—"the most intimate, the truest history." Perhaps
it is a doing, a being, a rebirth in the world of flesh which opens us to the fact that
"[t]wo kingdoms exist in this world,"[152] one which passes with time, the other
which—unconditioned by time—repeats *what was and is* eternally and begs for
infinite rereading.[153] (As Kearney writes, "Resurrection is to be understood … as
the event that returns us to the world, to the *secula seculorum*, so that we may live
more abundantly."[154] It is "the embodiment of infinity in the finite, of transcendence, of eschatology in the now."[155])

That Nietzsche views life as work of literature—as a novel in which we, the
characters, have the ability (the prerogative) to fashion ourselves—is a reading
not original to me but one that I find compelling.[156] In his novella, Unamuno
suggests something similar:

> for all I know, perhaps I created real, actual beings, independent of me,
> beyond my control, characters with immortal souls. For all I know,
> Augusto Perez in my novel *Mist* was right when he claimed to be more
> real, more objective than I am, I who thought I had invented him.[157]

Might such an understanding of our engagement with the world shine new light
upon the notion of eternal recurrence (and, likewise, resurrection)? What is
eternal recurrence but the insistence that the story of one's life is worth telling
and retelling again and again in the divine novel of eternity?

In *The End of the Affair*, Graham Greene employs a similar analogy:

> Always I find when I begin to write there is one character who obstinately
> will not come alive. There is nothing psychologically false about him, but
> he sticks, he has to be pushed around, words have to be found for him,
> all the technical skill I have acquired through the laborious years have to

be employed in making him appear alive to my readers.... Every other character helps, he only hinders.... I can imagine a God feeling in just that way about some of us. The saints, one would suppose, in a sense create themselves. They come alive. They are capable of the surprising act or word. They stand outside the plot, unconditioned by it. But we have to be pushed around. We have the obstinacy of nonexistence. We are inextricably bound to the plot, and wearily God forces us, here and there, according to his intention, characters without poetry, without free will, whose only importance is that somewhere, at some time, we help to furnish the scene in which a living character moves and speaks, providing perhaps the saints with the opportunities for *their* free will.[158]

What would it mean to be such a saint, to no longer be "bound to the plot," to "stand outside" time, "unconditioned by it," to "create" oneself, truly exercising one's "free will"?

Maurice Bendrix, Greene's narrator, depicts Sarah, the novel's saint, as someone who has "no doubts," someone defined by "surrender," "abandonment," "love."[159] In a passage oddly reminiscent of Manoussakis,[160] Bendrix reflects on the *abandonment* of Sarah, a word used to describe, at once, "the strange sad angry cry" of her orgasm,[161] the selflessness with which she loves Bendrix,[162] and her desire to give up everything for the sake of God.[163] For Sarah, "The moment only mattered. Eternity is said not to be an extension of time but an absence of time and sometimes it seemed to me that her abandonment touched that strange mathematical point of endlessness, a point with no width, occupying no space."[164] ("Thus, for a moment, *Psyche ist ausgedehnt*—not any more.")[165]

As someone capable of standing "outside the plot," "outside history," Sarah operates—at least at times—in an ever-present moment, a timeless time of freedom and love.[166] Bendrix, on the other hand, does not share Sarah's "capacity for love."[167] He "sticks," he "will not come alive,"[168] because he can never let go of "the I, I, I"[169]—the prison of himself.[170] That Bendrix has "always found it hard to feel sexual desire without some sense of superiority" is telling.[171] (Indeed, even as Sarah abandons herself in lovemaking, Bendrix clings to his superiority, emphasizing his ability to make her orgasm—something that her husband, "Poor Henry," has never been able to do, "not in the whole ten years" of their marriage.)[172] His love is not love but, as he repeats time and again, "hate." That is, "ordinary human love" (sadism, Thanatos) which is "jealous," seeks possession, would rather see the beloved dead "than with another man."[173] Bendrix does not love with recklessness, with abandonment, surrender. He is incapable of existing at "the moment of absolute trust and absolute pleasure, the moment when it [is] impossible to quarrel because it [is] impossible to think."[174] That moment— "a moment [which] might well be eternity long"[175]—is reserved for those who live "outside history," outside chronology, in the eternal present of a love made manifest *here and now*.

Still, Greene suggests, such a moment is not beyond our reach. It is, in fact, open to us at every instant—even in the depths of our depravity. (As *Time* magazine so aptly put it, "Adultery can lead to sainthood.")[176] Commenting on the salacious events of the celebrated Bolton Case, Parkis—the private eye employed by Bendrix to follow Sarah—describes how he once unexpectedly uncovered a love triangle: "It made a great stir, sir, at the time. Lady Bolton, her maid and the man, sir. All discovered together... It's all human nature, sir, isn't it, and human love. Though I *was* surprised. Not having expected the third."[177] *The third*—his presence is indeed a surprise, that which upends our human nature and unsettles our human love.

Two pages on, we read in Sarah's diary of another *ménage à trois*—one in which Sarah unknowingly participated, one between Bendrix, herself, and God: "even the first time, in the hotel near Paddington, we spent all we had. You were there, teaching us to squander, like you taught the rich man, so that one day we might have nothing left except this love of You."[178] Nothing but the love of God (*jouissance*). A love which is a squandering, an abandoning, a death of all that one has and all that one is: "If I begin to love God ... [i]f I ever loved like that, it would be the end of everything.... I'd cease to be Bendrix. Sarah, I'm afraid."[179]

Notes

1 See, Augustine, *On the Trinity*, (8.2.3–8.8.12).
2 Ibid., (9.2.2).
3 As CS Lewis writes,

> the words "God is love" have no real meaning unless God contains at least two Persons. Love is something that one person has for another person.... [Christians] believe that the living, dynamic activity of love has been going on in God forever and has created everything.... [I]n Christianity God is not a static thing ... but a dynamic, pulsating activity, a life, almost a kind of drama.
>
> *(Mere Christianity, 142–143)*

4 Augustine, *On the Trinity*, (9.2.2).
5 Kearney, "The Shulammite's Song," 312.
6 Balthasar, *Theo-drama, vol. 5*, 91.
7 Sweeney, "Bodily Love and the *Imago Trinitatis*," 117.
8 Kearney, "The Shulammite's Song," 309.
9 Žižek, "The Fear of Four Words," 38.
10 Kearney, "The Shulammite's Song," 309.
11 Žižek, "The Fear of Four Words," 31. For Balthasar, this would mean that "God is entangled in the world process ... that God 'needed' the world process and the Cross in order to become himself" (Balthasar, *Theo-drama, vol. 4*, 322–323). As CS Lewis rightly points out, this would mean that God is not love: "Love is something that one person has for another person. If God was a single person, then before the world was made, He was not love" (*Mere Christianity*, 142–143).
12 Balthasar, *Theo-drama, vol. 4*, 323.
13 Ibid.
14 Ibid., 324.
15 Ibid., 324–325.

16 Ibid., 325.

17 Cf.

> The union between the Father and the Son is such a live concrete thing that this union itself is also a Person.... What grows out of the joint life of the Father and Son is a real Person, in fact the Third of the three Persons who are God.... this spirit of love is, from all eternity, a love going on between the Father and the Son.
>
> *(Lewis,* Mere Christianity, *143–144)*

18 Balthasar, *Theo-drama, vol. 4*, 324.

19 Ibid., 331.

20 Ibid., 326.

21 Ibid., 327.

22 Cooper, "The Story of God and *Eros*," 95.

23 Ibid., 100.

24 Balthasar, *Theo-drama, vol. 4*, 324.

25 Augustine, *Confessions*, (11.8.10–9.11)

26 Nancy, *Corpus II*, 93.

27 Manoussakis, "Dying to Desire," 133.

28 Ibid.

29 Ibid., 125.

30 Nancy, *Corpus II*, 93–94.

31 Manoussakis, "Dying to Desire," 124.

32 Freud as quoted in ibid., 131.

33 Ibid., 126.

34 Ibid., 131.

35 Ibid., 120.

36 Ibid.

37 Lewis, *The Four Loves*, 86–90. If this distinction is maintained, it soon becomes evident just how unerotic, even anti-erotic, pornography actually is. The allure of porn depends upon the depersonalization of the persons on screen, the reduction of individuals to a means by which the viewer can achieve his orgasm. Which is why it is a common experience for porn-viewers to find that porn has become boring, stale. Viewers don't settle on a given video, they are not satisfied by viewing one porn star, but keep "clicking through" until climax is reached.

38 Manoussakis, "Dying to Desire," 126.

39 Ibid.

40 Ibid., 133.

41 "And what else is an Other who has turned into an object if not a corpse?" Ibid., 131.

42 Žižek, "The Fear of Four Words," 62.

43 "As regards active algolagnia, sadism, the roots are easy to detect in the normal. The sexuality of most male human beings contains an element of *aggressiveness*—a desire to subjugate." Freud, *Three Essays on Sexuality*, 157.

44 Lacan, *Encore: Seminar XX*, 72. It goes without saying that women too can possess (be possessed by) this destructive form of love just like, as we noted in Chapter 5, the church—including its male members—is essentially feminine. As Lacan says, "Everyone knows there are phallic women" (Ibid., 71) just as

> one is not obliged, when one is male, to situate oneself on the side of $\forall x \Phi x$. One can also situate oneself on the side of the not-whole. There are men who are just as good as women. It happens. And who also feel just fine about it. Despite—I won't say their phallus—despite what encumbers them that goes by that name, they get the idea or sense that there must be a *jouissance* that is beyond. Those are the ones we call mystics.
>
> *(Ibid., 76)*

45 Manoussakis, "Dying to Desire," 131.

46 Ibid., 128.

47 Whether, as Nietzsche says,

> Sexual love betrays itself most clearly as a lust for possession: the lover desires unconditional and sole possession of the person for whom he longs; he desires equally unconditional power over the soul and body of the beloved; he alone wants to be loved and desires to live and rule in the other soul as supreme and supremely desirable.
>
> *(Nietzsche,* The Gay Science, *[§14])*

48 Girard, *When These Things Begin*, 70.

49 Cf. "In the Incarnation, the triune God has ... disclosed himself in what is most deeply his own." Balthasar, *Mysterium Paschale*, 29.

50 Ibid., 28.

51 Ibid., 20.

52 Ibid., 22.

53 Ibid., 28.

54 See,

> If philosophy is not willing to content itself with, either, speaking abstractly of being, or with thinking concretely of the earthly and worldly (and no further), then it must at once empty itself in order to "know nothing ... except Jesus Christ and him crucified" (1 Corinthians 2,2). Then it may, starting out from this source, go on to "impart a secret and hidden wisdom of God, which God decreed before the ages for our glorification" (ibid., 2, 7). This proclamation, however, rises up over a deeper silence and a darker abyss than pure philosophy can know.
>
> *(Balthasar,* Mysterium Paschale, *66)*

55 Nietzsche, *The Anti-Christ*, (§28).

56 Ibid., (§32).

57 Ibid., (§30).

58 See: "*Instinctive exclusion of all aversion, all enmity, all feeling for limitation and distancing*: consequence of an extreme capacity for suffering and irritation which ... knows blessedness (pleasure) only in no longer resisting anyone or anything, neither the evil nor the evil-doer—love as the sole, as the *last* possibility of life." (Ibid.)

59 Ibid., (§32). Cf. "Whatever is done from love always occurs beyond good and evil." Nietzsche, *Beyond Good and Evil*, (§153).

60 Nietzsche, *The Anti-Christ*, (§32).

61 Ibid.

62 Ibid.

63 Ibid.

64 Lacan, *Encore: Seminar XX*, 68.

65 Nietzsche, *The Anti-Christ*, (§32).

66 Ibid., (§29).

67 "Civilization," Manoussakis writes, is

> the symptom of man's perversion. I believe that if we were able to look at civilization from the outside, that is, from what may be called a 'natural' point of view, we would be struck by how unnatural and how abnormal our society and every human being really is.
>
> *("Cracked," 60)*

68 Nietzsche, *The Anti-Christ*, (§29).

69 Ibid., (§33).

70 Anticipating our earlier discussion of the "unforgivable sin," Nietzsche tells us that the man who loves with the love of Christ shares Christ's unitive "instinct": "Under no circumstances, not even in the case of proved unfaithfulness, does he divorce his wife." Ibid.

71 "Inherent in [God's] love is an absolute renunciation: he will not be God for himself alone." Balthasar, *Theo-drama, vol. 4*, 324.

72 Nietzsche, *The Anti-Christ*, (§29).

73 Ibid., (§41).

74 Ibid., (§29).

75 Ibid., (§33).

76 "Jesus said to his Jews: 'The law was for servants—love God as I love him, as his son! What are morals to us sons of God!'" Nietzsche, *Beyond Good and Evil*, (§164).

77 Nietzsche, *The Anti-Christ*, (§27).

78 Ibid.

79 Ibid.

80 Ibid., (§39).

81 Ibid.

82 See, "States of consciousness, beliefs of any kind, holding something to be true for example … are a matter of complete indifference." Ibid.

83 Ibid., (§33).

84 Ibid.

85 Ibid., (§35).

86 Ibid., (§33).

87 Ibid., (§35).

88 Ibid.

89 Ibid.

90 Ibid., (§39).

91 Ibid.

92 Ibid.

93 Nietzsche, *Beyond Good and Evil*, (§30).

94 See Ibid., (§290).

95 Ibid., (§289).

96 Ibid.

97 Ibid., (§40).

98 Nietzsche, *The Anti-Christ*, (§41).

99 Ibid., (§36).

100 See, "the crowd adored a god—and that 'god' was merely a poor sacrificial animal." Nietzsche, *Beyond Good and Evil*, (§269).

101 Ibid.

102 Nietzsche, *The Anti-Christ*, (§33).

103 Ibid., (§34).

104 Balthasar, *Theo-drama, vol. 4*, 329.

105 Balthasar, *Mysterium Paschale*, 22.

106 Gregory of Nyssa, as quoted in ibid., 20–21.

107 Nietzsche, *The Anti-Christ*, (§39).

108 Balthasar, *Mysterium Paschale*, 29.

109 Nietzsche, *Beyond Good and Evil*, (§269).

110 See,

> I want to learn more and more to see as beautiful what is necessary in things; then I shall be one of those who makes things beautiful. *Amor fati*: let that be my love henceforth! I do not want to wage war against what is ugly. I do not want to accuse; I do not even want to accuse those who accuse. *Looking away* shall be

my only negation. And all in all and on the whole: some day I wish to be only a Yes-sayer.

(*Nietzsche*, The Gay Science, *[§276]*)

111 Nietzsche, *The Anti-Christ*, (§32).
112 Ibid., (§40).
113 Nietzsche, *Ecce Homo*, "Thus Spoke Zarathustra," (§6).
114 Nietzsche, *Beyond Good and Evil*, (§184).
115 Ibid., (§225).
116 Ibid., (§212). Cf. "Foxes have dens and birds of the sky have nests, but the Son of Man has nowhere to rest his head" (Matthew 8:20).
117 Nietzsche, *The Anti-Christ*, (§41).
118 Nietzsche, *Beyond Good and Evil*, (§225).
119 Kearney, "God Making," 3.
120 Ibid., 4.
121 Nietzsche, *The Anti-Christ*, (§34).
122 Dostoevsky, *The Brothers Karamazov*, 299.
123 Ibid.
124 Ibid., 288–290.
125 Ibid., 289.
126 Ibid., 303.
127 Nietzsche, *The Anti-Christ*, (§29).
128 Ibid., (§33).
129 Ibid., (§34).
130 In another work on Nietzsche, I offer the following reading of his notion of eternal recurrence:

> Heidegger reminds us that, from the moment of birth, each of us carries with him his own mortality. Death is at every instant the possibility of the end of all possibilities, the unrealized reality that lies at the heart of things.... [Death is] a fate not reserved for some far-off *tomorrow* but ever present, the inner-most reality of our being. Yet this is only a sliver of a much larger truth. Not just death, but life—all of life, every encounter, every experience, the whole drama of existence—is contained within this very instant. From the moment we are born, each of us carries with him all that has been and all that will be—a cosmos unfolded and unfolding in the stillness between each breath. All that has happened has happened exactly as it had to in order to bring about this present moment. Everything has aligned to make this moment that is. Within this moment, all that has been subsists. Within this moment, the whole of the past recurs once more in the eternity of right now. That is why at odd times a memory will come, uncalled for, unprovoked. A memory not remembered but relived. A memory of what is rather than what was—the past made present in a present that forever bears witness to its past, that carries its past along with it, that makes of its past a repetition forward, an eternal recurrence, repeated again and again at every instant, every day. But it is not just the past that returns to us eternally. Like women who, at birth, already house within themselves the ova that will one day be their children, all that will happen, all that is to come—already *is*. The present is a present pregnant with the future. The future remains latent, hidden within. Prophets and seers of all ages have attested to this fact. Their gifts are the fruits of a future ever with us, a future gathered together with the past in this moment, here and now, at the still point of the turning word.
>
> (*Clemente*, "Disciple of a Still Unknown God," *161–162*)

This reading is not the only possible interpretation of Nietzsche's eternal recurrence, nor is it the one that I hope to put forward in this text. But it is related to the one that I hope to put forward.

131 Nietzsche, *The Anti-Christ*, (§41).

132 Rambo, "Trauma, Resurrection, and the Anatheistic Wager," 240.

133 Ibid., 248.

134 Nietzsche, *Ecce Homo*, "The Birth of Tragedy," (§2).

135 As translated in Unamuno, *Saint Manuel Bueno, Martyr*, 257.

136 See, "There is no other life but this, no life more eternal." Unamuno, *Saint Manuel Bueno, Martyr*, 283.

137 Ibid., 276.

138 Ibid., 264.

139 Ibid., 266.

140 See, "as we were walking along beside the lake he said 'There lies my greatest temptation ... a temptation to commit suicide.... How that water beckons me with its deep quiet!'" Ibid., 280.

141 Ibid.

142 Ibid.

143 Ibid., 265.

144 Ibid.

145 Augustine, *Confessions*, (1.6.7).

146 Unamuno, *Saint Manuel Bueno, Martyr*, 270.

147 Ibid., 273.

148 See,

> if Don Manuel ... had confessed [his] convictions to the people, they ... would not have understood. Nor, I should like to add, would they have believed [him]. They would have believed in [his] works and not [his] words. And works stand by themselves, and need no words to back them up.... one makes one's confession by one's conduct.
>
> *(Ibid., 294)*

Manuel himself seems to agree: "Dip your finger in holy water, and you will end by believing." Ibid., 276.

149 Ibid., 294.

150 Ibid., 288.

151 Lewis, *Mere Christianity*, 137.

152 Unamuno, *Saint Manuel Bueno, Martyr*, 282.

153 Cf.

> Another time ... we caught sight of a country girl, a goatherd, standing tall, on the crest of a mountain slope overlooking the lake and she was singing in a voice fresher than the waters. Don Manuel stopped me, and pointing to her said: "Look, it's as though time had stopped, as though this country girl had always been there just as she is, singing the way she is, and it's as though she would always be there, as she was before my consciousness began, as she will be when it is past. That girl is a part of nature—not of history—along with the rocks, the clouds, the trees, and the water."
>
> *(Ibid., 280–281)*

154 Kearney, *Anatheism*, 69.

155 Ibid., 166.

156 See, Nehamas, *Nietzsche: Life as Literature*.

157 Unamuno, *Saint Manuel Bueno, Martyr*, 293.

158 Greene, *The End of the Affair*, 154–155.

159 Ibid., 36–39.

160 "The distance that splits our consciousness ... is overcome at the moment of orgasm or prayer." Manoussakis, *The Ethics of Time*, 109.

161 Greene, *The End of the Affair*, 38.
162 Ibid., 39.
163 Ibid., 41.
164 Ibid., 39. CS Lewis, offering an analogy which bears a striking resemblance to the idea that Unamuno and Greene are attempting to articulate, describes (Boethian) eternity thus:

> Our life comes to us moment by moment. One moment disappears before the next comes along.... That is what Time is like. And of course you and I tend to take it for granted that this Time series—arrangement of past, present, and future—is not simply the way life comes to us but the way things really exist.... Almost certainly God is not in Time. His life does not consist of moments following one another.... [Every] moment from the beginning of the world is always the Present for Him.... That is difficult, I know. Let me try to give something, not the same, but a bit like it. Suppose I am writing a novel. I write "Mary laid down her work; next moment came a knock at the door!" For Mary who has to live in the imaginary time of my story there is no interval between putting down the work and hearing the knock. But I, who am Mary's maker, do not live in that imaginary time at all. Between writing the first half of that sentence and the second, I might sit down for three hours and think steadily about Mary. I could think about Mary as if she were the only character in the book and for as long as I pleased and the hours I spent in doing so would not appear in Mary's time (the time inside the story) at all.... God is not hurried along in the Time-stream of this universe anymore than an author is hurried along in the imaginary time of his own novel. He has infinite attention to spare for each one of us.
>
> (Mere Christianity, *137–138*)

165 Manoussakis, *The Ethics of Time*, 109.
166 See,

> I [Bendrix] felt that afternoon such complete trust when she said to me suddenly, without being questioned, "I've never loved anybody or anything as I do you." It was as if ... she was abandoning herself as completely as she had done [during her orgasm]. We most of us hesitate to make so complete a statement—we remember and we foresee and we doubt. She had no doubts. The moment only mattered.
>
> (Greene, The End of the Affair, *39*)

167 Ibid., 40.
168 Ibid., 154.
169 Ibid., 26.
170 See, "When I replied that I loved her too in that way, I was the liar, not she, for I never lose the consciousness of time." Ibid., 40.
171 Ibid., 17.
172 Ibid., 38.
173 Ibid., 43.
174 Ibid., 55.
175 Ibid., 55–56.
176 Ibid., viii.
177 Ibid., 69.
178 Ibid., 71.
179 Ibid., 152.

Bibliography

Augustine, *Confessions*, trans. Maria Boulding (New York: Vintage, 1998).

Augustine, *On the Trinity*, trans. Gareth B Matthews (Cambridge, UK: Cambridge University Press, 2002).

Balthasar, Hans Urs von, *Theo-Drama: Theological Dramatic Theory*, trans. Graham Harrison, vols. 1–5 (San Francisco: Ignatius, 1988–1998).

Balthasar, Hans Urs von, *Mysterium Paschale: The Mystery of Easter*, trans. Aidan Nichols (Edinburgh, Scotland: T&T Clark, 1990).

Clemente, M Saverio, "Disciple of a Still Unknown God or Becoming What I Am," in *misReading Nietzsche*, eds. Clemente, M Saverio and Bryan J Cocchiara (Eugene, OR: Pickwick Publications, 2018), 151–165.

Cooper, Adam, "The Story of God and *Eros*," in *God and Eros*, eds. Colin Patterson and Conor Sweeney (Eugene, OR: Cascade Books, 2015), 91–103.

Dostoevsky, Fyodor, *The Brothers Karamazov*, trans. Richard Pevear and Larissa Volokhonsky (New York: Farrar, Straus and Giroux, 2002).

Freud, Sigmund, *Three Essays on Sexuality*, in *The Standard Edition of the Complete Psychological Works of Sigmund Freud*, trans. James Strachey, vol. VII (London: Hogarth, 1953).

Girard, René, *When These Things Begin: Conversations with Michel Treguer*, trans. Trevor C Merrill (East Lansing: Michigan State University Press, 2014).

Greene, Graham, *The End of the Affair* (New York: Penguin, 2004).

Kearney, Richard, "The Shulammite's Song: Desire Descending and Ascending," in *Toward a Theology of Eros: Transfiguring Passion at the Limits of Discipline*, eds. Virginia Burrus and Catherine Keller (New York: Fordham University Press, 2006).

Kearney, Richard, *Anatheism: Returning to God After God* (New York: Columbia University Press, 2011).

Kearney, Richard, "God Making: Theopoetics and Anatheism," in *The Art of Anatheism*, eds. Richard Kearney and Matthew Clemente (London: Rowman & Littlefield, 2017), 3–28.

Lacan, Jacques, *Encore: The Seminar of Jacques Lacan Book XX: On Feminine Sexuality, the Limits of Love and Knowledge*, trans. Bruce Fink (New York: WW Norton, 1999).

Lewis, CS, *The Four Loves* (London: Fontana, 1963).

Lewis, CS, *Mere Christianity*, in *The Complete CS Lewis Signature Classics* (New York: HarperCollins, 2007).

Manoussakis, John, "Cracked: The Black Theology of Anatheism," in *The Art of Anatheism*, eds. Richard Kearney and Matthew Clemente (London: Rowman & Littlefield, 2017a), 49–66.

Manoussakis, John, *The Ethics of Time* (London: Bloomsbury, 2017b).

Manoussakis, John, "Dying to Desire: Soma, Sema, Sarx, and Sex," in *Somatic Desire: Rethinking Corporeality in Contemporary Thought*, eds. Sarah Horton, et al. (London: Lexington Books, 2019), 117–137.

Nancy, Jean-Luc, *Corpus II: Writings on Sexuality*, trans. Anne O'Byrne (New York: Fordham University Press, 2013).

Nehamas, Alexander, *Nietzsche: Life as Literature* (Cambridge: Harvard University Press, 1987).

Nietzsche, Friedrich, *The Birth of Tragedy*, trans. Walter Kaufmann (New York: Vintage, 1967).

Nietzsche, Friedrich, *The Gay Science*, trans. Walter Kaufmann (New York: Vintage, 1974).

Nietzsche, Friedrich, *Beyond Good and Evil*, trans. Walter Kaufmann (New York: Vintage, 1989a).

Nietzsche, Friedrich, *On the Genealogy of Morals and Ecce Homo*, trans. Walter Kaufmann (New York: Vintage, 1989b).

Nietzsche, Friedrich, *Twilight of the Idols and The Anti-Christ*, trans. RJ Hollingdale (New York: Penguin, 1990).

Rambo, Shelley, "Trauma, Resurrection, and the Anatheistic Wager," in *Richard Kearney's Anatheistic Wager: Philosophy, Theology, Poetics*, eds. Chris Doude van Troostwijk and Matthew Clemente (Bloomington: Indiana University Press, 2018), 239–249.

Sweeney, Conor, "Bodily Love and the *Imago Trinitatis*," in *God and Eros*, eds. Colin Patterson and Conor Sweeney (Eugene, OR: Cascade Books, 2015), 107–122.

Unamuno, Miguel de, *Saint Manuel Bueno, Martyr*, in *Basic Writings of Existentialism*, ed. Gordon Marion (New York: Modern Library, 2004).

Žižek, Slavoj, *The Puppet and the Dwarf* (Cambridge, MA: MIT Press, 2003).

Žižek, Slavoj, "The Fear of Four Words," in *The Monstrosity of Christ: Paradox or Dialectic?*, ed. Creston Davis (Cambridge, MA: MIT Press, 2009).

7

THANATOS

Descent into the Id

The perceptive reader will no doubt have noticed that toward the end of our last chapter a shift in the way of discussing "the Kingdom" of the present moment occurred as we transitioned from the works of Nietzsche, Dostoevsky, and Unamuno to the novel by Graham Greene. That shift—subtle though it may have seemed—actually represents the essential point, the point upon which everything hinges. For Nietzsche (and, to a lesser extent, Dostoevsky and Unamuno) the Kingdom of Christ is *within*. It is "hidden in each of us" and "will come ... in reality" only when we "wish" it to.[1] For Greene, however, the "abandonment" of Sarah—which touches "that strange mathematical point of endlessness," "eternity"[2]—is provoked from *without*. It is caused by a rupture, a trauma, which will not allow her to continue living in the "ordinary corrupt human love" she so desperately desires.[3] It is the appearance of the unexpected *third*—the intercession of God in her sex life (recall our discussion of Paul and his odd assertion that grace binds together as "one flesh," even those who copulate with prostitutes [1 Corinthians 6:16])—that leads her to sanctity.[4]

Žižek, we said, identifies "the shock of the external encounter" as that which defines the Jewish-Christian paradigm:

> the central feature of the Judeo-Christian tradition [is that] man's encounter with divinity is not the result of withdrawal into the depths of my inner Self and the ensuing realization of the identity of the core of my Self and the core of Divinity (*atman—Brahman* in Hinduism, etc.).[5]

Rather, while "both paganism and Gnosticism ... emphasize the 'inner journey' of spiritual self-purification, the return to one's true Inner Self, the self's 'rediscovery,'" Christianity—like Judaism before it—depends upon "an *external* traumatic encounter."[6] Unlike Nietzsche's Christ, who teaches us the inner-reality of a life lived in love, the God depicted by Greene is one who *violates* us from without: "You're a devil, God, tempting us to leap. But I don't want Your peace and I don't want Your love. I wanted something very simple and very easy; I wanted Sarah for a lifetime and You took her away. With Your great schemes You ruin our happiness like a harvester ruins a mouse's nest."[7]

The violence of God has always been a problem. (Think of what it means to say that "you [God] use pain to make your will known ... and even kill us lest we die away from you.")[8] Many Christians do not know what to do with it, which is why, as Kierkegaard notes, we seldom hear of it.[9] Yet if we are "to be sufficiently honest," he insists, we ought not to minimize what is "terrifying" about the divine in an attempt to "smuggle Christianity into the world."[10] We ought to recognize the horrible reality that "the one whom God blesses he curses in the same breath," that God's love is a love that "infringes" upon us, ruins our happiness.[11] Indeed, in spite of Nietzsche's protestations,[12] Christ himself insists, "I have come to bring not peace but the sword" (Matthew 10:34). And, as if to ratify the Žižekean point, he plainly states:

> Nothing that enters one from outside can defile that person; but the things that come out from within are what defile.... From within people, from their hearts, come evil thoughts, unchastity, theft, murder, adultery, greed, malice, deceit, licentiousness, envy, blasphemy, arrogance, folly. All these evils come from within and they defile."
>
> *(Mark 7:15–23)*

Love, Christ tells us, is not a condition of the heart. It is the heart that corrupts, the heart that perverts the Eros of God and turns it into the Thanatos of man. ("Because of the hardness of your hearts....") The Kingdom is not *within* you. It is "among you" (Luke 17:21), but not *of* you. (The meanness of man, as Ivan Karamazov points out, is crueler, more malicious than even the most savage of beasts.)[13] Indeed, as both Dostoevsky and Unamuno—contrary to the passages cited in our last chapter—suggest, paradise is found in the "birds, trees, meadows, sky,"[14] in "the rocks, the clouds, the trees, and the water,"[15] in the outside world, the strangeness, the otherness that encroaches—"that enters one"—from *without*.

The aesthetics of violence: Reading *Blood Meridian*

In the fifth episode of the first season of *True Detective*, Rust Cohle—the haggard, burnt-out ex-detective played by Matthew McConaughey—recounts the events that led to the discovery of the bodies of two small children who had been abducted and tortured by pedophiles in the Louisiana bayou. Reflecting on the absurd brutality of the crime, he says, "Someone once told me, 'Time is a flat circle.' Everything we've ever done or will do, we're gonna do over and over and over again. And that little boy and that little girl, they're gonna be in that room again and again and again forever." This realization alone is enough to shatter the "divine" vision of Nietzsche's eternal recurrence.[16] That the Kingdom of Heaven could be built upon the heads of murdered children is, as Ivan Karamazov so fervently argues, too monstrous to accept.

But if Nietzsche's eternal recurrence falls, so too falls the understanding of the resurrection, the "paradise" of the present moment, offered in our previous chapter. (As Flannery O'Connor so artfully testifies: "the kingdom of heaven suffers violence, and the violent bear it away" [Matthew 11:12].)[17] To that end, Cormac McCarthy's *Blood Meridian*—which depicts in harrowing detail the once profitable scalping trade that existed on the borderlands of America—reveals just how unbearable Nietzsche's "greatest weight" actually is. Written as if in response to Nietzsche's challenge that we "*crave nothing more fervently*"[18] than "to have *what was and is* repeated into all eternity,"[19] *Blood Meridian* never tires of showing us the insane and arbitrary nature of violence, the inhumanity that resides in each of our hearts. To do so, it doubles and triples and repeats again and again the same scenes of savagery, the same bloody massacres, over and over *ad infinitum*.

Just a few passages will serve to make the point: When the kid, the novel's main character, first sees the Glanton gang—the group of scalpers with whom he will butcher hundreds of American Indians—the gang is described as

> ... a pack of viciouslooking humans mounted on unshod ponies riding half drunk through the streets, bearded, barbarous, clad in the skins of animals stitched up with thews and armed with weapons of every description, revolvers of enormous weight and bowieknives the size of claymores and short twobarreled rifles with bores you could stick your thumbs in and the trappings of their horses fashioned out of human skin and their bridles woven up from human hair and decorated with human teeth and the riders wearing scapulars or necklaces of dried and blackened human ears and the horses rawlooking and wild in the eye and their teeth bared like feral dogs and riding also in the company a number of halfnaked savages reeling in the saddle, dangerous, filthy, brutal, the whole like a visitation from some heathen land where they and others like them fed on human flesh.[20]

Compare that description with the introduction of the Comanche—carrying "flutes made from human bones"—who the kid runs into as a member of Captain White's gang some thirty pages earlier:

> A legion of horribles, hundreds in number, half naked or clad in costumes attic or biblical or wardrobed out of a fevered dream with the skins of animals and silk finery and pieces of uniform still tracked with the blood of prior owners, coats of slain dragoons, frogged and braided cavalry jackets, one in a stovepipe hat and one with an umbrella and one in white stockings and a bloodstained weddingveil and some in headgear of cranefeathers or rawhide helmets that bore the horns of bull or buffalo and one

in a pigeontailed coat worn backwards and otherwise naked and one in the armor of a Spanish conquistador, the breastplate and pauldrons deeply dented with old blows of mace or sabre done in another country by men whose very bones were dust and many with their braids sliced up with the hair of other beasts until they trailed upon the ground and their horses' ears and tails worked with bits of brightly colored cloth and one whose horse's whole head was painted crimson red and all the horsemen's faces gaudy and grotesque with daubings like a company of mounted clowns, death hilarious, all howling in a barbarous tongue and riding down upon them like a horde from a hell more horrible yet than the brimstone land of christian reckoning, screeching and yammering and clothed in smoke like those vaporous beings in regions beyond right knowing where the eye wanders and the lip jerks and drools.[21]

These Comanche, falling upon their victims, set about

hacking and chopping at the bodies, ripping off limbs, heads, gutting the strange white torsos and holding up great handfuls of viscera, genitals, some of the savages so slathered up with gore they might have rolled in it like dogs and some who fell upon the dying and sodomized them with loud cries to their fellows.[22]

They do so in just the same way—with the same sadistic lust—as Captain White's gang preparing a recent evening's meal: "The skinners ... commenced cutting up the gutted antelopes in the floor of the wagon with bowieknives and handaxes, laughing and hacking in a welter of gore, a reeking scene in the light of the handheld lanterns."[23]

The repetitions in this text abound—the reader cannot go more than a few pages without hearing echoes from earlier in the work—and the scenes of savagery in particular recur so often that one must either put the book down or harden his heart, numb himself to them, and carry on. (The repetitions, however, are not limited to depictions of violence. For example, a beautiful echoing occurs in the first few pages which connects the suffering of the wandering kid—"walking the sand roads of the southern night alone, his hands balled in the cotton pockets of his cheap coat"[24]—with the suffering of the "Blacks in the fields, lank and stooped, their fingers spiderlike among the bolls of cotton." That the latter represent "[a] shadowed agony in the garden" reminds us that suffering is that which connects us not only to one another but also to the god who suffers.)[25] Why this recurrence? Why this onslaught of brutality?

In a 1992 interview with the *New York Times*, McCarthy tells us that "[t]he novel depends for its life on the novels that have been written."[26] A sentence later, he remarks that "good writers" are those who "deal with issues of life and death." That his criteria for assessing authors should echo the words of another author is telling. Is it merely a coincidence that Flannery O'Connor—to whom McCarthy is compared in that same article[27]—writes, in the Author's Note to the Second Edition of *Wise Blood* (notice the doubling in McCarthy's title): "That belief in Christ is to some a matter of life and death has been a stumbling block for readers who would prefer to think it a matter of no great consequence"?[28] Is it not more likely that, to borrow another phrase from O'Connor, the world depicted in *Blood Meridian*—in spite of all of its barbarism, senseless violence, and gore (or perhaps because of it)—is a thoroughly "Christ-haunted" world? (Why the title *Blood Meridian*? one might ask. The answer I believe lies in *The Cross*, a poem by John Donne, which finds in all created things an image of the crucified Christ: "Look down, thou spiest out crosses in small things;/ Look up, thou seest birds raised on crossed wings;/ All the globe's frame, and sphere's, is nothing else/ But the meridians crossing parallels.")[29]

Indeed, for all of the cruelty expressed therein, McCarthy's novel is filled with small, subtle, almost imperceptible gestures—of *kindness*. Some examples: when the kid is shot, he is nursed back to health by a "tavernkeeper's wife" who "attends him" and "carries out his slops;"[30] when he is alone in the wilderness, he is given food and "an old greenriver knife" by a group of cattle drovers so that he can fend for himself[31] (their act is explicitly called "kindness");[32] when he loses his mule, "a black"—who has no reason to help the white kid and plenty of reason to wish him ill—points him in the right direction;[33] when he is lost and dehydrated in a foreign land, he is given a drink of water by a group of Mexican bandits—who, again, have no cause to help him;[34] when he is imprisoned in a Mexican jailhouse,

> A woman brought [him] bowls of beans and charred tortillas on a plate of fried clay.... she had smuggled [him] sweets under her shawl and there were pieces of meat in the bottom of the bowl that had come from her own table;[35]

and on, and on. These moments of genuine human empathy are easily missed, swept away in the flood of violence. But they are there all the same, coming to the kid from *without*, as if inviting him to something better, something more. They watch him like the "eye" of God he sees painted on a wagon carrying "the host to some soul."[36] Chase him like the hound of heaven.[37] But will they catch him?

At times, the kid seems ready to respond in kind, ready to open his arms to the stranger, the other, those most in need. When one of his fellow scalpers is dying, "skewered through with a lance," he "wade[s] out of the water and approach[es] him," as if driven by an instinct for care;[38] when another "carried an arrow in his thigh, fletching and all, and none would touch it," he volunteers to pull it out;[39] and when he draws the short straw and is ordered to kill a wounded comrade, he refuses to murder the injured man and instead leaves him with a canteen full of water and a chance, however bleak, to survive.[40] Perhaps, then, *Blood Meridian* is a story of redemption, a testament to the fact that the darkness of this world is not enough to extinguish its light?

No, just the opposite. For the deeper we descend into this hellish tale, the more we recognize that "hell is nothing more and nothing less than the self itself—a self that has infected itself with the sickness unto death."[41]

The Judge within, or the self in hell

"Is it possible," Manoussakis asks, "to understand hell as a self-inflicted punishment?"[42] Augustine thinks so: "You do not want to be saved by [Christ]? Then you will be judged by yourself."[43] Indeed, for him one is not condemned to hell by God but, in wandering away from God, becomes a wasteland unto himself.[44] This understanding of damnation as a judgement that one passes upon oneself (is it CS Lewis who suggests that hell is locked from within?) is not without its bearing on our present conversation. From the first lines of *Blood Meridian*—which echo the opening of the *Inferno*: "In the middle of life's journey, I found myself in a dark wood"—we are aware that we are about to enter hell: "Outside lie dark turned fields with rags of snow and darker woods beyond that harbor yet a few last wolves."[45]

It is into these "darker woods" that the kid will soon venture, running away from home, yet unable to escape the darkness in himself:

> See the child. He is pale and thin, he wears a thin and ragged linen shirt.... He can neither read nor write and in him broods already a taste for mindless violence. All history present in that visage, the child the father of the man.[46]

That the kid—who will later be referred to as "the man"—already harbors *within* him a "taste for mindless violence," and that, at this moment, he prefigures all that he will be, his whole future, the entirety of his personal history, is a point that cannot be emphasized strongly enough. It is the key to understanding the rest of the novel.

We said above that the world of *Blood Meridian* is a Christ-haunted world. Yet there is another figure who looms over the work, a more pernicious figure, the figure of the Judge. In *The Wasteland*—another hellish work which undeniably influenced the writing of *Blood Meridian*[47]—Eliot's narrator makes it clear that we are living *after* the death of Christ, in a world devoid of divine presence, with nothing left to do but wait for death ourselves:

> After the torchlight red on sweaty faces
> After the frosty silence in the gardens
> After the agony in stony places
> The shouting and the crying
> Prison and palace and reverberation
> Of thunder of spring over distant mountains
> He who was living is now dead

We who were living are now dying
With a little patience.[48]

Yet even in this wasteland, even in this desert where "one can neither stand nor lie nor sit," there is the presence of a third.

Who is the third who walks always beside you?
When I count, there are only you and I together
But when I look ahead up the white road
There is always another one walking beside you
Gliding wrapt in a brown mantle, hooded
I do not know whether a man or a woman
—But who is that on the other side of you?[49]

The importance of this third, this man or woman who "will foller ye always even unto the end of the road,"[50] has been discussed at length above. What I want to draw our attention to here is the final line just quoted. Read it again: "—But who is that on the *other* side of you?" It is not the third who walks beside you, not Christ on the road to Emmaus, but a different figure, a more pernicious one.

Judge Holden is, if not a god, certainly a devil. His power extends beyond that of any mere human being. (Harold Bloom calls him "violence incarnate. The Judge stands for incessant warfare for its own sake.")[51] Power is what he lusts for, what he demands. "War," he tells us, "is the truest form of divination."[52] It is "a forcing of the unity of existence. War is God."[53] The Judge desires "to dictate the terms of his own fate," to "take charge of the world" such that "nothing [is] permitted to occur upon it save by my dispensation."[54] He is a philosopher, one whose pursuit of knowledge is a pursuit of power, a lust for control: "Only nature can enslave man and only when the existence of each last entity is routed out and made to stand naked before him will he be properly suzerain of the earth"—that is, the earth's "keeper or overlord."[55]

Yet what is most fascinating about the Judge is neither his preternatural intelligence nor his demonic charm. Taken as a character in himself, his appeal soon fades, his evil becomes if not banal then disgusting. (The allure of the Judge wears off right around the time that it is revealed he has a proclivity for small children. As *Lolita* has taught us, even the most literary of pedophiles is, at the end of the day, just a sad pedophile.) The most fascinating thing about him is his relation to the kid. For, what is Judge Holden if not the "visage" of "the man," the embodiment of the kid's "taste for mindless violence," his death-drive working at every moment for his destruction? (As Holden himself will say, "What do you think death is, man? … What is death if not an agency? And whom does he intend toward?")[56]

That the Judge represents something like man's collective unconscious—harboring within himself all of the knowledge accumulated and forgotten over the course of human history—is clear from the start. The notebook in which he sketches the items he collects as the gang makes its way across the frontier is used to "expunge" that which it documents "from the memory of man."[57] And as if to underscore the fact that *knowledge is destruction*—that is, in order to know something one must destroy the thing-in-itself, one must negate it and turn it into an object of thought—every time the Judge draws an item in his book, he subsequently destroys it. So it is with all things in the mind of man: "Men's memories are uncertain and the past that was differs little from the past that was not."[58]

The kid, who can "neither read nor write," whose father "quotes from poets whose names are now lost,"[59] finds himself both attracted to and repulsed by this man who is "a hand at anything," who is "clever," fluent in multiple languages, understands botany, geology, has read the classics.[60] Like the other members of the gang—all of whom claim to have "encountered that sooty-souled rascal in some other place"[61]—the kid has seen the Judge several times before. And the Judge has seen him. Indeed, he seems always to be watching him, as if directing him by his gaze, influencing his every choice with the look of his all-seeing eye.[62]

In the penultimate scene, the kid and the Judge meet in a tavern in Fort Griffin after years of being apart. The Judge asks the kid his reason for coming to the bar that night. "Everybody dont have to have a reason to be someplace," the kid replies.[63]

> That's so, said the judge. They do not have to have a reason. But order is not set aside because of their indifference.... Let me put it this way.... If it is so that they themselves have no reason and yet are indeed here must they not be here by reason of some other? And if this is so can you guess who that other might be?[64]

("—But who is that on the other side of you?") Who, if not the Judge? (*C'est le Diable qui tient les fils qui nous remuent!*) He is the "malign thing set against" man, the "power," the "force," Thanatos itself which governs this world and yet is *in* each of us: "Can [man] believe that the wreckage of his existence is unentailed?"[65]

That the kid—"father of the man"—has had "a taste for mindless [that is, *unconscious*] violence" brooding *within* him from the start reveals his affinity for the Judge, who eradicates understanding while provoking continued destruction. Indeed, he is not *like* the Judge, he *is* the Judge, or at least his offspring, who carries the worm of destruction in his heart. As the individual unconscious is grounded in the collective, as my Thanatonic drive toward annihilation is rooted in the Thanatos that lives in us all,[66] so the kid is made in the image and likeness of the Judge, is trapped in his own personal hell where he must stand as the judge for himself: "You do not want to be saved [from without]? Then you will be judged by yourself [from within]."

A reading too dark and awful

If the continuous carnage depicted in *Blood Meridian* is not enough to convince us of this fatalistic reading, if the synoptic chapter headings that open each chapter are not an indication that what will happen has already been predetermined from the start, orchestrated by some malignant "power" who sets the events in motion, then perhaps we ought to turn to the novel's ending, which has given rise to much speculation and which, I contend, underscores this point all the more. In the final scene, the kid—now the man—exits the tavern and makes his way down to the jakes to relieve himself. There, he opens the door and finds "The judge ... seated upon the closet. He was naked and he rose up smiling and gathered him in his arms against his immense and terrible flesh and shot the wooden barlatch home behind him."[67] We do not see what happens in the jakes. We only know that a short time later, two more men make their way down from the bar to the outhouse. When they do, they find that

> A third man was standing there urinating into the mud. Is someone in there? the first man said. The man who was relieving himself did not look up. I wouldnt go in there if I was you, he said. Is there somebody in there? I wouldnt go in. He hitched himself up and buttoned his trousers and stepped past them and went up the walk toward the lights. The first man watched him go and then opened the door of the jakes. Good God almighty, he said.[68]

"The prevailing interpretation of this enigmatic scene," writes Patrick Shaw, "is that Holden simply murders the unsuspecting kid."[69] It is typically assumed that what is found in the jakes is the mutilated body of the man which has been violated and left out in a public place for all to see. But a closer consideration of the text ought to give us pause before adopting this standard reading. First, who is "The man who was relieving himself" outside of the jakes? Why is he so unmoved by the horrific crime that lies within? Next, what are we to make of the fact that, immediately before the man enters the jakes, we are told that "[i] n the street men were calling for the little girl whose bear was dead for she was lost. They went among the darkened lots with lanterns and torches calling out to her"?[70] That girl is not mentioned again. Why is she brought in at this point? Finally, how should we interpret the kid's (apparent) impotency with the "dark little dwarf of a whore" prior to his exiting the bar to the jakes?[71]

Now, the mere fact that the "third man" standing by the jakes is referred to as "the man" is enough to raise our suspicions. That we are told that he "buttoned his trousers" a single page after the kid "pulled his trousers up and buttoned them" is striking too. Would it be too much to suggest that what is found in the outhouse is not the kid but what the kid left behind, not his mutilated body but the body he mutilated? Would it be too much to posit that the degradation of the missing "little girl" is that which is too dark and awful to show? (If it is true that

"The novel depends for its life on the novels that have been written," then one could not miss the parallel to another little girl desecrated and "locked all night in the outhouse.")[72]

This, we must remember, would not be the first child who—having been murdered by the man—has had her body manipulated. After being shot by the man, the young boy Elrod is discovered "lying on his back with his hands composed upon his chest."[73] Might the lost girl have been "composed" in a manner too atrocious to depict? That is, might the embrace of the Judge represent not a literal, physical embrace but a succumbing of the man to the darkness, the mindless violence within? (In Kierkegaardian terms might it represent his "qualitative leap" into the sinfulness that already exists in him through heredity?) He is now in the Judge's clutches. He has given himself over to him.

"I'd have loved you like a son," the Judge tells the kid.[74] But in the end, the kid is revealed to be more than the Judge's son. He is the one who sits "in judgement on [his] own deeds," "the person responsible," the one who bears "witness against [himself]."[75] He cannot escape the condemnation of his own judgements, he stands as "a thing already accomplished,"[76] already lost. At the novel's end, the kid has become the Judge (of) himself, "Dauphin," heir to a monstrous throne.[77] In his dream, he sees the Judge with "another man," a "man he could never see in his entirety but he seemed an artisan and a worker in metal."[78]

> The judge enshadowed him where he crouched at his trade but he was a coldforger who worked with hammer and die, perhaps under some indictment and an exile from men's fires, hammering out like his own conjectural destiny all through the night of his becoming some coinage for a dawn that would not be. It is this false moneyer with his gravers and burins who seeks favor with the judge and he is at contriving from cold slag brute in the crucible a face that will pass, an image that will render this residual specie current in the markets where men barter. Of this is judge judge and the night does not end.[79]

Who is this other "man," this "false moneyer," ever seeking "favor with the judge"? Who if not the kid himself—the kid who, prior to entering the jakes, is "enshadowed" by the Judge's "great corpus";[80] who uses a "chit," "a stamped brass token," to enter the dance that night;[81] who is no more than the "false coin" flung by the Judge into "the darkness beyond … the firelight" only to return "back out of the night" at the Judge's command? "The arc of circling bodies is determined by the length of their tether, said the judge. Moons, coins, men."[82]

And yet, if the kid is condemned from the start, caught in the hell of the Judge's (his own) snares, so too are all of us. We all live in a world ordered by the death-drive, a world of "false coins" (cf. Matthew 22:20–21) in which power is bought with violence and violence is "the truest form of divination," the means by which we seek to make ourselves *like gods*. Each of us is, to follow the suggestion of Nietzsche, an anti-Christ. Each sets himself up in opposition to the God of powerlessness, the God of love. That the kid succumbs to the Judge's disturbing predilection—that he ends by debasing a child—ought not to surprise us. Indeed, it is the logical conclusion of the pursuit of power. Power, in all of its forms, ends with the victimization of the weak and vulnerable, the destruction of the "little ones" (Matthew 18:6), the degradation of the "least of these" (25:40). (Think of Herod's massacre of the holy innocents and its consequents that continue to this day—a good reason to be leery of every movement [religious or political] that seeks to preserve power or calls for future *empowerment*.)

If this realization is unsettling, *Blood Meridian* seems to suggest, that by no means makes it untrue. The book opens with an epigraph that quotes from a report in the *Yuma Daily Sun*: "Clark, who led last year's expedition to the Afar region of northern Ethiopia, and UC Berkeley colleague Tim D. White, also said that a re-examination of a 300,000-year-old fossil skull found in the same region earlier showed evidence of having been scalped."[83] It ends with the image of the Judge, naked and dancing, "[t]owering over" a room full of dancers.[84] "They *are* dancing," we are told.[85] Not *were*. Are. "He is a great favorite, the judge."[86] He has always been a great favorite, from the moment the first man attempted to bring about his own divinization. And he still is today: "He is dancing, dancing. He says that he will never die."[87]

Thanatos reconsidered: On being *all Id*

It is fitting at this point that we should return to the understanding of the death-drive offered earlier and attempt to develop it a bit further. In our first chapter, we spoke of the feeling of oceanic oneness, the regression to the unboundedness of infancy, the desire to return to a state of limitlessness, eternity, undifferentiated unity. This, we said, is the experience that man's Thanatonic drive seeks to recapture, the original stasis which it longs to repeat. (It is by no means an accident that the Judge speaks of war as "a forcing of the unity of existence."[88] As Dostoevsky's Grand Inquisitor notes, it is in the service of "communality"—that is, unity, "universal worship"—that men "have destroyed each other with the sword.")[89] Yet the desire for such a primordial unity is, we have also said, illusory: "nostalgia is the desire to return, to go back to an idealized past that never was."[90] (That the Judge is described as a being devoid of "history," as being "something wholly other" than "his antecedents," arising out of "a void without terminus or origin" is not accident either.)[91] This desire, this destructive impulse, exists in all of us. It is the inescapable sin at the heart of the human condition. And, as McCarthy's novel so aptly depicts, it is there from the start.

To this end, Augustine tells us that "The only innocent feature in babies is the weakness of their frames; the minds of infants are far from innocent."[92] Why the minds? In our first chapter we discussed how "Augustine's emphasis on the literal meaning of infancy, as his 'unspeaking stage' in life" reveals man's "fundamental experience of a primordial separation"—that is, the separation caused by time and space.[93] To this understanding of the "sinfulness of infants" our foregoing discussion forces us to add another. Is it not the case that the minds of infants are sinful because, as Freud would say, they are *infantile*—that is, oceanic, believing that they constitute the whole of existence? Does not the infant see himself as God? Or, said differently, isn't the infant all Id?

In a recent paper which draws upon the work done in his 2018 book *Ça n'a rien à voir*, Falque writes, "death is not only the destruction of the self, but also an entry into the 'Id.'"[94] It is a descent into chaos, meaninglessness, "eternal contradiction, father of all things."[95] Thus to enter the Id is to "succumb to self-oblivion," to lose the *"principium individuationis,"* to plunge headlong into the depths of the "primal unity," the "hidden substratum of suffering," "[e]xcess revealed ... as truth."[96] It is to be, as Augustine would say, "at odds with myself, fragmenting myself,"[97] to become a "disintegrated self."[98] (Anyone who has been present during the death of another can attest to the meaningless character of such a descent. The dying person, he will tell you, was unmade, fragmented before his very eyes.) Yet, as infancy reveals, death is man's primal state: "The infant without words and without image is formless: asemic. [He] remains submerged in an undifferentiated and absolute whole which, to the extent that [he] knows of no difference, allows him no identity."[99] (Hence, life is "but a dying.")[100]

What is interesting for Augustine (and for Freud) is that upon leaving the disordered (that is, formless, chaotic, deathlike) stage of infancy, man seeks to return to it again and again. Thus we hear in Book II of the *Confessions* of how the pubescent Augustine—"intent on pleasing myself" and spurred on by "restlessness," the desire for "excesses," "the frenzy of lust," "the floodtide of my nature"[101]—ends by pursuing the most destructive of impulses. In recounting the famous story of his theft from a neighbor's pear tree, Augustine meditates on the absurdity and meaninglessness of sin.

> Enable my heart to tell you now what it was seeking in this action which made me bad for no reason, in which there was no motive for my malice except malice. The malice was loathsome and I loved it. I was in love with my own ruin, in love with decay: not with the thing for which I was falling into decay but with decay itself, for I was depraved in soul, and I leapt down from your strong support into destruction, hungering not for some advantage to be gained by the foul deed, but for the foulness of it.[102]

Reversing the Ancient assumption that evil is only committed out of ignorance—that sin is merely the confused pursuit of a false good in place of a true one—Augustine asserts that man desires evil "for its own sake."[103] "To do what is wrong simply because it was wrong" represents "a seduction of the mind," "a craving to do harm for sport and fun."[104]

Yet if this "craving" compels us to leap down into destruction "for no reason," still, Augustine asserts, it does represent a kind of "mimicry" of God (sadism).[105] Such "a perversion of the human being who is not and cannot be God"[106] can only be achieved by attempting—under the influence of the death-drive—to return to the (imaginary) oneness of infancy, to submerge oneself in the undifferentiated and absolute whole, to descend into the Id. ("It would be possible," Freud writes, "to picture the id as under the domination of the mute but powerful death instincts, which desire to be at peace and (prompted by the pleasure principle) to put Eros, the mischiefmaker, to rest.")[107]

But here a question arises: if at bottom we human beings are *all Id* such that "the ego" is merely "that part of the id which has been modified by the direct influence of the external world";[108] if, as Lacan's mirror stage posits, prior to being formulated as a subject by seeing his reflection, the infant is "nothing," a "formless" mass that "knows of no difference," has "no identity;"[109] what then is man's Eros if not Thanatos called by a different name?

In *The Ego and the Id*, Freud likens the ego—"in its relation to the id"—to "a man on horseback." "The ego," he writes, "is in the habit of transforming the id's will into action as if it were its own."[110] Who could fail to hear the resonances with Plato's *Phaedrus* in which the soul is compared to a chariot being led by two winged horses? It is up to the charioteer, Plato tells us, to struggle with the horses, transforming their wills into action in order to direct them upward toward the ideal realm of the gods (246a–254e). This is the erotic ascent, the striving of man's Eros toward truth and light. Yet, as Freud's repetition of this metaphor makes clear, it is not the (rational) charioteer who is in control: "Often a rider, if he is not to be parted from his horse, is obliged to guide it *where it wants to go*; so in the same way the ego is in the habit of transforming the id's will into action *as if* it were its own."[111] The ego guides the Id where *it* wants to go. But where does the Id want to go? The answer is clear: "If we may accept as an observation without exception that every living being dies for *internal* reasons, returning to the inorganic, then we can only say that *the goal of all life is death*, and, looking backwards, that the nonliving existed before the living."[112] Eros too is Thanatos. For, at bottom, we are *all Id*—incapable of ascent.

We would do well, I think, to remember that even Plato's erotic ascent is predicated on the soul's separation from the body "after death" (256b).

Notes

1 Dostoevsky, *The Brothers Karamazov*, 303.
2 Greene, *The End of the Affair*, 39.
3 Ibid., 71.
4 "God," Bendrix observes with surprise, "makes his saints out of such material as we are;"

> if even you [Sarah]—with your lusts and your adulteries and the timid lies you used to tell—can change like this, we all could be saints … if *you* are a saint, it's not so difficult to be a saint. It's something He can demand of any of us, leap.
>
> *(Ibid., 47 and 159 respectively)*

5 Žižek, "The Fear of Four Words," 37.

6 Ibid. On this point, like on so many others, Žižek bears witness to his indebtedness to Chesterton:

> Only the other day I saw in an excellent weekly paper of Puritan tone this remark, that Christianity when stripped of its armour of dogma ... turned out to be nothing but the Quaker doctrine of the Inner Light. Now, if I were to say that Christianity came into the world specially to destroy the doctrine of the Inner Light, that would be ... very much nearer to the truth.... Of all conceivable forms of enlightenment the worst is what these people call the Inner Light. Of all horrible religions the most horrible is the worship of the god within.... Christianity came into the world firstly in order to assert with violence that a man had not only to look inwards, but to look outwards, to behold with astonishment and enthusiasm a divine company and a divine captain. The only fun of being a Christian was that a man was not left alone with the Inner Light, but definitely recognized an outer light, fair as the sun, clear as the moon, terrible as an army with banners."
>
> (Chesterton, Orthodoxy, 73–74)

7 Greene, *The End of the Affair*, 159.
8 Augustine, *Confessions*, (2.2.4).
9 See, Kierkegaard, *Fear and Trembling*, 72.
10 Ibid., 72–73.
11 Ibid., 65. Speaking of the virgin birth of Jesus, Kierkegaard asks: "Has any woman been as infringed upon as was Mary?"
12 "Such a faith is not angry, does not censure ... it does not bring 'the sword'—it has no idea to what extent it could one day cause dissention." Nietzsche, *The Anti-Christ*, (§32).
13 See, "people speak sometimes about the 'animal' cruelty of man, but that is terribly unjust and offensive to animals, no animal could ever be so cruel as a man, so artfully, so artistically cruel." Dostoevsky, *The Brothers Karamazov*, 238.
14 Ibid., 289.
15 Unamuno, *Saint Manuel Bueno, Martyr*, 281.
16 Nietzsche, *The Gay Science*, (§341).
17 Quotation modified to match the famous O'Connor novel *The Violent Bear It Away*.
18 Nietzsche, *The Gay Science*, (§341).
19 Nietzsche, *Beyond Good and Evil*, (§56).
20 McCarthy, *Blood Meridian*, 82–83.
21 Ibid., 54–55.
22 Ibid., 56.
23 Ibid., 46.
24 Ibid., 5.
25 Ibid., 4.
26 Woodward, "Cormac McCarthy's Venomous Fiction."
27 "Like Flannery O'Conner, he sides with the misfits and anachronisms of modern life against 'progress.'" Ibid.
28 O'Connor, *Wise Blood*, 1.
29 Donne, *The Complete English Poems*, 326.
30 McCarthy, *Blood Meridian*, 4.
31 Ibid., 22.
32 Ibid., 16.
33 Ibid., 29.
34 Ibid., 67.
35 Ibid., 75.
36 Ibid., 79.

37 As the Reverend Green insists, Christ never leaves you, not even in the whorehouse:

> he couldnt stay out of these here hell, hell, hellholes right here in Nacogdoches. I said to him, said: You goin take the son of God in there with ye? And he said: Oh no. No I aint. And I said: Dont you know that he said I will foller ye always even unto the end of the road? Well, he said, I aint askin nobody to go nowheres. And I said: Neighbor, you dont need to ask. He's a goin to be there with ye ever step of the way whether ye ask it or ye dont. I said: Neighbor, you caint get shed of him. Now. Are you goin to drag him, him, into that hellhole yonder?
>
> *(Ibid., 6)*

38 Ibid., 163.
39 Ibid., 167–168.
40 Ibid., 218.
41 Manoussakis, *The Ethics of Time*, 134.
42 Ibid.
43 As quoted in Balthasar, *Dare We Hope*, 89.
44 See, Augustine, *Confessions*, (2.10.18).
45 McCarthy, *Blood Meridian*, 3. The wolf, which for Dante symbolizes man's greed, reappears again and again throughout this book.
46 Ibid.
47 Compare McCarthy's

> Climbing up through ocotillo and pricklypear where the rocks trembled and sleared in the sun, rock and no water and the sandy trace and they kept watch for any green thing that might tell of water but there was no water
>
> *(Ibid., 65)*

   with Eliot's "Here is no water but only rock/ Rock and no water and the sandy road" (Eliot, *The Complete Poems*, 47).
48 Eliot, *The Complete Poems*, 47.
49 Ibid., 48.
50 McCarthy, *Blood Meridian*, 6.
51 Pierce, "Harold Bloom on Blood Meridian," <www.avclub.com/harold-bloom-on -blood-meridian-1798216782>
52 McCarthy, *Blood Meridian*, 261.
53 Ibid.
54 Ibid., 207–208.
55 Ibid., 207.
56 Ibid., 343.
57 Ibid., 147.
58 Ibid., 344.
59 Ibid., 3.
60 Ibid., 128–141.
61 Ibid., 130.
62 See, for instance, the scene in which the kid draws the short straw described above:

> When the kid selected among the shafts to draw one he saw the judge watching him and he paused.... He let go the arrow he'd chosen and sorted out another and drew that one. It carried the red tassel.
>
> *(Ibid., 214)*

63 Ibid., 341.
64 Ibid., 342.

65 Ibid., 343.

66 Cf. the description of the Judge near the end of the book:

> he was among every kind of man, herder and bullwhacker and drover and freighter and miner and hunter and soldier and pedlar and gambler and drifter and drunkard and thief and he was among the dregs of the earth in beggary a thousand years and he was among the scapegrace scions of eastern dynasties and in all that motley assemblage he sat by them and yet alone as if he were some other sort of man entire.
>
> *(Ibid., 338)*

67 Ibid., 347.

68 Ibid., 347–348.

69 Shaw, "The Kid's Fate, the Judge's Guilt," 102.

70 McCarthy, *Blood Meridian*, 347.

71 See,

> Let's go, she said. I got to go.... You cant lay there. Come on. I got to go. He sat up and swung his legs over the edge of the little iron cot and stood and pulled his trousers up and buttoned them and buckled his belt.... You need to get down there and get you a drink, she said. You'll be all right.
>
> *(Ibid., 345–346)*

72 Dostoevsky, *The Brothers Karamazov*, 242.

73 McCarthy, *Blood Meridian*, 336.

74 Ibid., 319.

75 Ibid., 318–319.

76 Ibid., 322.

77 Ibid., 340.

78 Ibid., 322.

79 Ibid., 322–323.

80 Ibid., 340.

81 Ibid., 345.

82 Ibid., 257.

83 Ibid., 1.

84 Ibid., 348.

85 Ibid.

86 Ibid., 349.

87 Ibid.

88 McCarthy, *Blood Meridian*, 261.

89 Dostoevsky, *The Brothers Karamazov*, 254.

90 Manoussakis, *The Ethics of Time*, 108.

91 McCarthy, *Blood Meridian*, 322.

92 Augustine, *Confessions*, (1.7.11).

93 Manoussakis, *The Ethics of Time*, 81.

94 Falque, "Psychoanalysis and Philosophy," 9.

95 Nietzsche, *The Birth of Tragedy*, (§4).

96 Ibid.

97 Augustine, *Confessions*, (8.10.22).

98 Ibid., (2.1.1).

99 Manoussakis, "Dying to Desire," 127.

100 Augustine, *Confessions*, (1.6.7).

101 Ibid., (2.1.1–2.3.8).

102 Ibid., (2.4.9).

103 Ibid.

104 Ibid., (2.6.14–2.9.17).
105 See, "All those who wander far away and set themselves up against you are imitating you, but in a perverse way." Ibid., (2.6.14).
106 Manoussakis, "Cracked," 60.
107 Freud, *The Ego and the Id*, 62.
108 Ibid., 18–19.
109 Manoussakis, "Dying to Desire," 127.
110 Freud, *The Ego and the Id*, 19.
111 Ibid. (emphasis mine).
112 Freud, *Beyond the Pleasure Principle*, 77.

Bibliography

Augustine, *Confessions*, trans. Maria Boulding (New York: Vintage, 1998).

Balthasar, Hans Urs von, *Dare We Hope: "That All Men Be Saved"?*, trans. David Kipp and Lothar Krauth (San Francisco: Ignatius, 1988).

Chesterton, GK, *Orthodoxy* (Louisville: GLH Publishing, 2016).

Donne, John, *The Complete English Poems* (New York: Penguin, 1996).

Dostoevsky, Fyodor, *The Brothers Karamazov*, trans. Richard Pevear and Larissa Volokhonsky (New York: Farrar, Straus and Giroux, 2002).

Eliot, TS, *The Complete Poems and Plays: 1909–1950* (San Diego, CA: Harcourt, 1971).

Falque, Emmanuel, *Ça n'a rien à voir: Lire Freud en philosophe* (Paris: Les Éditions du Cerf, 2018a).

Falque, Emmanuel, "Psychoanalysis and Philosophy: Perspectives and Issues," trans. Brian Becker, presented at Lesley University on November 3, 2018b.

Freud, Sigmund, *The Ego and the Id*, trans. Joan Riviere (New York: WW Norton, 1960).

Freud, Sigmund, *Beyond the Pleasure Principle*, trans. Gregory C Richter, ed. Todd Dufresne (Peterborough, ON: Broadview Editions, 2011).

Greene, Graham, *The End of the Affair* (New York: Penguin, 2004).

Kierkegaard, Søren, *Fear and Trembling*, trans. Howard Hong and Edna Hong (Princeton, NJ: Princeton University Press, 1983).

Manoussakis, John, "Cracked: The Black Theology of Anatheism," in *The Art of Anatheism*, eds. Richard Kearney and Matthew Clemente (London: Rowman & Littlefield, 2017a), 49–66.

Manoussakis, John, *The Ethics of Time* (London: Bloomsbury, 2017b).

Manoussakis, John, "Dying to Desire: Soma, Sema, Sarx, and Sex," in *Somatic Desire: Rethinking Corporeality in Contemporary Thought*, eds. Sarah Horton, et al. (London: Lexington Books, 2019), 117–137.

McCarthy, Cormac, *Blood Meridian or the Evening Redness in the West* (New York: Vintage, 1992).

Nietzsche, Friedrich, *The Birth of Tragedy*, trans. Walter Kaufmann (New York: Vintage, 1967).

Nietzsche, Friedrich, *The Gay Science*, trans. Walter Kaufmann (New York: Vintage, 1974).

Nietzsche, Friedrich, *Beyond Good and Evil*, trans. Walter Kaufmann (New York: Vintage, 1989).

Nietzsche, Friedrich, *Twilight of the Idols and The Anti-Christ*, trans. RJ Hollingdale (New York: Penguin, 1990).

O'Connor, Flannery, *Wise Blood: A Novel* (New York: Farrar, Straus and Giroux, 2007).

Plato, *Phaedrus*, trans. Alexander Nehamas and Paul Woodruff (Indianapolis: Hackett, 1995).

Shaw, Patrick W, "The Kid's Fate, the Judge's Guilt: Ramifications of Closure in Cormac McCarthy's 'Blood Meridian'," in *The Southern Literary Journal*, vol. 30, no. 1 (Fall, 1997), 102–119.

Unamuno, Miguel de, *Saint Manuel Bueno, Martyr*, in *Basic Writings of Existentialism*, ed. Gordon Marion (New York: Modern Library, 2004).

Woodward, Richard, "Cormac McCarthy's Venomous Fiction," in *The New York Times* (April 19, 1992, Sunday, Late Edition). Available at: https://www.nytimes.com/books/98/05/17/specials/mccarthy-venom.html. Accessed: October 20, 2018.

Žižek, Slavoj, "The Fear of Four Words," in *The Monstrosity of Christ: Paradox or Dialectic?* ed. Creston Davis (Cambridge, MA: MIT Press, 2009).

8

RESURRECTION EX NIHILO

From nothing to all things made new

To return now to the question with which we began our last chapter—the question of violence: man's violence and the violence of God—we should first reiterate that it is by violence, by destruction, by will to power and the pursuit of death that man seeks to make himself God. Thanatos, the sadistic lust for mastery and control, is man's means of self-divinization—perverse and futile as it may be. This insight finds an excellent expression in a recent novel by Donald Ray Pollock: Willard, one of the main characters in *The Devil All the Time*, begins offering sacrifices to God in hopes of curing his wife's cancer. At first, he presents small offerings: prayers, fasts, bodily mortifications. Then he collects the carcasses of dead animals—roadkill and the like—to nail to crosses he has constructed in his backyard. But when his prayers (his demands) go unanswered, he begins to increase his use of violence in an attempt to force the will of the divine. He moves from sacrificing small animals to killing his son's dog and ultimately ends by murdering another human being and painting the crosses with the dead man's blood. Still, try as he might, he cannot make God's will conform to his own. No matter what he does—"it don't work."[1]

Yet if the perverse desire to be God accounts for the sadistic cruelty of man, how then should we understand the violence of God? John Donne, in one of his memorable *Divine Meditations*, prays: "Batter my heart, three-personed God."[2] After begging the deity to "o'erthrow me," "to break, blow, burn, and make me new," he concludes: "Except you enthral me, never shall [I] be free,/ Nor ever chaste, except you ravish me."[3] In this chapter we will suggest that, if it is by violence that man seeks to make himself God, it is by violence that God makes himself man and makes man anew. The insertion of the divine into the human condition, the entrance of God from *without*, cannot but be met with conflict, resistance.[4] Even Mary, perhaps the best suited to receive grace, felt "greatly troubled" by the prospect of finding "favor with God" (Luke 1:29–30). Grace *as such* is always felt to be an act of violation, a traumatic intrusion into what is most intimately mine—my self-willed defilement, the hardening of my heart—one which demands of me a radical conversion, a rebirth. Grace, as Graham Greene so eloquently depicts, ruins our happiness. It destroys "our old self," crucifying it along with the crucified God (Romans 6:6).

CS Lewis speaks of grace as confronting us with a new kind of life, one which is "not only different" but "actually opposed" to life as we know it.[5] "The natural life in each of us is something self-centered, something that wants to be petted and admired, to take advantage of other lives, to exploit the whole universe."[6] It is the life of Thanatos, the life that seeks death as its secret goal. And it "wants to be left to itself" because "[i]t knows that if the spiritual life gets hold of it, all its self-centeredness and self-will are going to be killed."[7] The grace of God is the destruction of that self. It is the descent of the divine into our fallen, fragmented condition. Such a descent undoes man's Thanatos from within, sowing seeds of life into the inorganic clay from which we were made and to which we long to return.[8]

Descent into the Id

In his recent work on Freud, Falque tells us that to be "submerged in the Id" is to "sink into the inorganic," to enter a "quasi-mineral or lapidary human state."[9] Comparing such an experience to that of "sloth"—the oft-forgotten deadly sin— he quotes from the 16th century thinker Charles de Bovelles: "sloth throws man down to the very lowest rank and makes him similar to minerals (*sicut mineralia*)."

> In fact, like minerals (*mineralia*), which are placed in the last rank, [such men] possess nothing else but being itself. To those, it is not permitted to exercise any natural operation or to move on their own. Whomsoever this dreadful monster of sloth possesses in this manner, firmly passes away into a permanent sleep (*assiduo ferme somno consopescunt*). They are deprived of any act and operation (*ab actu omni et operatione remittuntur*), they persevere unmoved like stones (*immoti ut lapides perstant*), as if mother nature had only granted them a simple being, without any obvious strength or any capacity for laudable actions.[10]

Recalling our earlier discussion of the connection between death and the Id—"death is not only the destruction of the self, but also an entry into the 'Id'"[11]— we are now prepared to approach the mystery of death in a new light. What does it mean to enter into the Id? What does it mean to exist in a "quasi-mineral" state?

In his exceedingly accessible little book *Life Out of Death*, Balthasar tells us that

> Death is the withdrawal of all life and its functions; it is, therefore, not nothingness or mere annihilation, although we cannot imagine this state of having life withdrawn as such, this state in which the body returns to

the earth, and the life to God who gave it.… It is like God breathing out and breathing in again.[12]

"The dead person," Balthasar insists, "is not nothingness."[13] Nor is he, *à la* Plato, an immortal soul which will be judged and deemed worthy of reward or punishment. Rather, he descends into the mineral, the inorganic, the chaos of clay which is not annihilated but rather decomposed, dispersed, scattered about. He is in Sheol, the Judaic underworld from which "one does not return."[14]

Citing extensively from scripture, Balthasar informs us that "[t]o existence in death there belong darkness … and even eternal darkness," "dust," "silence"; "No activity goes on there," "there is no joy," "no knowledge of what happens on earth"; "There is no more praise of God."[15] "Deprived of all strength and vitality (Isaiah 14:10), the dead are called *refa'im*, the powerless ones. They are as if they were not (Psalm 39:14; Sirach 17:28). They dwell in the country of forgetfulness (Psalm 88:13)."[16] Said another way, death is an entry into the inorganic, the lifeless, disordered flux that grounds our existence. (Philosophers who would speak of death would do well to consider the principle of mass conservation. If the matter that assembles itself into a human person cannot be destroyed, only broken down and dispersed—what then does this suggest about the psyche that arises from such matter?) Death is not the obliteration of the self but the self's decomposition, its unmaking, its descent into the Id "which is by definition the end from which [one] cannot return."[17]

And yet for Falque, the Id is precisely where God meets man. God is with us, he says, "*dans le Ça*"—in the Id.[18] Christ's descent into our humanity means that he descends to its darkest depths. According to Balthasar, "to become man is for [Christ], in a most hidden yet very real sense, already a humiliation—yes, indeed, as many would say, a deeper humiliation than the going to the Cross itself."[19] For, it is a complete self-emptying, a complete abandonment of what it is to be divine. "For God, the Incarnation is no 'increase,' but only emptying."[20] It is an emptying of the Godhead into the chaos of the Id, the mindless violence of the human heart. If Plato would have us ascend from Thanatos to Eros, from the filth and contamination of this world to the purified realm of the gods (a movement which, as Freud has shown, is never really possible), Christ introduces a new path, a narrow path—the descent of Eros into Thanatos, into the Id, the inorganic, the shit of this world,[21] the meaninglessness of death. Yet it is by making such a descent, by building his home in the chaos that we are (cf. John 1:14), that Christ introduces life into the very heart of death. It is by his death that Eros crucified resurrects our Eros anew.[22]

Anti-Oedipus: The new Adam

In their landmark work *Anti-Oedipus: Capitalism and Schizophrenia*, Deleuze and Guattari criticize "the incurable familialism of psychoanalysis" which "enclose[es] the unconscious within Oedipus."[23] Noting that "Freudian psychoanalysis made a somewhat intensive use of the family"[24] and lamenting how the "trinitary formula" of father–mother–child leads the individual, "forced and constrained, back to Oedipus" by convincing him that "getting well amounts to getting oedipalized,"[25] the duo suggest that what is needed—rather than a *return* that would bring us from "the rupture with families ... back again to families"[26]—is the opening of the individual to the outside world:

> There is no Oedipal triangle: Oedipus is always open in an open social field. Oedipus opens to the four winds, to the four corners of the social field (not even 3 + 1, but 4 + *n*). A poorly closed triangle, a porous or seeping triangle, an exploded triangle from which the flows of desire escape in the direction of other territories.[27]

Such is the revolutionary vision of a desire finally freed from the oppression of the oedipal model: "The revolutionary is the first to have the right to say: 'Oedipus? Never heard of it.'"[28]

And yet—whence such freedom? Who among us is revolutionary enough to escape the bonds into which he is born, the strictures of heredity? In our opening chapter, we sought to establish a link between the first man and the oedipal subject, suggesting that the complex is as inescapable as—if not identical to—man's fallen nature, original sin. Following this logic, we have argued that (human) desire is synonymous with the desire for death: "desire is the desire of *Thanatos*."[29] Otherness—at least from the solipsistic perspective of a fallen world—is impossible. (On this point, we are in agreement with as seemingly divergent of thinkers as Augustine, Nietzsche, Freud, Lacan, and Manoussakis.) Who then is capable of opening himself "to the opening of the world"?[30] Who can expose himself to "the four winds," make himself vulnerable to the otherness that encroaches from *without*, become "a porous or seeping triangle, an exploded triangle from which the flows of desire escape in the direction of other territories"?

"The very form of the Cross," Balthasar observes, "extending out into the four winds, always told the ancient Church that the Cross means solidarity: its outstretched arms would gladly embrace the universe."[31] In language oddly reminiscent of Deleuze and Guattari, Balthasar tells us that "the Cross explodes all systems."[32] (Including the oedipal?) It is perhaps unsurprising that we should suggest here that the only one truly capable of reversing the complex so ingrained in our nature is the one who descends into our humanity in order to experience "the human condition 'from within,' so as to re-direct it from inside."[33] Indeed, it is on the cross that Christ reveals himself as the true revolutionary,[34] anti-Oedipus incarnate. (If, as was suggested in our previous chapter, each of us is an anti-Christ, then it follows that Christ—the new Adam—is, as it were, an anti-Adam.)

Articulated in the most basic of terms, the Oedipus complex can be summarized as the individual's desire to kill his father and reclaim unrestricted access to his mother. In a stunning reversal, the Gospels tell us of Christ's submission to his Father to the point of death (Matthew 26:39; Mark 14:36; Luke 22:42), a death which deprives him of access to his mother and instead opens his mother to us all:

> When Jesus saw his mother and the disciple there whom he loved, he said to his mother, "Woman, behold, your son." Then he said to the disciple, "Behold, your mother." And from that hour the disciple took her into his home.[35]
>
> *(John 19:26–27)*

Such an opening of the followers of Christ to a world beyond the confines of their (self-inclosed) oedipal family structures is emblematic of the revolution realized by Christ on the cross—a revolution he calls for again and again, one which is misrepresented or ignored by those who lack the ears to hear it. Not only does the nuptial unity of two made one-flesh discussed at length in this work entail a breakdown of the narrow "familialism" decried by Deleuze and Guattari—"For this reason a man *shall leave his father and mother*" (Mark 10:7)— Christ constantly challenges us to open ourselves to that which is truly other. Seemingly incomprehensible statements—such as his insistence that, "If any one comes to me without hating his father and mother, wife and children, brothers and sisters, and even his own life, he cannot be my disciple" (Luke 14:26) and, similarly, "Whoever loves father or mother more than me is not worthy of me" (Matthew 10:37)—take on a new tone and tenor when read as an undermining of the oedipal structure, a breaking of the complex that perverts our Eros and fills us with a lust for violence and death.

On the cross, Christ reveals to us how "the flows of desire" (Eros) can extend outward rather than turning back in on the self (Thanatos). The masturbatory aim of man's will to power is reversed in what might be called Christ's *will to powerlessness*. Offering himself, emptying himself, giving up his will to the will of another, Christ reconciles the world to himself (2 Corinthians 5:19) by pouring himself out for the world, "making peace by the blood of his cross" (Colossians 1:20). If "whoever does the will of my heavenly Father is my brother, and sister, and mother" (Matthew 12:50), that is because "in love" the will of the Father has "destined us for adoption" (Ephesians 1:5). The "familialism" which continues the oedipal cycle by allowing every Oedipus to marry (the image of) his mother and reproduce offspring who inherit his complex (sin) can only be overcome when those "born not by natural generation nor by human choice nor by a man's decision" are granted the "power to become children of God" (John 1:12–13). And this can only happen when the Eros of God is "richly poured out on us," when his blood becomes "the bath of rebirth" (Titus 3:5–6).

Coincidence of opposites: God and the abyss

Speaking of the "exclusive and unique" character of Christ's death—which is, in one sense, "inclusive" in that it is experienced in "solidarity with the dead" and yet remains unique in that it spares the dead "the integral experience of death"—Balthasar tells us that Christ took "the whole experience [of death] upon himself" and, in so doing, revealed himself "as the only one who, going beyond the general experience of death, was able to measure the depths of that abyss."[36] What are those depths? How deep does Christ's descent go? To answer this, we must be willing to approach "a deeper silence and a darker abyss than pure philosophy can know."[37] Indeed, if we grant that "the Redeemer placed himself ... in the supreme solitude"—unthinkable to the likes of man—then we will have to admit that such an inquiry goes "beyond what [even] theology can affirm."[38] Nevertheless, such reflections are "not prohibited as a form of pious contemplation" and thus we will offer some brief speculations, not committing ourselves but suggesting what we take to be a reasonable hypothesis all the same.[39]

Falque opens *The Guide to Gethsemane* with a meditation on Matthias Grünewald's iconic Isenheim altarpiece which depicts in graphic detail the ugliness of the crucifixion. For Falque, Christ's "repulsive appearance demands simply that we see, or dare look at, what a mutilated body really is."[40] The hideousness of Christ—recalling Isaiah 52:14: "so marred were his features, beyond that of mortals his appearance, beyond that of human beings"—"shows us 'exposure' rather than 'purification,' ... his face swollen, neck broken, skin distended, muscles wasted, articulations dislocated, and skin cracked open."[41] The cross is the icon of ugliness, the incarnation of everything that is putrid and unclean:

> the crucifixion stands as a universal metaphor for injustice, torture and death. These are among the chief moral and physical evils of the human condition that repel us in their ugliness.... A "scandal" to the Greeks and an "absurdity" to reason (1 Cor. 1:23), [the cross] seems devoid of the power to delight. This is because it seems devoid of symmetry and intelligibility.[42]

Writing, albeit it in a different context, on the essence of "ugliness," Manoussakis tells us that

> a body is less naked when nude. Nakedness—"that real nakedness" as Levinas explains—"is not absence of clothing, but we might say the absence of forms." "A form is that by which a thing shows itself and is graspable."[43]

But the exposure of Christ on the cross is not something graspable, not intelligible, not a thing to be known. The "visibility of the flesh" laid bare, striped of its forms, robbed of its meaning, left utterly naked, exposed, reveals not a "catharsis for our transgressions"[44] but simply humiliation, degradation, death. "Stripped of one of the highest forms, the form of beauty, [such a] body is form-less and, thus, 'humble, bare and ugly.'"[45] It is a meaningless body, one which can hide behind no signifier, which cannot be made sense of, cannot be clothed in human understanding.

This "body stripped of its bodily forms," this "body without properties,"[46] is not unlike the egoless infant who has yet to see himself in the mirror: "that which the mirror reflects ... prior to its reflection," Manoussakis writes, is "nothing."[47] But it is not just nothing. Paradoxically, it is *nothing* and *everything*: the nothing of disorder—"That ineffable and unrepresentable *sarx*, that 'fragmented body,' as Lacan calls it"[48]—the everything of oceanic oneness, infinity, likeness to God. (Hence the desire to return to the infantile state.) It is here that I would like to posit an idea that I am not committed to and one which is not easy to explain: Is it possible that Christ on the cross is both nothing and everything? The coincidence of opposites taken to its utmost extreme? The identity of beauty and ugliness? The overcoming of good and evil? The unity of Eros and Thanatos? The overfullness of God poured out into an endless abyss?

It is "in the uttermost form of a slave," Balthasar tells us, that "the Son's glory breaks through."[49] But I want to propose something more: Is it not at the moment of the crucifixion, at the moment of his hideous death, when Christ has surrendered his will completely to the will of the Father ("not my will but yours be done" [Luke 22:42]), that he has become so identical with the Father that he no longer exists?[50] Much has been written on the last words of Christ as recorded in the Gospels of Matthew and Mark: "My God, my God, why have you forsaken me?" Often this is read as an acknowledgement that Christ was abandoned by the Father. ("Death-of-God" theology takes its point of departure here.) Yet what if Christ's last words signal not abandonment *by* but identity *with* the Father—the unity of the two which collapses into oneness, swallowing up distinction, eradicating difference, erasing otherness completely? What if on the cross, Christ and the Father become so perfectly aligned that one has become the other and the other has disappeared?

To grasp what is being proposed here, one must keep two seemingly contradictory thoughts in mind: first, that Christ's death represents "the supreme obedience of the Son towards the Father"—that is, it is the Father whose will is accomplished through the Son on the cross in love.[51] Second, that that same death represents—simultaneously and paradoxically—"the 'realisation' of all Godlessness ... ordained from the beginning by God ... so it is really God who assumes what is radically contrary to the divine, what is eternally reprobated by God."[52] Said differently, the Son—who is the revelation of the Father (Matthew 11:27)—reveals that he and the Father "are one" (John 10:30) at the very moment that he is made "to be sin" (2 Corinthians 5:21), at the moment when "God himself is forsaken by God because of man's godlessness."[53] "In the humility of his obedient self-lowering to the death of the Cross he is identical with the exalted Lord."[54] *Identical.* (As Karl Barth asks: "Where and when is [Christ] not both the humiliated One and the Exalted One: already exalted even in his humiliation, and still the Humiliated One even in his exaltation?")[55]

"Evil," Augustine tells us, "is nothing but the diminishment of good to the point where nothing at all is left."[56] But what can "the plunging down of the 'Accursed One' (Galatians 3:13) far from God, of the One who is 'sin' (II Corinthians 5:21) personified, who, falling where he is 'thrown' (Apocalypse 20, 14), 'consumes' his own substance" be but the complete *excarnation* of the incarnate God to the point where nothing at all is left? What can the *personification of sin* be but the extreme unmaking of him who is unmade, him who is personhood itself?

> If Jesus Christ, as the doctrine teaches, was both man and god, should we not conclude that it was not merely Christ's human nature, but at least 'One of the Trinity' (*eis tès triados pathoon*)—hence God himself—who suffered and died on the cross? According to a Syrian Monophysite formula 'God has been dead.' Nietzsche's madman, then, only uttered the distant echo of something already found at the origins of Christianity.[57]

No, not merely the origins but the heart of Christianity, the heart of God himself: "the Son's Cross is the revelation of the Father's love"[58] (cf. John 15:9), a love which is nothing but "folly and weakness,"[59] which epitomizes "God's self-abnegation,"[60] which descends to the depths and, in so doing, shows that "love is strong as death, longing is fierce as Sheol" (Song of Songs 8:6)—a "Love that stoops down."[61]

After the death of God

And yet ... the cautious reader would be right to point out that we may have inadvertently stumbled—albeit in the opposite direction—into the same error we warned against in Chapter 6. There, you will recall, we proclaimed: "Anything that eliminates otherness or refuses the possibility of communion with the other in love"—that is, anything that denies that unity can be accomplished without fusion or dissolution—"constitutes a sin against love, an unforgivable sin which denies that salvation comes from without, comes from the other." How then ought we to proceed?

Even before the First Council of Nicaea rejected the docetist heresy, the death of God was a contentious subject. It still is today. Balthasar, for instance, sees the death of God as "the wellspring of salvation"[62] only in so far as it is understood "in light of the event of Easter."[63] For others, however, God's death alone is enough to bring about a kind of salvation—one experienced *here and now*, not after this life but lived within it. Žižek, for instance, tells us that it is in the death of Christ "that human freedom is grounded."[64] "It is neither as payment for our sins nor as legalistic ransom, but by enacting [an] openness that Christ's sacrifice sets us free."[65] The freedom of which Žižek speaks is the openness left by the absence of God, an empty space which man alone can fill. (We might recall here Kearney's observation that "the Lord did not make anything on the seventh day, leaving it free for humans to complete."[66] Such freedom, Žižek seems to say, *is* the death of God, freedom is occasioned for us by his loss.) In God's stead, we must "become gods" (to quote Nietzsche) and see to the completion of the "divine creation" which has been left to us as our inheritance.

As if responding directly to the challenge levelled by Ivan Karamazov against the Boethian solution to the problem of theodicy—

> if everyone must suffer, in order to buy eternal harmony with their suffering, pray tell me what have children got to do with it? ... I absolutely renounce all higher harmony. It is not worth one little tear of even one tormented child[67]

—Žižek insists that

> Christ's death on the Cross means that we should immediately ditch the notion of God as a transcendent caretaker who guarantees the happy outcome of our acts, the guarantee of historical teleology—Christ's death on the Cross is the death of *this* God, ... it refuses any "deeper meaning" that obfuscates the brutal reality of historical catastrophes.[68]

Christ—who refuses to remain "wholly transcendent," a "supreme Creator who knows and directs everything and thus has no need to get involved in earthly accidents with partial passion"—"intervenes in creation as an engaged and combative figure," following the logic of abandonment to the most extreme of ends.[69] In so doing, he shows us that (*à la* Ivan)

> we should pass this gap that separates the entire harmonious picture from the stains it is composed of in the opposite direction—not withdrawing from meaningless stains to the wider harmony, but moving forward from the appearance of global harmony to the stains that compose it.[70]

We should descend like the God who descends, embracing the messiness of the world, of human existence in all of its strangeness and beauty, excluding neither the heights nor the depths of the sacredly profane.[71]

If, Žižek continues, we are "still too frightened today to assume all these consequences,"[72] if we seek "support in the authority of some presupposed figure of the 'big Other,'"[73] preferring "to stay with the comfortable image of God sitting up there, benevolently watching over our lives ... or, even more comfortably, just with some depersonalized Higher Force,"[74] that is because "what really frightens [us] is that [we] will lose the transcendent God guaranteeing the meaning of the universe, God as the hidden Master pulling the strings."[75] Yet it is *here*—in our fear and brokenness—that Christ meets us and helps us to confront the anxiety that enslaves:

> When we are afraid of something (and fear of death is the ultimate fear that makes us slaves), a true friend will say something like: "Don't be afraid,

look, I'll do it, what you're so afraid of, and I'll do it for free—not because I have to, but out of my love for you; I'm not afraid!" He does it and in this way sets us free, demonstrating in *actu* that it can be done, that we can do it too, that we are not slaves.... This is the way Christ brings freedom: confronting him, we become aware of our own freedom.[76]

For Žižek, Christ represents

a God who abandons [his] transcendent position and throws himself into his own creation, fully engaging himself in it up to dying, so that we, humans, are left with no higher Power watching over us, just with the terrible burden of freedom and responsibility for the fate of divine creation, and thus of God himself.[77]

And yet, Ivan might rebuff, it is not the fear of death but of a fate more awful than death that enslaves man:

Did you forget that peace and even death are dearer to man than free choice in the knowledge of good and evil? There is nothing more seductive for man than the freedom of his conscience, but there is nothing more tormenting either.[78]

Indeed, Ivan has not forgotten about Christ and the price he paid in blood; "on the contrary, I've been wondering all the while why you hadn't brought him up for so long, because in discussion your people usually trot him out first."[79] (Can we group Žižek together with Alyosha—and perhaps ourselves?—as the "people" who trot Christ out to bolster an argument?) Against such readings of the death of God as that which ushers in an age of unparalleled freedom, Ivan's Grand Inquisitor challenges Christ:

You want to go into the world, and you are going empty-handed, with some promise of freedom, which they in their simplicity and innate lawlessness cannot even comprehend, which they dread and fear—for nothing has ever been more insufferable for man and for human society than freedom![80]

If, as Žižek contends, fear makes us slaves, what could be more oppressive than "the terrible burden of freedom and responsibility for the fate of divine creation"? How will we handle such freedom? How have we been handling it thus far? Are we not, after the death of God, condemned to a world in which the only God is the "innate lawlessness" of the human heart, "the lust for power, for filthy earthly lucre, enslavement" in the extreme?[81] This is the world of *Blood Meridian*, a world devoid of Christ in which the redeeming power(lessness) of Christ plays no part, in which the Eros of God has accomplished nothing by its descent into the Thanatos of man:

> You desired the free love of man, that he should follow you freely, seduced and captivated by you. Instead of the firm ancient law, man had henceforth to decide for himself, with a free heart, what is good and what is evil, having only your image before him as a guide—but did it not occur to you that he would eventually reject and dispute even your image and your truth if he was oppressed by so terrible a burden as freedom of choice? They will finally cry out that the truth is not in you, for it was impossible to leave them in greater confusion and torment than you did, abandoning them to so many cares and insoluble problems. Thus you laid the foundation for the destruction of your own kingdom.[82]

Aesthetics as first philosophy:[83] Nietzsche and the anatheistic return

Freedom is an ethical category. As such, it has posed countless philosophical problems for those who would judge God by ethical standards. Questions of punishment and reward, free will and predestination, the arbitrary or meaningful nature of suffering, the problem of evil, etc., are all rooted in the assumption that God is primarily an ethical deity. But perhaps the time has come to revaluate the criteria by which we judge the divine? Perhaps our emphasis on the goodness and justice of God have obscured our vision, prevented us from seeing him in all of his ugliness and beauty?

Nietzsche began work on *The Birth of Tragedy* only weeks before heading to the frontlines as a medical orderly in the Franco-Prussian War. He finished it shortly after returning home, having contracted diphtheria and dysentery at the front, and having witnessed the carnage of war with his own eyes, having held the wounded and dying in his hands. "Life," he understandably asserts, "is something essentially amoral."[84] War had taught him as much. Yet in a surprising move, he does not use the brutal and senseless nature of the world to justify an argument against the existence of God. (The problem of theodicy—like the problem of freedom—is an ethical one: "If God is *wholly good*, why then does he allow for the existence of *evil*?") Nor does he uphold a nihilistic worldview, bemoaning the utter meaninglessness of life, the need to—as Silenus would advise—"die soon."[85] Rather, he suggests that there is perhaps

> an artistic meaning and crypto-meaning behind all events—a "god," if you please, but certainly only an entirely reckless and amoral artist-god who wants to experience, whether he is building or destroying, in the good and in the bad, his own joy and glory—one who, creating worlds, frees himself

from the *distress* of fullness and *overfullness* and from the *affliction* of the contradictions compressed in his soul.[86]

For Nietzsche, "the existence of the world is *justified* only as an aesthetic phenomenon." It is art that gives life its *meaning*, its *value*—note that these are aesthetic, as
opposed to ethical, categories—"art, and *not* morality, is … the truly *metaphysical*
activity of man."[87] If man is made in the image and likeness of his God, Nietzsche
contends, he is made to be an artist, not a moralist, a creator of worlds, not one of
"the good and the just," "the saints of Israel."[88] God, he insists, is not the God of
"absolute standards."[89] He is rather the "true author" of this world, the one who
writes the drama of our lives. Employing an analogy which we have identified in
the works of Greene, Unamuno, and CS Lewis—and which appears in everyone
from Augustine[90] to Aquinas[91] to Kierkegaard[92]—Nietzsche writes:

> The entire comedy of art is neither performed for our betterment or edu-
> cation nor are we the true authors of this art world. On the contrary, we
> may assume that we are merely images and artistic projections for the true
> author, and that we have our highest dignity in our significance as works of
> art—for it is only as an *aesthetic phenomenon* that existence and the world are
> eternally *justified*—while of course our consciousness of our own signifi-
> cance hardly differs from that which the soldiers painted on canvas have of
> the battle represented on it. Thus all our knowledge of art is basically quite
> illusory, because as knowing beings we are not one and identical with that
> being which, as the sole author and spectator of the comedy of art, prepares
> a perpetual entertainment for itself.[93]

Yet even if "we are not one and identical" with "the sole author" of our novelistic
lives, still, Nietzsche tells us, the individual artist, "in the act of artistic creation,"
can access "the eternal essence of art" by drawing near to the "primordial artist
of the world."[94] The more closely I imitate my creator, the more creative, and
thus like him, I become.

Recently, Kearney's work has developed along similar lines. Speaking of art
as the realm of "divine-human interplay,"[95] he writes, "This play of mutual recreation between human and divine … involves creatures cocreating with their
Creator."[96] "Artists often speak of feeling as though they are called to compose,
as if they are giving themselves over to something deeper, higher, stranger. Their
works are called into being, inspired by some inexpressible otherness, and they
themselves are the vessels through which that mysterious surplus [*jouissance*]
enters the world."[97] This quasi-mystical experience of creating a work of art has
been understood since the time of the Greeks as a making that makes manifest
the divine. (It is easy to see how Nietzsche settled upon his interpretation of
Greek tragedy.) It is referred to as "theopoetics"—the divine (*theos*) made manifest in and through making (*poiesis*).

For Kearney, there is an "ongoing double creation" at work in the world: "God making mortals and mortals making God."[98] "In this view, God codepends on us so that the promissory word of Genesis may be realized in embodied figures of time and space, image and flesh, art and action."[99] Like Nietzsche—who sees the creative impulse as being driven by God's "*overfullness*" (*jouissance*) which inspires in man "joy, strength, overflowing health, overgreat fullness"[100]— Kearney asserts that it is God's kenotic desire to empty himself and overflow into creation that gives rise to man's desire to make: "in forming the human, God bore witness to a gap within divinity, a sabbatical cleft or crack from which the life-drive of Eros could emerge as desire for its other.... Creation is a love affair. God is cracked about us. Theopoetics is theoerotics."[101]

This linking of the artistic impulse to divine desire is a furthering of Nietzsche's refutation of the old Platonic moralism: "In truth, nothing could be more opposed to the purely aesthetic interpretation and justification of the world which are taught in this book than the Christian [read, Platonic] teaching, which is, and wants to be, *only* moral and which relegates art, *every* art, to the realm of *lies*; with its absolute standards, beginning with the truthfulness of God, it negates, judges, and damns art."[102] (Here, perhaps, we begin to appreciate Dostoyevsky's enigmatic statement: "if someone were to prove to me that Christ was outside the truth, and it was really the case that the truth lay outside Christ, then I should choose to stay with Christ rather than with the truth"[103]—especially if we couple it with his oft-quoted maxim, "Beauty will save the world.")

Yet if Kearney, like Nietzsche, is ready to "abandon the old God of sovereignty and theodicy,"[104] if he agrees that after the death of God we must "become gods," we must be artists, we must create, he goes one step further still, pushing "Godlessness to the point of a return to Godliness."[105] The death of God, he writes, "gives birth to the God of life."[106] Anatheism is not simply a return *to* God after the death of God but, more profoundly, the return *of* God after the death of God. Here the problem with Žižek's freedom is overcome. For, if in dying Christ sets us free, in rising he reveals the meaning of our freedom: "to follow Christ the God-Man in completing the 'New Creation.'"[107] Descending into the "innate lawlessness" of our hearts, he turns our perversion into a wellspring of life. Dying, he destroys our death-drive. Rising, he resurrects our Eros anew.

Such an extreme remaking cannot but entail violence. Rebirth, like birth, demands the outpouring of blood. (To paraphrase Barthes, the birth of us characters must be ransomed by the death of our Author.) Out of nothing, God originally made us. But that first creation demanded a second—"creation again (*ana*)."[108] So into the nothing Christ descended. And on the third day, he rose again, showing us that the way to life is through death, the way to love is through surrender, and out of nothing—*resurrection ex nihilo*—all things can be made new (Revelation 21:5).

Notes

1 Pollock, *The Devil All the Time*, 68.
2 Donne, *The Complete English Poems*, 314.
3 Ibid., 314–315.
4 As Marion argues in his recent work on the related topic of Revelation,

> Resistance stems from the fact that no one is ever immediately prepared for, supportive of, or committed to a Revelation, but everyone, at least initially, becomes hostile to it since it redefines the entire field of possibility. It belongs to Revelation *as such* to appear intolerable and inadmissible, precisely because it is given as absolute and thus, *to our eyes*, seems intolerant, and thus intolerable. Moreover, the revealed character of a religion, to the extent that Revelation comes from *elsewhere*, confers on it only a very ambiguous privilege, even a mark of infamy: it can certainly claim an exterior authority and be supposedly superior to the human condition, but this exteriority and superiority itself arouses resistance only to the extent that the possible receivers of its arrival can acknowledge it.
> *("Thinking Elsewhere," 18)*

5 Lewis, *Mere Christianity*, 145.
6 Ibid.
7 Ibid.
8 See,

> Looking at this from the divine perspective, if God wished to "experience" … the human condition "from within," so as to re-direct it from inside it, and thus save it, he would have to place the decisive stress on that point where sinful, mortal man finds himself "at his wit's end." And this must be where man has lost himself in death without, for all that, finding God. This is the place where he has fallen into an abyss of grief, indifference, darkness, into the "pit" from which he cannot escape by his own powers.
> *(Balthasar,* Mysterium Paschale, *13)*

9 Falque, "Psychoanalysis and Philosophy," 10.
10 Bovelles as quote in ibid., 10–11.
11 Ibid., 9.
12 Balthasar, *Life Out of Death*, 50–51.
13 Ibid., 51.
14 Balthasar, *Mysterium Paschale*, 161.
15 Ibid.
16 Ibid., 161–162. (Biblical references have been standardized for consistency.)
17 Ibid., 50.
18 Falque, *Ça n'a rien à voir*, 146.
19 Balthasar, *Mysterium Paschale*, 23.
20 Ibid., 25.
21 I am thinking of Milan Kundera's famous quip on "the incompatibility of God and shit":

> Shit is a more onerous theological problem than is evil. Since God gave man freedom, we can, if need be, accept the idea that He is not responsible for man's crimes. The responsibility for shit, however, rests entirely with Him, the Creator of man.
> *(The Unbearable Lightness of Being, 245–246)*

22 See,

> It would be possible to picture the id as under the domination of the mute but powerful death instincts, which desire to be at peace and (prompted by the pleasure principle) to put Eros, the mischiefmaker, to rest; *but perhaps that might be to undervalue the part played by Eros.*
>
> *(Freud,* The Ego and the Id, *62 [emphasis mine])*

23 Deleuze and Guattari, *Anti-Oedipus*, 92.
24 Ibid., 93.
25 Ibid., 91.
26 Ibid., 89.
27 Ibid., 96.
28 Ibid.
29 Manoussakis, "Dying to Desire," 126.
30 Deleuze and Guattari, *Anti-Oedipus*, 96.
31 Balthasar, *Heart of the World*, 13.
32 Balthasar, *Theo-drama, vol. 4*, 319.
33 Balthasar, *Mysterium Paschale*, 13.
34 See,

> And now let the revolutionists choose a creed from all the creeds and a god from all the gods of the world, carefully weighing all the gods of inevitable recurrence and of unalterable power. They will not find another god who has himself been in revolt.
>
> *(Chesterton, as quoted in Žižek, "The Fear of Four Words," 48)*

35 In its official commentary on this passage, the United States Conference of Catholic Bishops (USCCB) tells us that this scene is meant to be interpreted symbolically: "Now that the hour has come (Jn 19:28), Mary (a symbol of the church?) is given a role as the mother of Christians (personified by the beloved disciple)." <www.usccb.org/bible/jn/19:26#51019026-1>
36 Balthasar, *Mysterium Paschale*, 168.
37 Ibid., 66.
38 Ibid., 181.
39 Ibid.
40 Falque, *The Guide to Gethsemane*, xx.
41 Ibid., xxi.
42 Fields, "The Beauty of the Ugly," 173.
43 Manoussakis, "Dying to Desire," 122.
44 Falque, *The Guide to Gethsemane*, xxi.
45 Manoussakis, "Dying to Desire," 122.
46 Ibid.
47 Ibid., 127.
48 Ibid.
49 Balthasar, *Mysterium Paschale*, 29.
50 See,

> With Christ, the very relationship between the substantial divine content and its representation changes: Christ does not represent this substantial divine content, God, he directly is God, *which is why he no longer has to resemble God*, to strive to be perfect and 'like God.' ... Buddha, Socrates, etc., *resemble* gods, while Christ

is God. … we are dealing with the singularity of a pure event, with contingency brought to its extreme.

(Žižek, "The Fear of Four Words," 81)

51 Balthasar, *Mysterium Paschale*, 52.
52 Ibid., 51–52.
53 Balthasar, *Theo-drama, vol. 2*, 194.
54 Balthasar, *Mysterium Paschale*, 79.
55 As quoted in ibid., 80.
56 Augustine, *Confessions*, (3.7.12).
57 Doude van Troostwijk, "The Still Born God, Again," 254.
58 Balthasar, *Mysterium Paschale*, 140.
59 Ibid., 82.
60 Ibid., 25.
61 Ibid.
62 Ibid., 49.
63 Ibid., 189.
64 Žižek, "The Fear of Four Words," 82.
65 Ibid.
66 Kearney, "God Making," 4.
67 Dostoevsky, *The Brothers Karamazov*, 244–245.
68 Žižek, "The Fear of Four Words," 55.
69 Ibid., 85.
70 Ibid., 96.
71 Kearney speaks of "Beauty" as "the extraordinary in the ordinary, the more in the less, transcendence in immanence, otherness in everyday 'thisness.'" Beauty, he says,

> embraces the splendour and pungency … of flesh. I believe this is a central aspect of the sacred often ignored in contemporary religion, which tends to observe a puritanical apartheid between sacred and profane, even in Christianity, which is supposed to be based on the radical incarnation of *logos* as *sarx*. The poetics of sacred carnality is, I believe, indispensable…. Poetics responds to the sacred that shines and seduces through the flesh. It's a form of sacred seduction.
>
> *("Theism, Atheism, Anatheism," 25)*

72 Žižek, "The Fear of Four Words," 25.
73 Ibid., 101.
74 Ibid., 25.
75 Ibid.
76 Ibid., 82.
77 Ibid., 25.
78 Dostoevsky, *The Brothers Karamazov*, 254.
79 Ibid., 246.
80 Ibid., 252.
81 Ibid., 260.
82 Ibid., 255.
83 For a thorough treatment of Nietzsche's prioritizing of aesthetics, see, Cocchiara, "Aesthetics as First Philosophy," 4–16.
84 Nietzsche, *The Birth of Tragedy*, "Attempt," (§5).
85 Ibid., (§3).
86 Ibid., "Attempt," (§5).
87 Ibid.
88 Nietzsche, *The Anti-Christ*, (§27).
89 Nietzsche, *The Birth of Tragedy*, "Attempt," (§5).

90 See,

> Some, in order to find God, read books. But the very appearance of creatures is a kind of book: behold those above you and those below you! Note! Read! God, whom you wish to know, did not make letters with ink; rather, he has placed before your eyes these things that he did make. Who could seek for a greater voice? Heaven and earth call out to you: God made me!
>
> *(as quoted in Bauerschmidt, "God as Author," 575)*

91 See *Summa theologiae* 1.22.2.
92 See Kierkegaard, *Sickness Unto Death*, 74.
93 Nietzsche, *The Birth of Tragedy*, (§5).
94 Ibid.
95 Kearney, "God Making," 3.
96 Ibid., 4.
97 Kearney and Clemente, *The Art of Anatheism*, vii.
98 Ibid., viii.
99 Kearney, "God Making," 4.
100 Nietzsche, *The Birth of Tragedy*, "Attempt," (§4).
101 Kearney, "God Making," 4–5.
102 Nietzsche, *The Birth of Tragedy*, "Attempt," (§5).
103 As quoted in Williams, *Dostoevsky: Language, Faith, and Fiction*, 15.
104 Kearney, *Anatheism*, 52.
105 Ibid., 70.
106 Ibid., 69. Cf.

> out of that evacuated space, out of what Eckhart calls the empty bowl, the vacant (a-theist) womb, a new divinity can give birth to itself through us, can begin again out of nothing, its nothing, our nothing. The God after God gives birth to itself through the void.
>
> *(Kearney, "Theism, Atheism, Anatheism," 31)*

107 Kearney, "God Making," 6.
108 Ibid., 3.

Bibliography

Augustine, *Confessions*, trans. Maria Boulding (New York: Vintage, 1998).

Balthasar, Hans Urs von, *Heart of the World*, trans. Erasmo S Leiva (San Francisco: Ignatius, 1979).

Balthasar, Hans Urs von, *Theo-Drama: Theological Dramatic Theory*, trans. Graham Harrison, vols. 1–5 (San Francisco: Ignatius, 1988–1998).

Balthasar, Hans Urs von, *Mysterium Paschale: The Mystery of Easter*, trans. Aidan Nichols (Edinburgh, Scotland: T&T Clark, 1990).

Balthasar, Hans Urs von, *Life Out of Death: Meditations on the Paschal Mystery*, trans. Martina Stockl (San Francisco: Ignatius, 2012).

Bauerschmidt, Frederick C., "God as Author: Thinking Through a Metaphor," in *Modern Theology*, vol. 31, no. 4 (October, 2015), 573–585.

Cocchiara, Bryan, "Aesthetics as First Philosophy: Nietzsche, the Artist, and His Work," in *misReading Nietzsche*, eds. M. Saverio Clemente and Bryan J. Cocchiara (Eugene, OR: Pickwick Publications, 2018), 4–16.

Deleuze, Gilles and Felix Guattari, *Anti-Oedipus: Capitalism and Schizophrenia*, trans. Robert Hurley, et al. (New York: Penguin, 1977).

Donne, John, *The Complete English Poems* (New York: Penguin, 1996).

Dostoevsky, Fyodor, *The Brothers Karamazov*, trans. Richard Pevear and Larissa Volokhonsky (New York: Farrar, Straus and Giroux, 2002).

Doude van Troostwijk, Chris, "The Still Born God, Again: Overcoming the Aporia of Anatheopoetics," in *The Art of Anatheism*, eds. Richard Kearney and Matthew Clemente (London: Rowman & Littlefield, 2017), 251–262.

Falque, Emmanuel, *Ça n'a rien à voir: Lire Freud en philosophe* (Paris: Les Éditions du Cerf, 2018a).

Falque, Emmanuel, "Psychoanalysis and Philosophy: Perspectives and Issues," trans. Brian Becker, Presented at Lesley University on November 3, 2018b.

Falque, Emmanuel, *The Guide to Gethsemane: Anxiety, Suffering, Death*, trans. George Hughes (New York: Fordham University Press, 2018c).

Fields, Stephen, "The Beauty of the Ugly: Balthasar, the Crucifixion, Analogy and God," in *the International Journal of Systematic Theology*, vol. 9, no. 2 (April, 2007), 172–183.

Freud, Sigmund, *The Ego and the Id*, trans. Joan Riviere (New York: WW Norton, 1960).

Kearney, Richard, *Anatheism: Returning to God After God* (New York: Columbia University Press, 2011).

Kearney, Richard, "God Making: Theopoetics and Anatheism," in *The Art of Anatheism*, eds. Richard Kearney and Matthew Clemente (London: Rowman & Littlefield, 2017), 3–28.

Kearney, Richard, "Theism, Atheism, Anatheism: A Conversation with James Wood," in *Richard Kearney's Anatheistic Wager: Philosophy, Theology, Poetics*, eds. Chris Doude van Troostwijk and Matthew Clemente (Bloomington: Indiana University Press, 2018), 7–39.

Kearney, Richard and Matthew Clemente eds., *The Art of Anatheism* (London: Rowman & Littlefield, 2017).

Kierkegaard, Søren, *The Sickness unto Death*, trans. Howard Hong and Edna Hong (Princeton, NJ: Princeton University Press, 1983).

Kundera, Milan, *The Unbearable Lightness of Being*, trans. Michael Henry Heim (New York: Harper & Row, 1984).

Lewis, CS, *Mere Christianity*, in *The Complete CS Lewis Signature Classics* (New York: Harper Collins, 2007).

Manoussakis, John, "Dying to Desire: Soma, Sema, Sarx, and Sex," in *Somatic Desire: Rethinking Corporeality in Contemporary Thought*, eds. Sarah Horton, et al. (London: Lexington Books, 2019), 117–137.

Marion, Jean-Luc, "Thinking Elsewhere," in *The Journal for Continental Philosophy of Religion*, vol. 1, no. 1 (April, 2019), 5–26.

Nietzsche, Friedrich, *The Birth of Tragedy*, trans. Walter Kaufmann (New York: Vintage, 1967).

Nietzsche, Friedrich, *Twilight of the Idols and The Anti-Christ*, trans. RJ Hollingdale (New York: Penguin, 1990).

Pollock, Donald Ray, *The Devil All the Time* (New York: Doubleday, 2011).

Williams, Rowan, *Dostoevsky: Language, Faith, and Fiction* (Waco, TX: Baylor University Press, 2011).

Žižek, Slavoj, "The Fear of Four Words," in *The Monstrosity of Christ: Paradox or Dialectic?*, ed. Creston Davis (Cambridge, MA: MIT Press, 2009).

AFTERWORD

Eschaton: A theopoetic

For my love

Batter my flesh.
Do with me what thou desireth.
The body is a prison? No.
A tomb in which you sow
Seeds fallen and left unbloomed
Until the springtime
Of your decomposition
Feeds life anew.

CONCLUSION

Eternal recurrence of the new:
A repetition forward

Paul tells us that women are saved through childbirth (1 Timothy 2:15). This saying is hard. To me, it has always been a profound mystery. How can salvation come through the birth of a child? And if childbearing is a means of salvation, why is it offered exclusively to women? What role, if any, do men play in the salvific work of creating new life? These questions have been of particular interest to me for the past nine months as my wife has been pregnant with our first child. It was only three days short days ago, however, that I received my first real insight into the depth of this great mystery. As I witnessed my wife labor through childbirth, I was reminded of Paul's words and began to consider their meaning. Admittedly, the connection between her suffering and the work of salvation was not initially my own. Rather, she sparked in me the following reflections and they have not left me since.

When we arrived at the hospital, she looked to me with sorrow in her eyes and said, "I'm so anxious. I can't imagine how Jesus felt in the Garden." As I tried to comfort her, I remembered the words Christ used to teach his disciples about his impending crucifixion: "When a woman is in labor, she is in anguish because her hour has arrived; but when she has given birth to a child, she no longer remembers the pain because of her joy that a child has been born into the world" (John 16:21). The analogy struck me and I kept it in mind as my wife's labor progressed through the night and into the next day. With each passing hour, I was reminded more and more of the cross and the sufferings of Christ. When my wife woke me with tears after I had fallen asleep at her bedside, I remembered the disciples who could not keep watch for a single hour (Matthew 26:40). When her contractions grew progressively more intense, each one worse than the last, I remembered the scourging at the pillar and thought of how each blow must have been felt more deeply than the last (John 19:1). When she begged me to rub ice over her parched lips, I remembered Christ's cry from the cross—"I thirst" (John 19:28). When she abandoned herself and poured out her blood, I remembered how Christ shed his for the sins of the world (Matthew 26:28). And when, seeing our baby for the first time, she cried, "My son! My son!" I remembered that we are no longer slaves (John 15:15) but sons of the living God (Galatians 3:26).

Bearing witness to the immense suffering and the immense joy of childbirth has given me a new appreciation for the mystery of the cross, for the distinctively feminine capacity to suffer and die for the sake of another. If Eros as we know it longs to grasp, to subjugate, to control, Eros crucified—the Eros of the cross and the canvas and the birthing bed—desires nothing more than to pour itself out, to empty itself of itself so that another may live. As any artist will tell you, death is essential to the work of creation. Art demands sacrifice. It demands that the artist be willing to die. So says the primordial author of this world: "Amen, amen, I say to you, unless a grain of wheat falls to the ground and dies, it remains just a grain of wheat; but if it dies, it produces much fruit" (John 12:24). We are that fruit. We are works of art. And with each new life, another work is born, waiting to be made anew, ready to become a child of God.

"Amen, I say to you, unless you turn and become like children, you will not enter the kingdom of heaven"

(Matthew 18:3)

MSC
Westborough, Massachusetts
October 23, 2015

INDEX

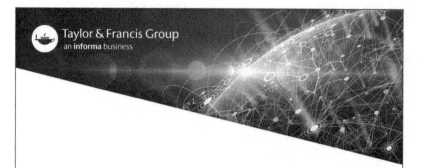